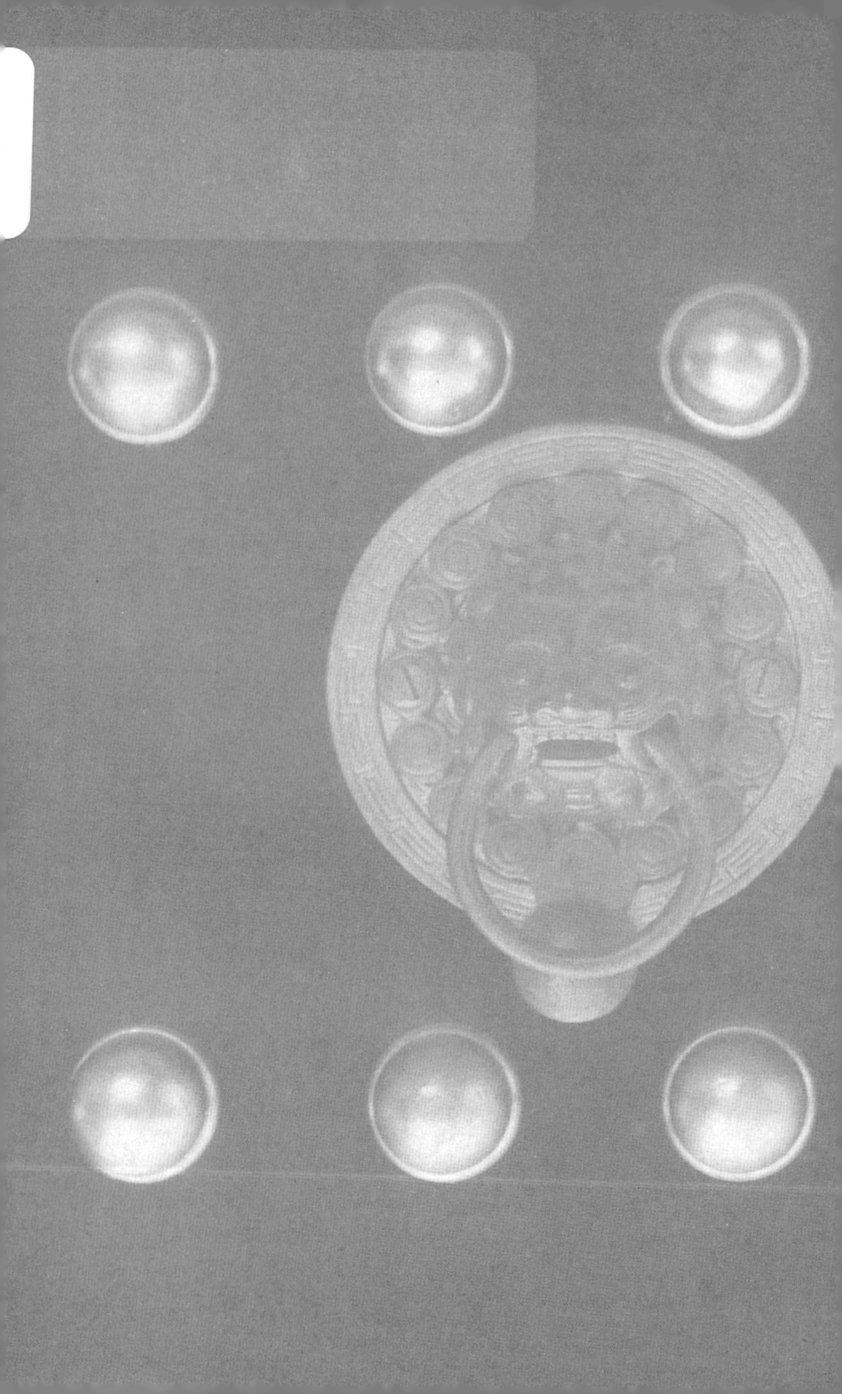

Tales of the Qing Court

Tales of the Qing Court

Written by

Fu Hu

Translated by

George Meng

Hai Feng Publishing Co.

ISBN 962-238-167-7

Written by
Fu Hu

Translated by
George Meng

Published by
Hai Feng Publishing Co.
Rm.1502,Wing On House
71 Des Voeux Rd., Central
Hong Kong

Printed by
Friendly Printing Co., Ltd.
Flat B1, 3/F Luen Ming Hing Ind. Bldg.
36 Muk Cheong St., Tokwawan
Kowloon, Hong Kong

First Edition January 1990
Second Edition November 1992
Third Edition August 1993
Fourth Edition October 1995
Fifth Edition July 1997

HF-141-P

Publisher's Note

The Qing Dynasty lasted 267 years, from the Emperor Shun Zhi ascended the throne in Beijing in 1644 until Xuan Tong was forced to vacate it in 1911. A total of 10 emperors occupied the throne during the dynasty, but perhaps this number should be extended to 12 to include Nuerhachi, who founded the state of "Later Jing" in 1616, and Huangtaiji, who changed the name of the state to "Great Qing" in 1626. As less than a century has gone by since the end of the Qing Dynasty, it is still fresh in people's minds. It is natural that a period which brought a brief period of peace and prosperity as well as a great deal of humiliation and misfortune, should still attract considerable attention.

It is the concern of historians to study the dynasty's imperial edicts, records, and notes on imperial life, and examine the merits or demerits of a sovereign. The general reader has no need to know what was really said in the many documents safely put away in secret repositories. Nor does he need to inquire into the authenticity of these materials. What is it to him if Yong Zheng's claim to the throne was legitimate or not, or whether Emperor Qian Long was of Han or Manchu stock?

This book *Tales of the Qing Court* makes no pretensions to historical accuracy. It is based on the folklore which surrounds the imperial family, and so must be regarded as partly factual and partly imaginary. These are tales of laughter, tears, love and hate in the lives of emperors, empresses, imperial ladies, generals, ministers, and courtiers. These tales are presented to the reader for recreation and perhaps illumination.

Forword

In his poem "To the Departing Maid" the Tang poet Cui Jiao laments:

The Marquis' mansion has walls
As high as the sea is deep.
Once you step into its halls,
I became a stranger who weeps.

In feudal times, the rank of marquis was second highest in the kingdom. To leave the home of a marquis was difficult as diving deep into the sea. If a man's sweetheart was taken, perhaps involuntarily, into a noble's mansion, they would eventually become strangers, for communication of love between them would be forever impossible. The walls surrounding the isolated world of an emperor, the supreme ruler of the land, were even higher. To keep palace affairs from disclosure, strict rules were laid down by the ruling house. As a result, few inside stories leaked to the outside world. Such stories, however, are of great significance in gaining a true understanding of a dynasty.

Fortunately, there have always been people who are curious and have no "respect for the secrets of the respectable." Through written records and by word of mouth they have provided us with a window through which to peep at the inside halls and chambers of the palace. We see scandals, evil deeds, struggles for power, desperate love affairs, the refined works of artists and scholars, or acts of revenge by heroic men and women against the despotic leaders. These scenes vividly reveal the hypocrisy and sincerity, beauty and ugliness, tears and joy, loyalty and betrayal of the times. The curtain has long since fallen on these scenes of tragedy, comedy, farce or serious drama. What remains for us to see is nothing more than the empty, silent halls that were once all tinsel and gilt. But through the written word, we can recreate these scenes from the past.

It is true that most of our tales have never found their way into authorized histories, but they nevertheless constitute an indispensable addition to such histories. Their value must not be ignored. We therefore present *Tales of the Qing Court*, which provide a glimpse of the often curious lives of some of the supreme rulers of the land. We hope they will stimulate an interest in one of the most important dynasties in Chinese history.

The book contains 100 tales which are independent of each other, but contain many common themes. These tales have their origin in unofficial histories, anecdotes, and popular legends. They cover a span of time from the mythical beginnings of the Manchus to the last emperor of the Qing Dynasty. The heroes and heroines of these tales are the Qing Emperors and their wives, concubines, children, other members of the imperial house, high ranking courtiers, or favourite attendants.

In the course of compiling this book I have consult a number of histories, anthologies of popular stories, and literary works, to whose authors I owe my sincere thanks.

Fu Hu

Contents

Legends of the Chinese Queue

When talking about braids, people tend to think of women's hair style. However, for a long period of time in Chinese history men also wore a single braid down their back. It was to foreigners a distinguishing feature of the Chinese. This impression has certainly been erased today. But who knows?

Why did Chinese men wear queues at all? The reason lies deep in Chinese history. Here is one story.

The Han nationality, which accounts for most of the Chinese population, traditionally wore long hair in ancient times. Their ancestors taught them that one's body including skin and hair all came from one's parents and so should be well protected from any damage. Doing otherwise would be considered unfilial and neither women nor men dared to cut so much as a lock of hair. Traditionally the Han male coiled his hair on top of his head and covered it with a cap. That tradition changed however when the Manchu nationality took power in China in 1644.

Hair style has been many changes, but is now an entirely private matter of taste. But the Manchu feudal rulers attached great importance to what people did with their hair. A man's forehead should be shaved to represent the crescent moon, while the remaining hair should be allowed to grow and braided into a queue at the back of the neck. Wherever the Manchu held sway, the people were forced to follow the Manchu hair style for men. In battles against the Ming Dynasty army of Han, the Manchu's first demand on ordering the Han soldiers to surrender was to shave their foreheads or they would be killed. The degenerate Ming army was no match for the domineering Manchu and soon collapsed. With unquestionable victory, the Manchu troops took power and established the Great Qing Dynasty.

The victorious Manchus intended to force all males in China to shave their foreheads and grow queues. However, out of their expectation, this policy brought strong opposition from the majority Han people and as the new state power was not strong enough and the north and south of the country remained divided, the Manchu rulers decided to postpone the policy and adopt a long term strategy. They gave in and declared that those surrendered Ming Dynasty officials who did not want the Manchu hair style could keep the Ming style and their traditional hats and gowns with long sleeves covering the hands. When the emperor held court, the Manchu officials stood on the right side and the Han on the left, each in their own hair style and costume. Though awkward the compromise helped to establish a short period of peaceful cooperation and harmony.

By the summer of 1645 a former Ming official by the name of Sun Zhixie had his forehead shaved and grew a queue in order to show his loyalty to the new Manchu rulers. When he changed over to the right side and stood on the side of Manchu officials at court, contrary to his expectation he was not welcomed by the Manchu officials and was pushed out of their ranks. And so the fake Manchu official had to return to his Han ranks. But they too pushed him out for posing as a Manchu. After the court session, humiliated and annoyed, Sun Zhixie submitted the following memorial to the throne: "Your Majesty, now that you have conquered the whole country, everything should be done in accordance with the new rules. It seems inappropriate to allow the Han to retain their hair style and go on wearing their traditional costume. Such would give the impression that Your Majesty was forced to yield to Han tradition and not vice versa. I sincerely hope the throne will soon reverse this edict."

The memorial naturally pleased the Manchu ruler and his court though they were surprised that a former Han official should make such a suggestion. Still, the imperial court in fact ordered all males to shave their foreheads and grow queues in Manchu style. The order read: "The emperor is the father of the people. Father and son should resemble each other in style and manner or they would seem alienated and thus harmful to the reign." The order also stipulated: "All male subjects in the capital and surrounding areas should have their foreheads shaved within ten days of the time this order was issued. Those in outlying areas of the country are required to do this within ten days of the arrival of the order. Those who obey are considered good subjects of the Qing Dynasty, while those who do not obey will be considered rebellious and subject to severe punishment." A popular saying among the people at that time was that to let your front hair grow would cause you to lose your head and to keep the head, you must shave the hair. Barbers suddenly became very powerful, going along with barbering equipment on shoulder poles inspecting male heads and forcing improper ones to shave. The barbers were empowered to behead anyone who dared to disobey on the spot. This head would be hung on the barber's pole as a warning to others. From that time barbers in China kept a pole at their stand, unlike the barber pole of the west. The episode resulted in queues for men becoming identification as subjects of Qing Dynasty.

Qing was China's last feudal dynasty, and the queues on the napes of Chinese males gradually disappeared following the victory of the 1911 Revolution led by Dr. Sun Yatsen. However, the successes and failures of the Qing Dynasty deserve in-depth study.

Most of us however, are not satisfied with reading the official history as the only means of understanding an epoch or historical figures and episodes. Perhaps we would like to be shown into a host's bedroom or even bathroom after being shown his lounge, kitchen and garden, the aim not being to probe into our host's privacy but to understand the family better.

And so I have written this *Tales of the Qing Court*. As most have been gleaned from handed-down tales, not all necessarily accord with episodes as recorded in official history books. The Qing Dynasty is now long gone, and what I have written is mostly hearsay about events in the Manchu court. Of course the tales may very well contain certain factual truth.

The Origins of the Manchu People

Long long ago there lived in heaven three fairy maidens who were sisters. The three girls led a very comfortable but lonely life in the Celestial Palace. One day the youngest of the three, Fu Kulun, said to her two elder sisters: "Today both our royal father and mother have gone to the Peach Festival. Why should we be left behind? Let's go out too."

"I agree, and how about you, eldest sister?" asked the second, Zeng Kulun.

"I agree, too," replied the eldest sister, En Kulun.

The three sisters thereupon dressed up and slipped out of the palace. They mounted the clouds and rode the mist, happy and excited at the beauty of what they saw.

Soon they discovered chains of snow-covered mountains beneath them, the snow so glistening that the girls could not so much as open their eyes. At the crest of the mountains lay a large lake, its blue water like a mirror. The sisters had never seen such a beautiful place and flew down one after another to enjoy it. They couldn't resist jumping into the water for a swim. It was such fun that they hoped to have another chance to visit the place.

"What's the name of the place and how can we find the lake when we come next time?" asked the second sister.

"Let's give it a name," the eldest sister said. "Look, what lofty white snow mountains! Let's call them Chang Bei Shan (Ever White Mountains). As for the lake, since we fairy sisters in heaven have been swimming here, let's just call it Tian Chi (Heavenly Pool). What do you think of that?"

The two younger sisters agreed and clapped their hands in excitement. "Superb!" they exclaimed. Since then the names Chang Bai Shan (Ever White Mountains) and Tian Chi (Heavenly Pool) have been handed down and are still used today.

Perhaps the swim in the lake made the youngest sister tired and hungry. She was about to look for something to eat when she suddenly saw a huge bird flying towards her. The shiny black bird held a red fruit in its beak. When flying above the girl's head, the bird uttered a sound and the fruit dropped onto the robe she had laid on the ground. The little sister ran to pick up the fruit. It smelled delicious. She tasted it gingerly at first and then swallowed it down, feeling quite heavy and warm afterwards. She came to feel love for the life in the human world, while everything in heaven seemed far away and inconsequential.

"Little sister, put on your robe. We must return to heaven," urged the eldest sister, awakening the little sister from her dreams. But now she had no desire to return to Celestial Palace.

The two elder sisters were astonished at this and reminded her that if she did not return home, the royal father would be angry.

"But my dear sisters, I now realize that my roots are here. This beautiful place can provide me with everything I need. And I don't care if my father is angry."

"But, what made you change your mind and want to stay here? You really surprise me," added the second sister.

The question put the young sister in an awkward

position and she hung her head in silence. Only after repeated interrogation did she whisper to her sisters that after swallowing the red fruit she had the feeling she was pregnant.

The two elder sisters were aghast at the news and realized that their little sister had no choice but to remain in the world of humans. But how could she survive by herself in those far-away mountains? They climbed to the top of a peak and saw beyond the dense forest, fields of wheat, sheep and pigs, and fish in the river. The elder sisters decided to take their younger sister to a field near the mountains. They descended and made a tree house for her to live in. After she was settled, the two elder sisters said a reluctant farewell to her.

In time the little sister gave birth to a son. Strangely enough, the child was very strong and could speak soon after birth. After a few years he was a robust and capable lad, very good at hunting and fishing. His mother gave him a Manchu name, Aisin Gioro Bukuli Yongshun and told him that he was sired by God and mandated to rule the troubled world.

His mother helped him to accomplish this mission as he matured. She told him that he should go downstream to a destination of his own. The mother then gave him a small boat and flew away.

Acting on his mother's instruction, the boy took the boat and drifted down the river to the designated place and there wove a willow twig and wormwood mat on which he sat on the river bank.

At that time there were three tribes fighting fiercely among themselves for the domination of the land. One day someone went to fetch water in the river and found the strange boy, Bukuli Yongshun, sitting on the river bank and returned to report this to his chiefs. The chiefs then went and found the strange but handsome young man. He was so clever and strong that the three tribes agreed to stop fighting and take the extraordinary young man as their leader. And so Bukuli Yongshun became the earliest ancestor of the Manchus, whose descendants were all good at hunting and fishing. The sheep, pigs and wheat his mother saw on the Chang Bai Shan (Ever White Mountains) became their means of subsistence for generation after generation.

Fishing and hunting perhaps contributed to the Manchu character of bravery and toughness, some say even mercilessness. Years later, when the tribes could no longer bear the ruthlessness of the descendants of Bukuli Yongshun, they rose in revolt and took brutal revenge.

In fact, the rebellion and others that followed left only one Manchu alive, and this one was pursued by dozens of mounted troops so that the fugitive, on hearing the uproar of his pursuers stopped and hid beside the road. Just then a magic bird swooped down and covered the boy with its huge wings. The mounted troops took the bird for an old log and passed by in their furious pursuit. The boy was thus spared and in time prospered. His descendants once again took power over the tribes and from that time on the Manchus highly respected the crow, for it was thought that it was a huge crow that saved their ancestor.

Stories of the Heroic General Nuerhachi

In the late 17th century a boy named Nuerhachi was born into one of the three main tribes of the Nuzhen nationality in Jianzhou province of northeast China. The eldest son of chieftain Dakeshi and his wife Xidaci was exceptionally strong and half again as tall as the others. As a child he walked about in huge leather boots. Xidaci died when he was ten and he was brought up by a stepmother named Nalashi. He often gathered pine nuts in the mountains and sold them in the city of Fushun. With little formal education, he was greatly influenced by the Chinese historical novels *Tales of the Three Kingdoms* and *Outlaws of the Marsh*, the former describing fierce and heroic battles among three ancient kingdoms, the latter peasant revolts and armed struggles. Thus taught, he chose the life of a soldier. As he grew up he was saddened by the Nuzhen tribes in China's northeast of killing for wealth and spheres of power, and this occurring even among brothers, friends and relatives. Nuerhachi lost his father in the tribal fighting, and when he reached the age of 24 he decided to bring his supporters together and take revenge on his killers. He first attacked the neighboring tribe of Nikan Wailan, launching a surprise attack on its capital city Tulun with a detachment of 13 armed men. They charged forward against the rain of arrows shot from above the city wall. Nuerhachi suddenly let out a mighty roar which struck the defending soldiers with panic so that his men were able to capture the city. They failed to seize Chieftain Nikan Wailan, however, who had fled to eastern Liaoning province. The frontier Ming Dynasty forces did not want to antagonize Nuerhachi and so handed Nikan Wailan over to Nuerhachi. Good relations were preserved between the imperial court and its vassal state. Nuerhachi had Nikan Wailan killed.

Nuerhachi thus conquered all the neighboring tribes within five to six years, going on to conquer other Nuzhen tribes. All these battles were colorful and legendary, involving a degree of mythology as in the instance of the troops of Yehe Hada who were reportedly defeated with the intervention of magical power.

Nine tribes then joined in a war against Nuerhachi, making concerted attacks with three converging columns. Nuerhachi responded by ordering his experienced general Wulikan to keep close watch on his enemy's movements. The general was leading a troop of mounted men eastward, when thousands of crows suddenly appeared before them, blocking their way over a mountain when the troops decided to retreat, the crows flew away. But when they turned to march on, the crows flew back again and blocked their way. Wulikan, puzzled, sent back a report to Nuerhachi, who ordered them to change their route. Wulikan accordingly led the troops in another direction and by evening they reached a riverside where they saw the fires of the enemy camp on the northern bank of the river. Wulikan sent a soldier in the middle of the night to report this news to Nuerhachi.

Nuerhachi was pleased at the news and said to his officers: "According to earlier information the Kingdom of Yehe would send troops to attack us. Now they have come at last."

He did not however believe that his enemy would cross the river by night. If he sent his troops ahead hurriedly by night, the enemy might be alerted, so he ordered his troops to rest well that night and start out early the next morning. Nuerhachi then himself fell into sound sleep. His wife, who was along with him, was worried about the attack and woke him up.

"The army of the nine states are approaching and you just sleep like a log. Are you scared or at a loss what to do?" she asked.

"What do you mean, scared?" explained Nuerhachi. "How could I sleep so soundly if I was scared? I have nothing to worry about because I haven't done anything wrong. I'm now fighting to unite the country and bring peace to the people in accordance with the will of heaven. The enemy troops should come to surrender instead of sending troops to attack me. God in heaven would not forgive them." He then fell asleep again.

Early next morning Nuerhachi called his troops together, prayed to heaven and then marched out. His troops, well rested, fought bravely against an exhausted army from nine different states. After only a few battles Nuerhachi defeated the 20,000 strong army, killing 4,000 and capturing 3,000 horses and over 1,000 suits of armor.

The victory over the army from nine states further consolidated Nuerhachi's force and his enlarged manor among the Nuzhen states of the Manchu. Nuerhachi's success aided the organizing of the Nuzhen states' forces in northeast China and prepared the way for unifying all Manchus.

A war hero, Nuerhachi led a very simple personal life. When he went hunting in the snow, he would roll up his robe in order to keep it from getting wet. His soldiers were often puzzled at his thrift. They once asked: "General, you have large territory and great power, why should you treasure such a trivial thing as a robe?"

The general said smilingly: "I treasure my robe not because I lack clothes, but because it represents man's labour. We have no right to waste. I hope all of you learn from this example."

Consequently, none of the officers and men in the Army of Eight Banners dared wear expensive clothes, or lead an extravagant life in any way.

Nuerhachi died at the age of 67. His eighth son the crown prince, Taiji succeeded to the throne and honoured his royal father as "Wise Emperor." Later he revered him as "Sacred Emperor" and finally as "Most Sacred and Benevolent Emperor."

An Emperor Shares His Power

When Nuerhachi died, his second son, Prince Dai Shan was expected to succeed to the highest position of Khan of the Manchu tribe in northeast China. Raised in a war-torn country, Dai Shan had become skilled with a bow and arrow as a child. Following his father, he had rendered outstanding service on both the northern and southern fronts. Sophisticated and tolerant, he was popular among members of the royal household and the high officials. Most of the royal court therefore agreed to support Dai Shan as heir to the throne.

However, a cousin by the name of Yuetuo Sahalian had a different opinion. He said to Dai Shan: "Brother, as an older prince, you are the rightful heir. What is more, you have made a great contribution during the war. In terms of all round civil and military ability, however, I would say that eighth brother Huangtaiji is a better candidate for the throne. What's your opinion?"

Prince Dai Shan pondered for a while and then nodded in agreement. At a meeting to discuss the succession, Dai Shan personally proposed that Eighth Prince Huangtaiji be the heir being a more competent and versatile person than himself. Those present realized Dai Shan's words were true and so a final decision was made.

Prince Huangtaiji proved to be a true hero. Once declared Khan, he led an army to unify the Nuzhen tribes in northeast China. During the war, his 14th brother Duoergun's troops succeeded in conquering the

Chahaer tribe.

Huangtaiji was told that the Chahaer chieftain's wife Sutai had brought an imperial seal with her and he dispatched his men to collect it. The seal was a national treasure, made of jade with two beautiful coiled dragons carved on its handle.

Huangtaiji was delighted by the seal, for it was the symbol of state power. Once in possession of this seal, he became more confident, believing that he had really been given the mandate of heaven to rule the country. Soon afterwards he designated himself emperor and changed the reign title from that of the Later Jin to the Great Qing.

Under the influence of his father, Huangtaiji had read many Chinese books since he was a child. He had a good knowledge of the history of the Liao, Jin and Yuan dynasties and enjoyed the popular novel *Tales of the Three Kingdoms*. He ordered that these books be translated into Manchu to enable the Manchu officials and the ordinary people to read them. Although he was influenced by Han culture, he was not as overbearing in his use of power as many of the Han emperors. He believed that since the throne had been offered to him by his brothers, he had no right to exercise supreme power alone. He decided to share power with his brothers, and ordered dragon chairs the same as his own be set up so that they might sit side by side with the emperor. As a result, Princes Dai Shan, Manguertai and a cousin named Amin sat next to the emperor during court sessions. This sharing of power continued for about five years.

On one occasion, Prince Manguertai drew a sword and threatened Huangtaiji. Some of the courtiers pointed out that it was therefore no longer appropriate for him to sit beside the emperor. Huangtaiji was also angered by his brother's sinister intentions, but nevertheless he said: "To stop this long-term practice of sharing power would lead to conjecture that I don't pay due respect to my brothers." Prince Dai Shan understood Huangtaiji's awkward position and suggested: "You are the emperor. During court sessions, you should sit in the middle facing south, and we should sit on each side facing east and west at the head of the courtiers and ministers." Huangtaiji agreed to this proposal and so ended the practice of sharing power with his brothers.

Although this unique practice was highly praised at the time, Huangtaiji's offspring had no intention of following his example. They resorted instead to fierce and bloody battles for the right to succeed to the throne.

Internal Strife Between the Princes

Greedy and ambitious, the fifth prince Manguertai refused to submit to his younger brother, Emperor Huangtaiji. He formed an alliance with Prince Degelei and made secret plans to overthrow Huangtaiji when the opportunity arose. Kneeling before a statue of the Buddha, they vowed not to betray their purpose under any circumstances.

One day, Manguertai persuaded his sister and sister-in-law Xiaonamu to invite Huangtaiji to a sumptuous banquet. During the banquet they tried to murder the emperor by poisoning his wine, but their plot was discovered and the conspirators were caught red-handed. Manguertai swore he had no part in their scheme, and declared that the banquet had been prepared by his son Gebilun. As a result, Gebilun was sentenced to death and his five brothers were banished as commoners.

Shortly after this incident, Manguertai died of a sudden illness. Years later Degelei also died. After the death of these two conspirators, Prince Shenlunji was in a state of suspense and decided to reveal the true story to the emperor. All the people involved in the conspiracy were eventually killed except Shenlunji.

Just as the curtain came down on this play, an even fiercer struggle began on the same stage.

After 17 years on the throne, Huangtaiji died at the age of 51. He died so unexpectedly that he had no time to appoint an heir, thus setting in motion a complicated series of events. Both the eldest prince

Haoge and the 14th prince Duoergun were in the prime of life, and each had his own powerful supporters and military forces.

As soon as Huangtaiji died, many courtiers and ministers gathered at Prince Haoge's mansion to discuss ways of ensuring his succession. Prince Duoergun, however, had an equal number of supporters. Prince Adali sided with Duoergun and vowed to devote his life to help him succeed to the throne. Prince Shuotuo sent messengers to inform Prince Duoergun that both the internal minister and the court general would support him, and urged Duoergun to seize the throne. In order to ensure their victory in the struggle, they also tried to win over Prince Dai Shan. Adali and Shuotuo told Dai Shan: "We've made up our minds to support Duoergun's claim to the throne and hope you'll side with us." With so many supporters, Duoergun was confident that he would win the battle.

However, all these secret schemes became known to the shrewd Empress Xiao Zhuang. The empress opposed both sides, planning to help her son Fu Lin win the throne.

She joined forces with Prince Dai Shan, and then frustrated Duoergun's plans by seducing him with her beauty. Aiming to defeat Duoergun, her first step was to have his powerful follower Adali arrested and strangled to death. Duoergun's real power was reduced when his title was changed to that of regent. Duoergun, however, did not give up his ambitions for the throne. He even declared publicly that he should be emperor and Fu Lin the prince.

When later Duoergun led an army to fight in northern China, he used the opportunity to expand his own power base, and bided his time to stage a comeback.

With the help of Empress Xiao Zhuang, Huangtaiji ascended the throne and established his capital in Beijing. By this time, Duoergun had accumulated greater power and became more arrogant. He proclaimed himself "uncle regent" and even "father regent." His words should have carried the weight of imperial edicts, but his dissipated life and notorious reputation embarrassed his supporters and enraged his opponents.

Years later, as Duoergun was on his way to attack a city which the Qing army had been unable to conquer for a long time, he died of a sudden illness. On hearing the news, his long-time opponents launched a surprise attack and killed his entire family. As a further punishment Duoergun's body was then burnt in public.

The Emperor and the Apple

Once upon a time, an old couple and their beautiful daughter lived on a boat on a large river. As a child the girl learnt how to catch fish from the river, dig for edible plants on land and take care of the household. By the age of 18, she was charming and as pretty as a flower.

One day, while washing clothes in the river, the girl suddenly noticed her own charming reflection in the water. The sight filled her with both joy and anxiety. As she continued to gaze at the flowing water, she saw leaves and flower petals drifting downstream. Suddenly, she also noticed a small ball floating towards her. As it came closer, the girl saw it was in fact a red apple, and since no one was around, she decided to take a bite. The apple was the most delicious the girl had ever tasted, and it filled her with a strange sense of excitement.

As time went by, the young girl's mother began to notice that her daughter had changed. The girl was less cheerful than before and often sat idly at the end of the boat gazing absent-mindedly into the flowing river.

Five months later, the girl's mother realized that her daughter was pregnant. One night, she decided to tell her husband of her discovery. He immediately flew into a rage, shouting: "What shame! Who is the scoundrel who seduced her?" "Don't make such a fuss," replied his wife. " You'd better think of a way out."

"What can I do? She'd better jump into the river and drown herself," the girl's father replied angrily.

"What a villain you are! She is our only daughter. Do you want to murder her? She's been living with us in this boat day and night. Do you have any evidence to prove that she has been living an immoral life?" retorted the mother.

The father was tongue-tied. As the couple could not think of a way to solve the problem, they let the matter take its own course.

Four months later, the girl gave birth to a shiny, fragrant red apple. As the apple rolled across the floor, it suddenly cracked open and out jumped a beautiful baby boy. The old couple were pleased to have a grandson, and took good care of him. However, when people asked where the baby had come from, they simply replied that he was their adopted grandchild.

At that time, the Manchu chieftain Huangtaiji was fighting the Ming army in the north and northeast of China. The small family on the boat, like many others, became refugees from the war, drifting from place to place to escape the calamity. One day, the family encountered a group of mounted troops in pursuit of the Ming army, and became separated from each other. Just as the young mother, with her baby in her arms, was wondering where to go, she suddenly came upon a heavy-set man on horseback leading a group of soldiers. The man was none other than the Khan of the Manchus.

"What a beautiful baby!" exclaimed Huangtaiji, who, although he had six children of his own, had never seen such a lovely child. He liked it so much that he began to envy the poor woman her good fortune. "Young lady, is this your son?" he asked, pointing at the baby.

"Yes, he is my son," she answered in terror.

"Good. But where are you going? Do you have a

safe place to live? If not, I'd like to adopt your son so that both you and the baby can live in my home. What do you think of the idea?"

The young lady did not know what to do, but not seeing any ill intention in his suggestion, and needing to provide a safe place for her baby, she decided to accept his offer. Huangtaiji then sent a group of soldiers to escort the mother and the son to Shenyang, the Manchu capital in northeastern China.

Empress Xiao Zhuang fell in love with the child immediately and devoted all her energy to raising her adopted son. Huangtaiji eventually returned home victorious and discussed giving the child a formal name with his wife. As the Khan tried hard to decide on a suitable name, the empress teased the child, saying: "My little honey, how lucky you are to have such an adopted father!" Huangtaiji suddenly inspired: "We'll call the child Fu Lin (good luck in Chinese)."

When Fu Lin was six years old his adopted father Huangtaiji died. The shrewd empress used all her resources to help her adopted son succeed to the throne. After many fierce battles in the royal court, Fu Lin was made emperor at the age of 13, adopting the reign title of Shun Zhi. He was the first Manchu ruler to establish his capital in Beijing. His first imperial edict commanded everyone to pay due respect to young ladies, an expression of his filial piety towards his young mother.

Emperor Shun Zhi and a Courtesan

General Hong Chengshou once led the Qing army to conquer the city of Nanjing in eastern China. After his victory, he discovered a rare beauty among the refugees. She was none other than the well-known singer Dong Xiaowan from the Qinhuai River area in Nanjing. General Hong wanted to take the girl as his concubine, but she flatly refused. Dong Xiaowan said that she was already married to a talented scholar by the name of Mao Xiang, but the couple had become separated as they fled the war and she was then captured by the Qing army.

The general was not too disappointed, but began to consider ways of using this beauty to his own advantage. Eventually, he decided to present her as a gift to the emperor himself, hoping to curry favour with the throne.

Having defeated the Ming army in the south, General Hong returned to Beijing with Dong Xiaowan. At a banquet to celebrate his victory, the general suggested that the girl should perform for their entertainment. Dong Xiaowan's elegant songs and dances delighted the audience and lit up the hall. Emperor Shun Zhi was startled, and stared at the beautiful dancing girl with unabashed delight. She was so elegant and charming that she seemed like a fairy maiden from heaven. General Hong, seeing what was on the emperor's mind, went over to him and whispered: "Your Majesty, she is the well-known artist Dong from Nanjing. I've brought her to Beijing especially for Your

Majesty." The emperor appeared not to notice the general's words and continued to gaze at the rare beauty. General Hong, forced to raise his voice to attract the emperor's attention, said: "Your Majesty, I have brought you the most charming artist Dong as a special gift." As if awakening from a dream, the emperor said: "Good. I'll give you an extra reward." General Hong was more delighted with the knowledge that the emperor would give him a reward other than with all his achievements in battle.

After the celebration banquet, Emperor Shun Zhi immediately held an audience with General Hong to find out more details about the girl. The emperor decided to keep her as one of his concubines, although this was forbidden according to the rules of the Qing court, which did not allow a Manchu emperor to take a Han woman as his concubine. Embarrassed, the emperor asked the general for advice. General Hong said complacently: "Your Majesty, please don't worry. I've already thought of a way out."

"What is it?" the emperor was eager to know.

"Your Majesty can first order Prince Donge to adopt the girl. As soon as she becomes a member of the royal family, she is entitled to be your imperial courtesan."

The emperor was overjoyed and asked the general to make the arrangements personally. It was arranged that Lady Dong should live in the beautiful and peaceful Lanxin Palace, attended by a trusted imperial maid.

Two days later, General Hong reported to the emperor that Dong Xiaowan had become Prince Donge's adopted daughter. Emperor Shun Zhi immediately issued an edict granting her the title of imperial courtesan and personally informed her of the news in Lanxin Palace. On hearing her fate, Lady Dong was overcome with fear, for she was a married woman, and would never betray her husband Mao Xiang.

Emperor Shun Zhi's personal life was unhappy. Soon after his father's death, his mother had married his uncle, Prince Duoergun. This marriage deeply humiliated and enraged him. He vented his anger on his wife who was a relative of Duoergun by banishing her not long after their marriage. This act of revenge, however, arosed a great deal of unfavourable comment and to some extent tarnished the emperor's reputation.

After the arrival of Lady Dong, the emperor changed a great deal, he no longer felt sad but confident and cheerful. He visited Lanxin Palace almost everyday to spend some time with Lady Dong. Dong Xiaowan, however, was depressed and cold towards him. She knew that the emperor was truly in love with her, but she felt compelled to tell him about her own life. With tears rolling down her cheeks, she said: "Your Majesty, it's most kind of you to grant me the title of imperial courtesan, but as a married woman I am not entitled to this honour." The emperor, misunderstanding her words said consolingly: "I don't mind whether you are married or not. What is important is that I truly love you." The emperor then tried to take her in his arms, which greatly frightened the lady. She hurriedly stepped back and said: "Your Majesty, please don't do that. As a married woman, I'll never betray my husband under any circumstances. I hope you will let me go so that I can be reunited with him." Greatly annoyed, the emperor retorted: "I am the emperor. Do you think I am no better than a poor scholar?"

"Your Majesty, I don't mean that, but my love for my husband is more precious than my life. True love cannot be won by power and wealth. If you force me to betray my husband, I'll die right now." To avoid this unhappy ending the emperor, deeply disappointed, ceased his demands. Hoping that Lady Dong would sooner or later change her mind, he sighed and left the palace.

In an attempt to win her heart, Emperor Shun Zhi sent Lady Dong many precious treasures. The lady, however, remained unmoved by his gifts. Her heart was heavy, and she had no desire to dress in fine clothes or make up her face. Instead she buried herself in her books, or gazed absent-mindedly through the window, often with tears rolling down her cheeks. One day the emperor ordered a eunuch to send her four pots of orchids. Dong Xiaowan was greatly pleased and asked the eunuch to extend her thanks to the emperor. Emperor Shun Zhi was rather puzzled by the lady's warm reaction, but presuming that she might at last have changed her mind, he hurried to Lanxin Palace to find out for himself.

Lady Dong welcomed the emperor warmly and again extended her thanks for the orchids. Surprised, the emperor said: "I have sent you many treasures, but you've never before expressed your gratitude. Why are the orchids so special?" Before the lady had time to reply, the emperor added triumphantly: "I know you'll change your mind in the end."

Lady Dong replied: "Your Majesty, my husband loved orchids more than any other flower. With the orchids in my room, I feel as though my husband and I were together. This is why I appreciated the orchids so much and extended my thanks to you."

Deeply disappointed the emperor pleaded: "Are you so hard-hearted that you remain completely unmoved by my true love?"

"Your Majesty, I will be faithful to my husband.

I've made up my mind that it is better to die than betray him," replied Lady Dong.

Deeply hurt the emperor said wryly: "Even with all the power and wealth of an emperor I cannot win a beauty's heart." He turned and said eagerly: "I really need you." Lady Dong was touched but replied: "I am very sorry, Your Majesty. If you truly love me, you must agree to my three conditions."

"What conditions?"

"Firstly, I want to have a Buddhist hall set up in Lanxin Palace so that I can pray and practice self-cultivation."

The emperor nodded in consent.

"Secondly, I will not involve myself in any state affairs."

The emperor nodded again.

"Thirdly, we will behave as man and wife in name only."

The emperor was reluctant to agree to the third condition. Sensing his hesitation, Lady Dong threatened: "If Your Majesty does not agree, I shall end my life at once."

The emperor therefore had no choice but to give his consent.

Although Dong Xiaowan accepted the title of imperial courtesan, she still pined for her husband day and night. Her husband Mao Xiang also sadly missed his wife. He wrote a letter to his uncle Qian Qianyi, who was a high official, asking him to help arrange a meeting with Dong Xiaowan in the palace. Minister Qian was sympathetic and asked a fellow townsman, an old eunuch, to work out a plan. Mao Xiang disguised as a eunuch was to follow the old eunuch into the palace. If the plot was discovered, then Mao Xiang would flee along a route already prepared in advance.

Three days later in the evening, the old eunuch took Mao Xiang to Lanxin Palace. He introduced the young man to an attendant and said: "Sir, I have something else to do. Please let this eunuch attend to the imperial courtesan in my place this evening." The old eunuch then hurried away.

Gazing through the window into the distance, Lady Dong suddenly heard familiar steps behind her. When she turned round, she was surprised to see a lowly eunuch, who looked very much like her husband. She thought it must be just an illusion, but as she looked more closely, she realized that it was indeed her dear Mao Xiang. She was almost about to cry out with joy, when her husband stopped her pointing out the attendant watching at the gate. Lady Dong hurriedly dispatched the old eunuch for a pot of flowers. As he departed on his errand, the long separated couple threw themselves into each other's arms weeping bitterly. As is always the case, time slipped by too quickly as the lovers enjoyed their happy reunion. The moon soon rose high in the sky, and the lovers knew that they must part. Unable to detain him any longer, Lady Dong assured him: "I am so happy that we were reunited tonight. We have shared an unforgettable moment. Don't be sad. I will be faithful to you forever. Wait until I can flee this miserable place."

Mao Xiang nodded and comforted her by saying: "I never doubt your loyalty. I will also remain faithful to you. Let's hope for a true reunion in the near future."

As the couple were exchanging their vows of love, the door of their room suddenly burst open. The empress dowager and the empress, who had long haboured great hatred for this imperial courtesan of Han nationality, forced their way in and shouted: "Have them arrested!"

"Wait!" Lady Dong shouted, threatening them with a candlestick. As the group stepped back, the lady urged her husband to flee.

Mao Xiang managed to escape, but the empress dowager then tried to force Lady Dong to confess her guilt. Lady Dong, however, resolutely denied everything and refused to say anything at all about the man who had fled. Flying into a rage, the empress dowager threw a piece of white silk to Dong Xiaowan, ordering her to commit suicide at once.

Lady Dong calmly stood on a chair, and throwing one end of the silk over a beam, formed a noose for her neck. Even at the last moment, she did not forget to say goodbye to her husband. With tears in her eyes, she said: "Dear Mao Xiang, I wish you a long life. I am leaving now." So saying, she kicked over the chair and hung herself.

Watching this awful spectacle, some of the attendants screamed in terror or wept sadly. The empress dowager was annoyed and shouted: "What are you weeping for?" She then swept angrily from the room

Shocked at the terrible news, Emperor Shun Zhi rushed to Lanxin Palace but found that Lady Dong was already dead. The emperor cried from his heart for his lover's miserable fate.

Deeply grieved, the emperor helped close the lady's eyes and straigtened her clothes as his last comfort to his beloved. He then ordered that she should be buried in a funeral ceremony befitting her station as an imperial courtesan. "What a cold-blooded world!" he exclaimed sorrowfully as tears rolled down his cheeks.

A Disillusioned Emperor Turns a Monk

Once, as he was returning from Lanxin Palace, Emperor Shun Zhi suddenly realized that his life had become meaningless. He could no longer find anything worth-while to believe in. His beloved mother had betrayed his father soon after his death. The most sacred imperial power was in tatters and being manipulated by powerful courtiers and ministers to their own selfish ends. His great love, Lady Dong, had been forced to commit suicide, and the immaculately dressed high officials, although preaching justice and virtue in public were in fact hypocritical and ruthless. To the emperor, the world seemed an evil, detestable place.

Filled with grief and indignation, the emperor went to his study and wrote the following lines:

What is the use of having supreme power and wealth,
If even the emperor cannot save a lady from a miserable fate.
In grief at her death, the lady's palace has become a desolate tomb.
A monk in the Western Hills fares better than this forlorn emperor.

Emperor Shun Zhi also wrote an edict declaring: "My third son Xuan Ye is heir to my throne." Putting his brush aside on the table, the emperor told the eunuchs and guards at the gate: "I have nothing for you this evening. You may leave immediately."

Early next morning, the courtiers, ministers and generals waited outside the Qian Qing Hall to attend the usual court session. Long past his usual time of arrival, the emperor had still not made an appearance. A leading general, Hong Chengshou, believing that something unusual must have happened, whispered to a group of courtiers, he then led a number of high officials to report to the empress dowager. On hearing the news, the empress dowager and the empress, accompanied by a group of high officials and imperial maids, went straight to the Qian Qing Hall. The empress dowager ordered a eunuch to open the door, but there was no sign of the emperor. In the bedroom, the empress dowager noticed that the quilts were in place, and the bed had obviously not been slept in.

"Here is a poem by the emperor!" cried the empress, picking up a sheet of paper from the desk and handing it to the empress dowager. The empress dowager read the poem, and with tears rolling down her cheeks, she passed it to the others in the room.

To their great surprise, the high officials learnt from the poem that His Majesty had made up his mind to abdicate the throne and become a monk. Panic-stricken, no one knew what to do. The experienced empress dowager, however, said calmly: "His Majesty has gone. You should try your best to find him."

"It seems from the poem as if His Majesty must be in a temple in the Western Hills," said the empress sadly. After carefully studying the poem for themselves, the officials all agreed with her. The empress dowager then ordered them to form two groups, one to go to the Western Hills in Beijing, the other to the Western Hills in Shanxi province. In the meantime, eight years old Prince Xuan Ye ascended the throne, according to the edict written by Emperor Shun Zhi.

Adopting the reign title of Kang Xi, he was the second emperor to rule since the Manchus assumed power.

As for Emperor Shun Zhi, he had disguised himself as a commoner and left the palace that same night. He entered Honglian Temple in the Western Hills outside Beijing, and told the abbot not to mention his existence to anyone. His only desire was to concentrate on self-cultivation according to the Buddhist doctrine. In order to abandon worldly affairs, the emperor began to eat wild fruits and drink spring water. He also selected a large stone which he used for exercising. He carried the stone from the foot of the mountain to the top, rolled it down, then carried it again to the top. He repeated this several times each day. After a long time, the large stone became a small round pebble, which was later called "the emperor's stone ball." This simple life and rigorous exercise strengthened his body and his mind. He later travelled to other parts of the country to enjoy the magnificent mountains and rivers, and lived for a long time on Wutai Mountain in Shanxi province. As an old man, he returned to the Western Hills in Beijing and later died in Bailian Temple, a few miles from Honglian Temple. It is said that at the time of his death the emperor lay on the ground with his head pointing to the southeast in the direction of the Forbidden City in Beijing.

A Search in the Mountains

As a child, Emperor Kang Xi was aware that his mother was unhappy, and sometimes even wept with sorrow when she was alone. He believed that the empress dowager was pining for his father, the former emperor, and Emperor Kang Xi himself often thought of him. When he grew up, he said to his mother one day: "Dear mother, I know you are lonely and always thinking of my father. If you can tell me where he's gone, I would like to look for him myself."

The empress dowager said: "I don't know exactly where he's gone, but your father was fond of travelling through forests and mountains and along large rivers. I often heard that he was particularly interested in the landscape and historical relics of the San Men Gorges. He might be in that part of the country."

Emperor Kang Xi made arrangements for state affairs to be managed in his absence, dressed himself as a scholar and set off for the San Men Gorges.

Kang Xi was amazed by the magnificent mountain scenery and torrential rivers. The area's natural beauty was so different from the imperial gardens, and he came to realize why his father was so fascinated with the mountains, forests and rivers. The emperor found himself lodgings, and then set off in search of his royal father.

One day, Kang Xi was wandering in the mountains when he heard the sound of horses galloping in the wild. It was only the wind in the forest, but it was growing dark and he was anxious to return to his lodgings. On the way back, however, he lost his way. Suddenly he came upon a mat and three sticks under a tree. The emperor was very tired, and sat on the mat to take a short rest. Looking up at the bright stars in the evening sky, Kang Xi soon fell asleep. The next day, he set out again to look for his father, but could find no trace of him. The emperor began to realize that it would be no easy task to find his father, and knew that he would have to return to the imperial palace to attend state affairs.

When Emperor Kang Xi returned home, he reported to his mother that he had failed in his mission. The empress dowager asked: "Did you find anything unusual?"

"Yes. One evening I lost my way in the mountains and saw a mat and three sticks under a tree. I slept on the mat over night."

The empress dowager thought for a while and then nodded: "I understand. Your royal father was there."

"How do you know?"

"I know because the Chinese characters for a mat and three sticks are the same as those for your father's name."

When the emperor realized what had happened, he regretted that he had not thought of it on the spot. What a pity to lose such a chance!

"Empress dowager, now that I know my father's whereabouts, I would like to look for him a second time. Even if I can't find him, I shall bring back his mat and three sticks to remind us of him."

Emperor Kang Xi set out a second time for the San Men Gorges. He went straight to the place where he had found the mat and the three sticks, but they were gone. With a sad heart, he rested for a while and then went on to search the neighboring mountains. The scenery of the next mountain seemed even more magnificent than the last and there were many birds singing in the dense forest. Emperor Kang Xi knew that his father must be much happier living in such a beautiful place than as emperor in the Forbidden City.

After his previous lesson, the emperor searched much more carefully for his father. He looked throughout the day but could find no trace of him. As the sun sank in the west and the mountains were enveloped in the glow of its rays, the whole of nature seemed sleepy, as if also tired after a hard day's work.

What could he do? As Kang Xi climbed higher, he saw dim lights in the forest half way up the opposite mountainside. He was overjoyed, like an exhausted swimmer at last catching sight of land. The emperor hurried towards the lights. When he reached them, he found a temple with *The Temple of Pa Sa* inscribed in four large characters on the front gate. The temple was empty except for a bed and a table. "This has nothing to do with my father," the emperor thought. Completely exhausted, he lay on the bed and was soon asleep. At about midnight, Emperor Kang Xi was awakened by a knock at the door. He rose to open it and found an old monk standing outside.

The monk seemed glad to see such a young man spending the night in his temple. The emperor asked him his name and where he came from. "My name is Pa Sa," the old monk replied, "and I am from the northern part of the mountain. And where are you from, sir?"

"From Beijing, the capital of the country."

"How are the crops in Beijing this year?"

"Very good. We have had good weather and a bumper harvest."

After a short pause, the old monk said: "You can

sleep here. I have another room." Emperor Kang Xi, thanking him repeatedly, said good night and was soon sound asleep.

After several days, the emperor had still not found any evidence of his lost father, and once again returned to the palace empty handed.

When she heard the emperor's story of his meeting with the old monk in the temple, the empress dowager sighed sadly and tears rolled down her cheeks. Puzzled, her son asked what had made his mother so sad.

The empress dowager said with a sob: "That old monk is your father, but you didn't recognize him even face to face. Isn't that sad?"

Even more puzzled the emperor asked: "How do you know?" The empress dowager replied: "The two characters pa sa mean father in the Manchu language. When he asked about the weather, he was referring to my childhood name, which no one knows except your father."

"Is this true? How stupid I was." The emperor fell into a chair and began beating his head with his fist. "I will go and look for my father a third time," he cried.

"Forget about it, my son!" said the empress dowager. "Your father has seen your filial piety twice. It seems he is determined to go his own way. Please don't bother him any more. Even if you go a third time, he would not choose to recognize you."

Emperor Kang Xi was persuaded to accept his mother's advice and gave up the idea of a third journey. Instead, he had the temple in the mountains rebuilt into a palace in honour of his father.

The Young Emperor Subdues His State Ministers

Emperor Kang Xi ascended the throne at the age of eight. His great-grand mother and the empress dowager, after consultation with important courtiers, appointed four state ministers, Suoni, Ebilong, Sukeshaha and Aobai, as advisors to the emperor on state affairs.

Aobai was an ambitious politician. He organized a secret sect to help him expand his own power in the hope of superseding the emperor when the time was ripe. His first step was to eliminate the other three ministers, beginning with Sukeshaha.

The Qing Dynasty had a military-administration system known as the Eight Banners. Aobai belonged to the deputy yellow banner, while Sukeshaha was a member of the pure white banner, which owned better land than that of the deputy yellow banner. In order to occupy fertile land and expand his territory, Aobai demanded that the pure white banner's land, which he claimed had originally belonged to the deputy yellow banner, be redistributed. Prime minister Sunahai, governor of Henan, Shandong and Shanxi provinces, Zhu Changzha and Wang Denglian, provincial military governor of Hebei province were opposed to Aobai's demands. Emperor Kang Xi held an audience with his four state ministers to discuss the matter.

During the discussions, Aobai fabricated charges against the other three ministers, accusing them of cheating the throne. He simply stated that "these three bad people should be killed for their unpardonable crime of defying the emperor."

Sukeshaha stood firm against Aobai, but the other two ministers gave way before his authority. Emperor Kang Xi disagreed with Aobai, but before he could express his opinion, Aobai seized the Emperor's brush and wrote an "imperial edict" ordering the death of all three ministers.

Confronted by the powerful Aobai, Sukeshaha, helpless and isolated, begged the emperor to let him resign and serve as a humble guard in the imperial tombs. Aobai disagreed, charging Sukeshaha with harboring evil designs and seeking only extricate himself from punishment. He demanded that the emperor kill Sukeshaha and his whole family at once. Emperor Kang Xi was shocked and asked Aobai: "Why do you hate Sukeshaha so much that you want to kill his whole family?" Aobai retorted: "It's for Your Majesty's sake. If he is not killed, other high officials and generals will follow his example in defying and even rising against you."

Emperor Kang Xi was furious at the charge and refuted it by saying: "I know very well who will rise against me. Sukeshaha is not that kind of man."

Aobai was so audacious that he even threatened to strike the emperor because of his disapproval. Emperor Kang Xi was frightened, but none the less argued: "Even if he should be punished, he does not deserve such a severe punishment."

Aobai replied: "Then have him hanged." Sukeshaha and his family were thus sent to their death by Aobai. From that time on Aobai's true nature became more and more evident.

Emperor Kang Xi came to realize that Aobai was a serious threat and should be got rid of without delay.

However, Aobai's henchmen were strategically placcd at court, and reported all the emperor's actions back to him. To allay Aobai's suspicions, Emperor Kang Xi recruited 100 teenagers from the Eight Banners to practice "Buku," (a kind of Manchu wrestling game) with him. These teenagers in fact acted as the emperor's bodyguards, protecting him both day and night. They practiced hard and became very skilled in martial arts.

Before long, news spread that Aobai had suddenly been taken ill and in fact was planning to launch a coup d'etat and kill the emperor. Emperor Kang Xi and his imperial bodyguards visited Aobai's home to enquire about his health. They found Aobai looking flustered and obviously only pretending to be ill. The resouceful emperor urged his guards to examine the patient. When one of the guards lifted the patient's quilt, he saw the glint of a dagger underneath. Caught red-handed, Aobai turned pale with fright. But Emperor Kang Xi said calmly: "It is an old Manchu custom to carry a sword day and night, there is nothing strange in this." Aobai felt somewhat relieved, not realizing that the emperor was now fully aware of his underhand schemes. Kang Xi then gathered together several young men from his martial arts group to arrest Aobai.

One day, the emperor invited Aobai to have a drink at the palace. Since the dagger incident, Aobai had been upset and feared that the emperor would take steps to arrest him. When he received the emperor's invitation, Aobai felt nervous and wondered if there would be any danger. Believing that the emperor had only a group of youngsters at his side and knowing his own skill in martial arts, Aobai decided he had nothing to fear. He went straight to the palace without hesitation. When he arrived at the imperial garden, he saw the emperor busy practicing martial arts with his young companions. Kang Xi barely noticed Aobai which enraged the minister. "What can I do for you, Your Majesty?" he shouted angrily.

Emperor Kang Xi turned and replied calmly: "I'd like to have a drink with you." He then ordered the young palace guards to offer Aobai a seat at the table. A guard gave him a chair, and without a word of thanks, Aobai lifted his robe and sat down. Instead of sitting on the chair however, he found himself flying flat on the ground, for one of the legs of the chair had been cut off in advance. According to the rules of the Qing court, a breach of etiquette by a minister in front of the emperor was a crime. Seeing Aobai on the ground Emperor Kang Xi cried: "You detestable fool, I offered you a seat, how dare you take such liberties before me!" "Come guards, arrest him!"

A group of young palace guards immediately rushed in and tied up Aobai hand and foot. "I didn't intentionally offend Your Majesty," the minister blustered. "Please pardon me."

"Intentionally?" Emperor Kang Xi replied mockingly."You savagely killed three ministers and hanged one of the founding fathers of the Great Qing Dynasty. Do you mean that all these actions were unintentional? What a traitorous criminal you are!"

Aobai again tried to deny his guilt but the emperor waved his hand and the guards dragged him off to prison. Aobai was tried and convicted of 13 crimes. He was sentenced to death, and subsequently all his followers were also punished.

The young palace guards who helped to arrest Aobai were later appointed to high official posts by the emperor. One of them, a man of great strength by the name of Han Dali, was even made a prince.

A Master of Calligraphy and Painting

Emperor Kang Xi was a man of great talent and bold vision. During his reign of 61 years, he made outstanding achievements in both civil and military affairs. The emperor was an avid reader, and skilled at Chinese calligraphy, painting and classical poetry.

In his leisure time, the emperor often practiced writing characters or drawing. When in a good mood, he would sometimes give his calligraphy or paintings to his favourite officials. A Manchu official by the name of Tan Dai was well versed in landscape painting. The emperor often invited him to the palace to discuss the painting, and eventually granted him the title of "painting master". As well as giving his calligraphy to those knowledgable about art and literature, he also rewarded officials of good moral character. During an inspection tour of Jiangsu province, Kang Xi met a local member of the gentry named Wang Wan. Wang Wan was an honest scholar highly respected in the village, and the emperor gave him a scroll in honour of his good deeds. More and more people came to seek the emperor's calligraphy as a symbol of honour. On this second inspection tour to Jiangsu province, the emperor was impressed by the devotion of Song Mou, the provincial military governor. The emperor decided to issue an imperial edict as a reward for his dedication. General Song Mou said to the emperor: "In the Song Dynasty, Emperor Xiao Zhong honoured a state minister by the name of Fan Chengda by giving him two Chinese characters 'Stone Lake' written in the emperor's own hand. As a result, the minister was able to call himself a lay Buddhist by the Stone Lake. I can't compare myself to Fan Chengda in terms of achievement, but I am much luckier than he, for we are now under the reign of a greater and wiser emperor. Your humble servant has opened a shop on the west hillside and sincerely implores Your Majesty to give the shop a scroll of your calligraphy."

The emperor laughed at this round about response, and agreed to give a scroll. He wrote two Chinese characters "West Hillside" to serve as a name for the shop. Thereafter many other officials followed Song Mou's example in seeking samples of the emperor's hand writing, either for their own glory or simply to show off.

“The Most Delicious Restaurant”

Emperor Kang Xi often disguised himself as a commoner to make private journeys in the capital. One day he arrived at a restaurant outside Fuchengmen Gate in the west of Beijing. “Honey Hall Restaurant” was a two storey building with private rooms upstairs reserved for rich and influential customers. Common folk could only eat on the ground floor. The emperor went upstairs and ordered food and a bottle of wine.

After a while, a group of young men, carrying caged birds and crickets and making a great deal of noise, swaggered into the restaurant. They were the sons of rich and powerful families belonging to the Manchu Eight Banners. One of them said his bird, which could catch money thrown into the air, was worth 50 taels of silver in the market. Another boasted that his cricket was the best and he would never sell even if offered ten taels of silver. The group ordered a great deal of expensive food and wine, and boasted and flattered each other in an outrageous manner.

The behaviour of these young people shocked the emperor. He remembered how their Manchu forefathers had fought bravely to win power, but now their offspring were leading decadent lives, and spending money without restraint. If the younger genenration behaved in this manner, there was no hope for the Manchu Dynasty. But what can we do about it? The emperor asked himself.

With a heavy heart, the emperor went downstairs and found the restaurant full of customers, most of them labourers in shabby clothes. They had bought steamed stuffed buns and were eating wherever they could find a space. The emperor couldn't understand why business on the ground floor was so good and asked someone the reason. The carter answered: "Honey Hall Restaurant is famous for its stuffed buns, because they are large, tasty and cheaper than other restaurants.' We workers all come here for the food."

The emperor then sought out the owner of the shop: "You sell steamed buns very cheaply, what about your profit?"

The shopkeeper sized up his customer, and feeling that he was an honest man, told him the truth. The owner said he used leftovers from the private rooms upstairs to stuff the steamed buns. In this way he could sell the buns cheaply and still make a profit. The labourers liked his buns and the restaurant had a good reputation. The emperor was impressed by the shopkeeper's business sense.

Next day, the Honey Hall Restaurant received a scroll in the emperor's handwriting from the imperial court, inscribed with the words "Most Delicious Restaurant". With great excitement, the shopkeeper recalled his customer of the previous evening. He was none other than the emperor himself! He hurriedly made the imperial inscription into a gold-lettered signboard, and the restaurant's business soon became even more brisk.

At the end of the year, Emperor Kang Xi wrote a scroll for those profligate sons of the Manchu Eight Banners. It read: "A bowl of rice or gruel comes from arduous labour; Cloth and clothing are made through hard work."

Emperor Kang Xi wanted to change the wasteful and extravagant way of life common in high society, but his efforts proved to be of little use. The Manchu ruling class and their offspring had been indulging in such an extravagant way of life for so long that they were unable to change.

Magic Sharpshooter

Most of the Manchu nationality were good horsemen as well as crack shots. This was one reason why they could defeat the Ming Dynasty army and take over the reign in central China. Emperor Kang Xi once said his forefathers had taken power on horseback. The emperor himself was expert in shooting and so was nicknamed the "magic sharpshooter." In his later years he liked to boast to his close senior officials that he had killed 135 tigers, 20 bears, 25 panthers, 10 lynxes and monkeys, 14 musk deer, 90 wolves, 132 wild boars and hundreds of other deer with his fowling piece and bow and arrow. He had even shot 316 hares in a single day, his highest hunting record.

Influenced by the emperor, most senior officials followed suit and went in for riding and shooting. Whenever the emperor went shooting there were a large number of ministers and generals accompanying, with fanfare and grand atmosphere.

One autumn, Emperor Kang Xi went hunting in Chengde, a summer resort in northern Hebei province. There were a number of spacious hunting grounds outside Chengde city with an area of 400 square kilometers. The emperor naturally took the lead galloping across the vast plain and soon leaving his senior ministers Jiang Chenmu and Chen Dianyong far behind. He looked around and proudly asked: "Where is minister Chen?"

"The minister couldn't catch up with Your Majesty," answered one of the emperor's bodyguards.

"Why?"

"Because he hasn't a good horse."

"Give him a good horse," ordered the emperor.

Minister Chen then changed his horse and tried his best to catch up with the emperor. After a while, Emperor Kang Xi asked Chen: "Can you tell the difference between a good horse and a bad one?"

"I know a little about horses," answered Minister Chen. "It's said a good horse usually has a strong back and small hoofs so it can keep steady while galloping."

The emperor nodded in agreement and asked another question: "Are you a good horseman?"

"I learned how to ride during my childhood, but I am no match for other senior ministers of the Eight Banners."

"Very well," said the emperor, satisfied.

During the hunt the emperor would sally forth over the grasslands four to five times a day, and sometimes he went into very rough places. But he never appeared tired. In the evening he would sit by a lamp reading official papers and dictating comments for the ministers to write on the documents.

In 1683, on an inspection tour of the western part of the Qing empire, the emperor encountered a tiger running in the forest not far from his camp. He immediately took up his bow and killed the tiger with only one arrow. The local people were relieved that the emperor had rid them of a danger. They designated the place as The Emperor's Tiger Killing Site in commemoration.

Investigations of a Mosque

In the Qing Dynasty, a supervisory commission was set up to keep watch on anti-Qing comments and actions by both other officials or common people. Its members were called imperial supervisors whose duty it was to search out such dissidents and secretly report them to the emperor.

One such imperial supervisor by the name of Wang, an ignorant but power-hungry person, was intent on catching dissidents in the hope of winning promotion for himself and making his fortune.

One day this official visited Niujie (Ox Street), an area in south Beijing exclusively inhabited by the Hui nationality. On seeing groups of people wearing white caps on their way to a large hall he thought such a crowd would either make trouble or even plot rebellion. He considered his chance to seize dissidents had come. "If I crack this criminal case, I'll be rewarded and promoted," he thought, beside himself with joy. Still, he knew such an important matter required evidence. He then approached the large hall and tried to get in but was stopped by the gatekeeper, for only people with white caps were allowed to enter. He loitered about for a while and finally asked a pedlar: "Do you know what those people in white caps are doing over there?"

"They're worshipping their god," answered the pedlar.

"God? Who is their god?"

"Mu. His name is Mu."

"Isn't he the reigning emperor himself?"

The pedlar looked at him with disdain and replied: "They never worship the reigning emperor!"

The official was so surprised that he couldn't believe his own ears. An area in Beijing under the emperor's own eyes should harbour people daring to worship a person called Mu as their god and not the reigning Emperor Kang Xi? Here was undoubtedly open rebellion. He turned to the pedlar and accused: "You know the truth and didn't report?" "Report what?" retorted the pedlar. "It's none of your business! Don't poke your nose into other people's business!"

"Other people's business indeed! Why, this is open rebellion!"

"Hush, don't talk nonsense! If they hear what you said, they would have your head cut off. They are united as one, and they will fight to the finish anyone who dares to insult them."

The imperial supervisor was convinced that those white-hatted people gathering together were out for rebellion. He hurried back to camp and wrote a memorial to Emperor Kang Xi as follows:

"A large number of people are gathering in Niujie for rebellion. They want to support a rebellious chief called Mu as their true god and will fight to the death against the Great Qing Dynasty. All the above is true as I have seen with my own eyes. Please send troops at once to wipe them out. This is urgent!"

Emperor Kang Xi was astonished to learn of this threat and called in his ministers and generals to discuss the matter. In an attempt to show their loyalty to the throne the ministers and generals expressed their bitter indignation and urged the emperor to send troops at once to besiege Nuijie and wipe out the rebels.

Emperor Kang Xi did not however take any hasty

action, but raised some questions. He asked: "Most of you live in town. Have you discovered anything abnormal recently in the area of Niujie?"

The ministers and generals looked at each other nonplussed, unable to answer the question. They were afraid if they gave a true answer they would be accused of failing to report what they had seen. If they said they saw nothing unusual they feared that they would be accused of covering up a rebellion if there really was a rebellion. The officials were all agape and tongue-tied. Emperor Kang Xi was annoyed and murmured "an utterly worthless bunch!"

Emperor Kang Xi finally decided to send some plainclothes guards to see what was going on, while the emperor himself put on a small white cap and street clothes to make a private investigation. Following behind a group of worshippers, Emperor Kang Xi entered the courtyard of the large mosque. Noticing that everyone entering the mosque took off their shoes, the emperor followed suit. When others knelt down, he did the same. When several people in long gowns and white turbans entered the mosque, Emperor Kang Xi guessed the chief called Mu must be among them. He opened his eyes wide. Next an old man with a beard made a speech and the others repeated aloud after him. Though the emperor couldn't understand what they said he imagined that these people were praying to a kind of god. The emperor was thoroughgoing and wanted to get all the facts straight. He then asked a moslem: "Sir, I couldn't hear clearly what the old man said just now. Would you please tell me what it was?" The fellow looked at him and said: "That was an imam. What he repeated was Allah Mohammed's teaching for the Moslems."

On returning to the palace the emperor ordered

some scholars to translate the Koran, in which he could find no words instigating rebellion. Then the emperor realized that the gathering the imperial supervisor reported was the Moslem religious rites and had nothing to do with rebellion.

The next day when the emperor held court he told his officals of his own investigation. Then he reprimanded the supervisor: "A high official, so ignorant as to give such false information as could have caused me to make a big mistake, should be removed from office and punished."

"Your Majesty, but..." the supervisor begged to explain.

"Get out!" retorted the irate emperor.

The supervisor's dream of getting a promotion thus ended satirically in punishment.

In order to help other officials to learn from this lesson, Emperor Kang Xi later issued an order: "Any official who deliberately gives false information and slanders minority national gatherings for personal ambition will be subject to the death penalty for slander."

Grain Seeds a Thousand Years Old

The rice produced in Yongji county, Jilin province was a special type well-known in China. It was snow white and very delicious in taste. The rice was however not a native product, and had a long history with many legends.

When Emperor Kang Xi made his second investigation tour to the province of Jilin, he was invited for a boat trip on the Songhua River by the local general Pahai. That day there were many racing boats on the river and among them the emperor caught sight of an exquisitely decorated large boat carrying a table of cakes, fruits and burning incense sticks.

"What is that boat for?" asked the emperor pointing at it.

General Pahai hurriedly knelt down and reported: "They are holding a ceremony of worship, Your Majesty."

"Worship what?"

"Worship the river demons."

The emperor frowned and demanded: "Where are the river demons?"

"Your Majesty, it's a long story. Allow me to tell it to you. Some time ago when my soldiers were felling some trees by the riverside, they dug up a stone jar which emitted bright light at night. Surprised, the soldiers reported and presented it to me. I then asked a monk to pray to the heavenly god for instruction. The god said it was a magic jar in which he had 500 river demons in custody. After 81 days in the jar, the river demons would no longer be able to make trouble. Now the people on the big boat are holding a ceremony of worship before releasing the demons."

"I see," said the emperor. But he didn't believe such superstitious tales, for the emperor had some knowledge of science. He then ordered: "Since it is a magic jar, I'd like to have a look at it with my own eyes. Send the jar to my palace camp."

General Pahai took the jar with reverence to the palace as ordered. The emperor stroked the jar gently and asked: "General, do you dare open it?"

In panic, General Pahai knelt down and pleaded: "Your Majesty! I dare not run such risks under any circumstances. In case the demons jumped out and hurt Your Majesty, I could not bear the responsibility, even though I were punished by death."

"Don't worry. As I am the son of heaven, no demons can hurt me."

"What if the demons hurt the common people?"

"General, didn't you request me to suppress the demons?"

"Then I'll ask the monk to open the jar."

"No. I'll open it myself," replied the emperor, and he set about opening the stone jar, causing panic among those standing by.

The emperor opened the jar and turned it upside down. Some fine grain poured forth. "What good grain it is!" cried the onlookers. General Pahai had closed his eyes in fear, but when he heard the sound of the grain he looked at it and felt great relief.

Emperor Kang Xi examined the stone jar closely and found the Chinese characters carved on it: "Grain of the Great Tang Dynasty."

"The Great Tang Dynasty! That was almost a thousand years ago!" Emperor Kang Xi marvelled. He then turned to General Pahai and asked: "General, where are your river demons?"

General Pahai turned pale in panic and prostrated himself before the emperor pleading for mercy: "I deserve to die for my crime, but please have mercy considering my old age."

"Rise!" the emperor ordered the general and turned to the people gathered round: "My subjects, I consider this a happy event, for heaven has sent us this precious grain for the benefit of our people. Now I hand over this grain for seed to be cultivated in your most fertile fields. In future both you and the army should have rich harvests of fine rice."

Ever since the reign of Emperor Kang Xi rice from the thousand-year-old grain seed has been sown not only in Jilin province but the whole of northeast China through the generations.

Tea Servant and the Magistrate

A subsidiary palace had been specially built for Emperor Kang Xi beside Baiyangdian Lake. It was in fact an elegant structure with a large balcony overlooking the lake. Its yellow bricks, green tiles, colourful painted corridor and pavilion reflected in the lake presented a picture of a veritable fairyland. Emperor Kang Xi would visit this palace once in summer, when he would watch water sports and enjoy the lake fish and shrimps. In winter he loved watching ice hockey.

On the night of the Lantern Festival (15th of the first lunar month) in 1679, the emperor came to watch fireworks. He sat on the balcony with a table of cakes, fruits and other delicacies before him as he enjoyed the display of fireworks and also entertainment by lovely singers and dancers.

Amid the festive atmosphere the emperor suddenly heard some sad cries and sent for the magistrate to inquire into their source. Magistrate Liu was a scholar who had climbed to officialdom by fawning on his superiors and was indifferent to the fate of ordinary people. When he was summoned by the emperor, the magistrate thought a good chance had come for him to show his talents before the throne so as to win promotion. Rushing in, he prostrated himself before the emperor.

Emperor Kang Xi however was not impressed by this show of humility and asked sternly: "Magistrate Liu, as the responsible official here do you know the conditions of the people you rule?"

"Yes, Your Majesty. Thanks to your great concern, we have an abundant harvest of all crops this year, and so the local people are well off with ample food and clothing."

"Is that true?" inquired the emperor doubtfully.

"Yes, Your Majesty," replied the magistrate.

But at that moment, a servant standing by with tea made a sign for the magistrate. The alert emperor noticed this and fixed his gaze on the tea servant. Magistrate Liu assumed that the servant had offended the emperor and ordered his guards to arrest the servant. At this the emperor stopped the proceedings and asked the servant, "Do you have anything to say?"

"No, I dare not say a word before Your Majesty."

"Don't worry. So long as you tell the truth you'll be rewarded," encouraged the emperor. Assured, the tea servant knelt and was bold enough to tell the following story.

"What the magistrate reported about the situation is not true. In fact, the local people's life is miserable. Not far from here a heart-broken mother is weeping over her son who starved to death not long ago."

"I see." The emperor glared at the magistrate, who promptly kowtowed before the emperor, trembling in panic.

The sobbing could still be heard in the distance. Disturbed by what he heard and had learned, the emperor lost all interest in the lantern and fireworks but turned to the tea servant. "You have told me the truth and will be rewarded." As for the magistrate, the emperor reprimanded him severely and ordered him to reduce the taxes and provide relief to the suffering people.

Years later, after Emperor Kang Xi died, the magistrate took revenge on the tea servant by ordering his guards to arrest and punish him. In despair, the tea servant jumped into the lake and was drowned. That night the magistrate's house was set afire and the magistrate was burnt to death in his sleep.

Emperor Kang Xi and the Enclosures

Emperor Kang Xi, while on a hunting trip in Jilin province in the northeast of China, came upon two lords fighting fiercely over a white deer. Even though locked in mortal combat one of the lords suddenly realized that the man on horseback watching them was none other than the emperor. He hurriedly moved away from his opponent and commanded in a low voice: "Stop fighting. Here comes the emperor!" The second lord turned to find the emperor watching them closely from the roadside. The two lords immediately cast aside their bows and arrows, and knelt down before the emperor. Following their masters' example, their bodyguards also laid down their arms and prostrated themselves on the ground.

"Your humble slaves were unaware of Your Majesty's arrival. We deserve to be severely punished for failing to welcome you. Please have mercy on us," pleaded the two lords as they kowtowed to the emperor.

"What were you fighting about?" he inquired.

"Your Majesty, this is my territory but his men have encroached on my land," said one of the lords.

"My white deer strayed onto his land. He captured it and refused to return it to me. When I insisted, he provoked a fight," said the other.

The two lords stood pointing their fingers at each other and quarrelling so fiercely that the fight seemed on the point of breaking out again.

The emperor rebuked them sternly saying: "What a shame you two lords fought each other merely over a deer. Go home at once and I will settle accounts with you later."

During his stay in Jilin, the emperor learnt that the land, including the mountains and forests, had all been enclosed by the princes, lords, generals, and rich and powerful families of the Eight Banners, and was now treated as their own private property. They acted like tyrants in the occupied lands, and often fought among themselves for more wealth and power.

Emperor Kang Xi realized that the enclosure of land must be stopped at once, or the internal struggles for wealth and power would eventually lead to disintegration of the whole nation. The state would no longer be able to ensure internal peace or resist foreign aggression. The consequences could be disasterous. What should he do? After much thought, the emperor decided that simply forcing them to give up their privileges was not enough. The emperor had only recently ascended the throne, while the princes, and generals had very powerful forces and were firmly established in the area.

The emperor turned over a number of plans in his mind. Finally he decided that the only solution was to show the princes and generals the disasterous consequences of the enclosures, in the hope that they would give up their privileges of their own accord.

The next day, Emperor Kang Xi invited the princes, lords and generals to a sumptuous banquet at the temporary palace. The emperor dressed with care in an imperial robe sewn with gold thread and inlaid with thousands of pearls. After wining and dining for a while, the emperor raised his cup saying: "Firstly, I propose a toast to you princes, lords and generals for your great contributions to the nation. I think I should reward you for what you have done for the country."

Then he took off his precious imperial robe, and holding it in both hands said: "I couldn't think of anything more valuable than this robe to reward you with so I have decided to cut the robe into pieces of different size and give them to each of you according to your contribution."

Surprised at the emperor's words, the lords looked at each other not knowing what to do. Then one white haired old lord knelt down and pleaded with the emperor saying: "Your Majesty, please don't cut this imperial robe into pieces, it is a rare national treasure." The others present also fell to their knees and joined in the old man's pleas to the emperor.

Emperor Kang Xi said with a smile: "You're quite right. This imperial robe is a precious national treasure. If it were cut into pieces, it would be ruined once and for all."

"What you say is true, our wise emperor," the lords chanted.

"Please rise. I have another question to ask you," said the emperor. As they seated themselves once again at the table, the emperor asked: "What other treasures do we own in addition to this imperial robe?"

"Ginseng."

"Pilose antler."

"Jade."

"Pearls."

"...." Replied the lords in quick succession.

Emperor Kang Xi nodded in agreement and then motioned them to be quiet.

"But what about our fertile land and beautiful countryside, are they not national treasures?" asked the emperor.

"Certainly they are," echoed the lords.

"Yes. They are our most precious treasures. Our

forefathers lived and worked on the land. They gave their lives for this land. My imperial robe by comparison is of little significance." The emperor paused for a moment and asked solemnly: "You couldn't bear to see my imperial robe cut into pieces, but some of you would stop at nothing to enclose the land. Such a practice is the same as dividing our precious country. What is more, you don't hesitate to fight each other as enemies over the enclosures." The emperor choked with emotion as he said these words.

The princes, lords and generals lowered their heads and did not reply. Some knelt as an expression of their remorse.

"It's good for you to understand your mistake. I won't blame you for what you've done in the past. But now I give you the following order: From now on, it will no longer be permissable to enclose the land in this province as private property or hunting estates. Anyone who dares to disobey will be severely punished."

Thereafter, all the land was placed under the jurisdiction of the generals of the province. Both the Han and Manchu people had the right to farm and raise animals on the land. The roads which had been destroyed as the land was enclosed were restored, and white stones were used to build roads linking different parts of the area. The roads were called "White Deer Roads" to commemorate the abolition of the enclosures.

Encounter in the Meditation Room

The Panshan Mountain was a celebrated beauty spot in Liaoning province. It was clad by peach, plum and other trees in which birds of all plumes chirped in harmony. On the mountainside stood a Buddhist monastery named Panshan Temple after the mountain. The abbot of the temple, called Zhipu, was a monk reputed to be literarily talented, unawed before the powerful, and very witty.

One year, Emperor Kang Xi with a group of attendants made a trip to the Panshan Mountain to see the views. When feeling tired from a long climb, the party went into the temple for a rest. No sooner had the emperor settled himself in a chair in a meditation room than he smelt a whiff of sweet perfume.

"Isn't this a kind of cosmetic scent only coming from the body of a woman?" the emperor wondered. "How can such a scent be in the air of a place of Buddhist worship? Surely no nun uses cosmetics. Then the monks here must be..." He felt shame to conjecture further, but was roused to a nameless anger and began to ponder on how to teach a lesson to the misbehaving monks who were supposed to be living under Buddhist vows.

Just then the abbot Zhipu came into the meditation room. In greeting the emperor, Zhipu made a deep bow instead of going down on his knees as was the usual manner in paying respects to a sovereign. This added to the emperor's displeasure. His Majesty decided to embarrass or insult the abbot by touching his sore spot. In an ironic tone he improvised two poetic lines:

From sacred room wafts powder scents,
And there's a lady in holy man's mind.

Refusing to take the royal insult lying down, Zhipu countered with lines of his own:

To palaces female squads are sent;
What's wrong with dames here to find?

The emperor was surprised at the quick repartee of the abbot who seemed to be living up to his reputation as a witty soul. Still trying to get the upper hand of his prideful verbal adversary, His Majesty quickly said:

"Now, then, you and I seem to be none the wiser for the humour. Aren't we worshipping the same Buddha?"

Giving no ground, Zhipu countered again:

"Since we are worshipping the same Buddha, as you say, we must be on an equal footing. Then should I kneel to greet Your Majesty?"

"It doesn't matter whether you kowtow to me or not," answered Emperor Kang Xi, feeling he was not getting any ground.

While this verbal encounter was going on without either party conceding defeat, a girl carrying a basket in her hand came out of a hall of the temple. And with her appearance, the powder scent became even heavier. Now the emperor began to realize the real source of the perfume. Coming over to the girl, he asked: "Young lady, why are you in this temple all by yourself? Don't you know you are too young to come here unescorted?"

"My father has fallen seriously ill," replied the girl. "I've come with my mother to burn incense to Buddha and pray for my father's speedy recovery."

"Where is your mother now?"

The girl turned away and pointed to an old woman

stepping out of the hall: "There she is."

After the departure of mother and daughter, Emperor Kang Xi felt the abbot had poked fun at him, and he had no reason to like that. With a stern look on his face, he asked Zhipu: "Is it true that dames could be found in this temple as you said a moment ago?"

"In this human world of ours," replied the abbot calmly, "things are at once true and untrue. Never take them too seriously. This humble monk has played a joke on you for fun, that's all."

"But how can you be so sacrilegious as to have played such a joke?"

"Well, Your Majesty's word is law," the abbot pointed out. "If I had gainsaid you too obviously I would have committed an unpardonable offense. As I could not refuse to answer your questions, my best way out was to play a joke."

"What a clever monk you are!" the emperor commended. "And you are brave at that."

Then referring to the book *An Account of the Panshan Mountain* written by Zhipu, the emperor said: "It's a work well done, rich in content and fluent in language. It serves very well to expound the Buddhist dharma. For your pains let me reward you with 10,000 taels of silver, which you may use for refurbishing the Panshan Temple."

Delighted, the abbot showed his thanks by bringing his palms together in the Buddhist manner.

Thereafter, everytime Emperor Kang Xi made an inspection tour to Liaoning province, he would come to the Panshan Temple for a visit with Zhipu. The two of them often exchanged poems flowing from their pens, and this became a story on everyone's lips.

An Inscription Written after Drinking

Once Emperor Kang Xi made a visit to the Lingyin Temple close by the West Lake at Hangzhou in Zhejiang province. When he was in the temple after drinking in the picturesque lake view of hills, waters, trees and flowers, he was in such exuberant spirits that he gave orders to hold a banquet to entertain a large company of his favourite officials.

As was the Buddhist rule, only vegetarian dishes were ever allowed on the temple table. But this time the emperor as host simply brushed aside the rule, much to the dismay of the monks, who had no choice but to bow to the imperial wish rather than protest against an insult to their faith. The air of the usually tranquil place of worship was being filled with the savory smell of wine and meat as well as with music and songs. Feeling hungry from the sightseeing exertion, the emperor made frequent use of his chopsticks and wine cup to enjoy the pleasures of a luxurious table. His guests were quick to follow suit.

The abbot of the temple found the emperor in cheerful spirits and had an idea to take advantage of it. He had known that His Majesty always delighted in writing poems or inscriptions. So he quietly moved close to the side of the prefect of Hangzhou and whispered in his ear: "Sir, this humble old monk wishes to ask His Majesty for an inscription to grace the temple. Do you think the idea all right?"

The prefect nodded his agreement, saying: "What a good idea! If His Majesty deigns to write an inscription bearing the name of your Lingyin Temple, as a local official I would feel greatly honoured as well." The head of Qiantang county beside them also chimed in: "At the moment the emperor is pretty much in wine. Our abbot's request for an inscription will surely be granted."

With the encouragement of these two local officials, the old abbot boldly stepped before the emperor and said in a kneeling position: "Your Majesty, may this humble monk beg you for an inscription bearing the name of our temple? For Buddha's sake, would Your Majesty be so kind as to favour us with it?"

The emperor granted the request graciously. With a writing brush saturated with ink, he wrote out with a flourish of the hand the upper part of the character "*ling*" which was the first of the three characters "*ling, yin, shi*" meaning Lingyin Temple. In the Chinese language, a character is a word usually written in a limited square space. The character "*ling*" is formed of three parts, upper, middle and lower. All these parts must be so written as to be well arranged in the square space. The upper part of the character "*ling*" is itself a character "*yu*" meaning "rain." This part of the character was written so large by the emperor that it took up the better part of the space, leaving insufficient room for the other two parts to crowd in. For a moment the emperor was uncertain what to do. The officials and monks crowding round the writing table all saw the emperor knitting his brow, but ventured not a word. Only one high courtier, Gao Jiangcun by name, came to the rescue. He wrote in his palm the characters "*yun*" and "*lin*" meaning "cloud" and "wood" respectively, and showed them to the emperor while pretending to smooth out the writing paper. As a matter of fact, the two-part character "*yun*" has the same upper part "*yu*" as in the case of the character "*ling*." The emperor was so delighted at the hint and forthwith wrote the four characters "*yun*, *lin*, *chan*, *shi*" meaning "Sacred Yunlin Temple" as a whole.

The abbot, being an honest soul, did not hesitate to point out the error as he said: "Your Majesty, our temple is called Lingyin Temple, not Sacred Yunlin Temple."

The emperor was quite displeased at the correction. Giving a cold stare at the abbot, he uttered an angry remark: "Nonsense!"

The abbot felt such a remark was an injustice to him, as he had only spoken the truth. But in face of the many disapproving eyes fixed on him, he had to refrain from making any more truth-defending remarks and step aside feeling unhappy.

To save his own face, the emperor posed a question to all present: "Don't you think it fitting and proper to call this place of worship Yunlin Temple, since there are clouds in the sky and woods on the ground?"

"Very proper, Your Majesty," the officials chorused their agreement. "Your Majesty's learning is as great as Heaven."

Indeed His Majesty was immensely tickled to hear these remarks of admiration. Then, on the orders of the prefect of Hangzhou, a new inscription board was soon put up over the temple gate to replace the old board bearing the inscription "Lingyin Temple."

Punishing a Corrupt Official

Emperor Kang Xi, disguised as a commoner, once made a tour of investigation in the southern part of China. One day he dropped in to a small restaurant which contained only a few wooden tables and chairs. Two customers were waiting at one of the tables.

"Waiter," called the emperor, but there was no answer. "Waiter!" he called again, but still received no reply.

"The waiters are all busy attending high officials in the next room,"said one customer who had been waiting to be served for some time.

The emperor crossed to the next room, and lifting the curtain over the doorway, peered inside. He saw a fat official being attended by a waiter as he wined and dined. Only after the official had finished his banquet and left the restaurant did the waiter serve the other customers.

The waiter apologized for the delay, and hurried to attend to those who had been waiting a long time. The emperor asked the waiter what kind of rules they had in the restaurant.

"Just now we were waiting at the table," he pointed out, "but no one came to help us. You only attended to that fat customer. Is that fair?"

"I couldn't help it," said the waiter. "You must be a stranger here, since you don't know who that fat customer is. He's the official in charge of local taxes. He has a tight hold on us shopkeepers. None of us dare to offend him."

"Has he been a customer for a long time?"

"Yes!"

"Does he pay for his food?"

"If he had to pay, he wouldn't come here so often."

"Then why don't you ask him to pay?"

With a wry smile, the waiter said, "You must be a stupid scholar always locked in your study to know so little about social affairs. Tax officials hold the power of life and death over businessmen, let alone a small shopkeeper like me."

"It sounds terrible. But surely the royal court has made rules and regulations about the collection of taxes?"

"What's the use of rules and regulations on paper? Officials have power. Whatever they say is the law. A few years ago, the same tax official ordered me to give him a chicken every month. I followed his orders and sent a chicken each month from January to October, but somehow I forgot in November. As a result, I was fined 50 taels of silver at the end of the year on a trumped up charge of evading taxation. What can a small restaurant owner like me do about such official punishment?"

On hearing this story, the emperor became very angry and pounded the table with his fist: "This is outrageous!" he cried. "Is everything that you have told me the truth?"

"Every word is true."

"Good. Bring me a brush and paper!" commanded the emperor.

Puzzled, the waiter brought him a brush and paper as he asked.

"I'll write you a note, and tomorrow you must take it to the magistrate who will take out a lawsuit against the tax official. The magistrate will take care of the case."

The customer spoke with authority, which made the waiter believe he must be someone of importance. The waiter asked: "Sir, may I ask, who you are?"

"I won't tell you now. When you go to the magistrate tomorrow you will know everything."

After the mysterious customer left the restaurant, the shopkeeper began to worry about going to the magistrate. If the tax official was found not guilty, he would suffer even greater disasters in the future. If he refused to make a case against him, he would probably lose a good chance. He finally decided to try his luck.

The next day, the shopowner went to the magistrate with his customer's note. When the secretary read the note, he was scared out of his wits. Trembling, he immediately ordered the guards to ask the magistrate to receive the emperor's edict.

Having read the emperor's note, the magistrate called the tax official to come at once to the county court. When the tax official entered the court, he saw the shopowner sitting to one side, and immediately understood what had happened. Without further ado, the tax official pleaded quilty and promised to pay back all the money he had received from the shopowner.

Only later did the shopkeeper learn that it was none other than Emperor Kang Xi who had helped him to punish the tax official.

A Clever Trick

In the northern part of Dengfeng county, Henan province, there was once an area of great natural beauty, with a chain of green mountains and clear flowing streams. In 495, Emperor Xiao Wen of the Northern Wei Dynasty (386--534 A.D.) ordered a monastery to be built at the foot of Wurufeng peak, to the north of Shaoshi Mountain. Shaolin Monastery later became the birth place of Zen Buddhism and the famous Shaolin boxing, but by the Qing Dynasty, over 1000 years later, the monastery had fallen into disrepair.

After careful renovations during the reign of Kang Xi, the monastery's front door appeared even more magnificent than before. The head monk Jinzai hired a carpenter to make a horizontal board from red sandlewood, and then invited several calligraphers to write on it the name of the monastery, but none proved satisfactory.

Before long, news came that emperor Kang Xi would visit the monastery. Monk Jingzai was overjoyed, because he knew that the emperor had excellent calligraphy. He was unsure, however, whether the emperor would agree to write an inscription for such an unknown monastery. He therefore decided to gain a sample of the emperor's handwriting by trickery.

One day, while Emperor Kang Xi was visiting the monastery, he saw two monks, one old, the other young, arguing heatedly about whose calligraphy was the best. Each boasted of his own handwriting and belittled the other's. The old monk, with a large brush in his hand, had just finished writing the name of the monastery on a sheet of paper. The Chinese characters were large enough, but looked clumsy and ill formed. The young monk's writing also appeared shapeless. They continued to argue so fiercely that they seemed on the point of fighting.

The strange quarrel attracted the emperor, who went over to the monks. They stopped quarrelling at once and hurriedly asked the emperor for his judgement.

"If I give my opinion about your handwriting, I hope you won't mind what I say."

"No, not at all," the two monks answered in chorus.

"To be frank, neither handwriting is good enough," the emperor commented.

"Good heavens! You must be a great calligrapher. Would you be kind enough to write the name of our monastery?" urged the two monks. Before the emperor could nod his assent, they rushed to get a better writing brush, ink stick, ink slab and paper. When the four treasures of the study were ready, the emperor used his brush to write the name "Shaolin Monastery" with vigorous strokes. As soon as the emperor laid down his brush, he found hundreds of monks lying prostrate before him with their palms together in a Buddhist greeting. The head monk Jingzai expressed his gratitude: "It is a great honour for us to have Your Majesty's calligraphy for our monastery." Emperor Kang Xi realized at last that he had been tricked, but he was not at all angry.

It is now more than 300 years since the emperor wrote the name of Shaolin Monastery, but the board, with a square imperial seal at the top, still hangs at the front door of the monastery.

A Discontented Scholar

During a journey to the lower reaches of the Yangtse River, Emperor Kang Xi one day came to a small town called Meihuali (plum blossom village) in Jiaxing county, Zhejiang province. It was early spring and the temperature in the area often changed abruptly. The emperor went for a stroll in the town and came to Plum Blossom Pond. On the southern bank of the pond, a group of sightseers were seated in a thatched pavilion. A man in his 50s was sitting on a wooden chair with the upper part of his body exposed to the sun. Emperor Kang Xi thought this quite strange and asked: "Old fellow, it isn't so warm, why are you sitting here with your shirt off?"

The man looked at the emperor, and gently stroking his stomach sighed: "I can't help it. I have too many books here in my stomach. If they are not exposed to the sun, they will turn rotten in the seasons to come."

The clever emperor at once realized that the man was actually complaining because his learning was not apprcciated. Kang Xi respected talented men and believed that if the man had real gifts then local officials should offer him a chance to display them.

When he returned to the capital, the emperor ordered the local officials of Jiaxing county to send the scholar to the palace for an interview. The man was overjoyed with the news and quickly prepared to leave for Beijing. As soon as he arrived in the capital, he was taken to meet the emperor. The emperor reminded him of the large number of books in his stomach, and said he would like to know what kind of books they were.

The man remembered how he had met the emperor in the thatched pavilion in early spring, and replied: "Thank you for your great concern, Your Majesty. I have brought with me 81 volumes of my books." He then presented them to the emperor, who glanced over a few pages and was surprised at the man's talent. The emperor then passed the books to his senior officials who also admired the scholar's learning. The emperor turned to the man and said: "You just stay in the capital and I'll give you many opportunities to serve the royal court with your knowledge."

The scholar, Zhu Yizun, for that was made an editor in the Imperial Academy and later became one of the most famous scholars of the Qing Dynasty.

Emperor Kang Xi and the Scholar Pu Songlin

Pu Songlin was a learned man of good character, but he failed several times to pass the imperial examinations, while less learned men were successful. His experiences made him aware of the corruption in official circles and the unfairness of the imperial examination system. Deeply disappointed, he grumbled: "This society is even more ugly and horrible than hell."

After the examination, he returned home full of bitterness, but dared not reveal his feelings. In the midst of his despair, he suddenly had a bright idea. Catching sight of a writing brush and paper on his desk, he thought: "Why shouldn't I write ghost stories to satirize those conceited officials who are even more ugly than ghosts?"

In order to collect materials, Pu Songlin opened a tea house in the village and put up a sign announcing that anyone who would tell ghost stories would be served tea free of charge. As news of the tea house spread people came from far and near to tell ghost stories, or simply out of curiosity. Pu Songlin wrote down all the interesting ghost stories and after three years published them in a book entitled: *Legendary Stories of Ghosts and Foxes*.

Zhu Liuzhi, one of Pu Songlin's fellow students, was then a senior official in the capital. Once when he returned home for a visit, he dropped in to see his old friend. He soon learned of Pu Songlin's book, and after reading a few pages, was absorbed by the fantastic stories. He insisted on borrowing the novel for further reading.

As soon as he returned to his post, Zhu Liuzhi started to read again. He was so absorbed that he forgot even to eat and sleep. One morning, when all the officials were waiting for the emperor's routine court session, Zhu took out the book to pass the time. He was so completely occupied that he didn't even notice the arrival of the emperor.

Kang Xi noticed that all the officials were patiently waiting in line, except for Zhu, who was buried in a book. The emperor found this strange and, tiptoing up behind Zhu, he glanced over his shoulder to see what he was reading. The other officials were worried about the incident, thinking that this time Zhu might be punished for his casual attitude at court.

"What is the book that attracts you so much?" said the emperor. Frightened, Zhu Liuzhi turned to find the emperor standing behind him. He hurriedly knelt and asked for mercy. The emperor calmed him down saying: "There is nothing wrong in using the time for reading, but what kind of stories absorb you so much? I'd like to have a look at them." The emperor then took the book and opened the day's court session.

A few days later, Zhu Liuzhi was summoned by the emperor who wanted to hear more about the author of the book. He asked why such an obviously learned man did not take the imperial examination.

"He did, Your Majesty, but he failed," replied Zhu Liuzhi.

"I see," sighed the emperor. He was nevertheless surprised, and ordered Zhu to bring the author to the capital where he would offer him a post in the palace. Zhu Liuzhi was overjoyed, and immediately returned to his hometown. He thought his friend would be delighted by the news, but Pu Songlin showed no interest and flatly refused to take a post at court. Zhu Liuzhi returned to the capital with a heavy heart, afraid that his friend would be punished for refusing an imperial command.

Emperor Kang Xi, however, was not angered by the refusal, and even decided to pay a visit to this upright scholar. Pu Songlin was greatly touched by the emperor's visit, but had no desire for an official post because of his disappointment with the imperial examination system. The emperor realized that some of the officials in charge of the examination were stupid and had deeply hurt talented people like Pu Songlin. The emperor looked around the scholar's poor study and asked: "Is this where you wrote your *Legendary Stories of Ghosts and Foxes*?"

"Yes, Your Majesty."

"Then I'd like to offer a suggestion about the title of your book," said the emperor.

"What do you suggest?"

"Just call it *Strange Tales from the Liao Zhai Studio*. Do you agree?"

"Yes," replied Pu Songlin, and expressed his gratitude to the emperor. The emperor wrote the new title of the book in his excellent calligraphy.

On returning to the palace, the emperor made inquiries about the examination in order to find out why such excellent scholars as Pu Songlin had not passed. He then summoned the six officials in charge of the examination and rebuked them saying: "Why did the author of such good stories fail the exam?"

Guiltily the officials prostrated themselves before the emperor, but dared not answer his question.

"Tell the truth, and your case might be handled leniently," commanded the emperor.

Zhang Wansheng, one of the chief examiners replied: "Pu Songlin wrote excellent articles in all three examinations, and should have been a successful candidate. He didn't pass because we were jealous of him. We have committed a most terrible crime."

Emperor Kang Xi flew into a rage at this confession. "You damned jealous officials. We trusted you to select man of talent, but you villains have been misled by your jealousy and caused great harm to the nation and the people. Guards! Take them to the Ministry of Punishments for trial," ordered the emperor.

At the trial, Zhang Wansheng was dismissed from office and became a commoner. The other five were sentenced to death.

Later, Pu Songlin wrote several stories about chief examiners who were punished in hell for their jealousy of talented candidates in the imperial examinations.

Searching for the Living Buddha Pu Xian

Emperor Kang Xi became very superstitious in his later years. He decided to visit the living Buddha Pu Xian, who lived on Emei Mountain in Sichuan province, in the hope of finding the secret of eternal life.

Although he was escorted by a large entourage, the emperor felt uneasy about travelling to Sichuan province. He ordered several people who resembled him to dress in similar clothes and travel in sedan-chairs like his own.

Monk Zhao Yu was the abbot of Pu Xian Temple, home of the living Buddha. One evening, the local wise man of the mountain, a white haired old man, came to inform Zhao Yu that the emperor would visit the temple the very next day to meet Pu Xian. He told the monk to get everything ready and also taught him how to answer difficult questions. For instance, if the emperor made inquiries about the living Buddha Pu Xian, he should reply that he had left for Zhao Jue Temple in Chengdu city, the capital of Sichuan province.

The white haired old man also told the monk that nine emperors would come to the temple. They would all be similar, but only one was the real emperor.

"But how will I recognize the real emperor since I have never seen him before,"Zhao Yu said anxiously.

"The one with a few pockmarks on his face is the real emperor," revealed the local wise man.

Early next morning, Zhao Yu ordered the monks to clean the temple thoroughly. After breakfast, the abbot led a group of monks to the front gate of the temple to await the arrival of the emperor. Before long, a group of people, including the nine "emperors" and their entourages arrived at the temple. Zhao Yu searched out the emperor with a pockmarked face, and prostrated himself before him, saying: "This humble monk of Pu Xian Temple warmly welcomes Your Majesty."

Emperor Kang Xi was furious that the monk had seen through his disguise so easily. He flew into a rage and ordered his bodyguards to arrest the head monk.

"Your Majesty, please have mercy on me, I am innocent," pleaded Zhao Yu.

"How did you recognize me?" demanded the emperor.

Zhao Yu repeated the words of the white haired local wise man.

"Where is the living Buddha Pu Xian?" demanded the emperor.

"The Buddha left for Zhao Jue Temple in Chengdu city to avoid any worldly involvement."

The emperor asked no more questions, but gave the order to set out for Zhao Jue Temple at once.

To prevent another failure, Emperor Kang Xi this time disguised himself as an old lay Buddhist.

The living Buddha Pu Xian knew that the emperor had been in power for more than 50 years. He suspected that Kang Xi sought the secret of eternal life in order to retain his hold on the throne. Pu Xian decided to disguise himself as a monk and play a trick on the greedy emperor.

"Master, could you tell me where the Buddhist Pu Xian is living?" asked Emperor Kang Xi.

"He is in the Pu Xian Hall."

The emperor entered the hall and found it deserted. "Master, there is no one in the hall," cried the emperor deeply puzzled.

"What's that?" said the monk, pointing at a Buddhist statue behind a table.

"But that isn't the living Buddha. It's only an idol carved from wood and moulded in clay."

"Then why do so many people worship him with such sincerity?" the monk retorted.

Now, Pu Xian, disguised as a junior monk was just on his way to the next hall. Emperor Kang Xi stopped him and asked: "Little master, do you know where the Buddha Pu Xian lives?"

"He is seeing a patient in the rear hall."

The emperor was pleased with the news, believing he would find the Buddha at last. He hurried to the rear hall, and saw an old monk with white eyebrows treating a patient with boils on one of his legs. He gazed at the monk for a while and then asked: "Old master, are you the living Buddha Pu Xian?"

"Am I a living Buddha? What do you mean? I am of course a living Buddhist, and have lived for over eighty years," retorted the old monk who was rather hard of hearing. Disappointed, the emperor left the rear hall.

As he was passing a kitchen, a cook stopped him and asked: "Master, who are you looking for?"

"I'm looking for the living Buddha Pu Xian."

"What do you want with him?"

"I'd like to ask him for some special medicine which will give me eternal life so that I may make a greater contribution to the nation."

The cook laughed and said: "You are looking for the wrong person. His medicine doesn't work."

"How do you know?"

"Master, the rich and powerful have tricked the

people of their wealth and many of them are now short of food and clothing and in a miserable state. The ordinary people have no wish for eternal life. Only high officials and those who are rich seek such medicine. But when so many poor, miserable people are cursing them day and night, how could such medicine save them from the fate of death?"

The monk's words struck the emperor with the force of a blow. Filled with rage, Emperor Kang Xi was ready to flare up, but had to control his anger for fear of revealing his true indentity. Disappointed, he had to return to the capital empty handed.

A Scheme for Usurping the Throne

Emperor Kang Xi had originally appointed his second son Prince Yin Reng as his successor. However, after 33 years of observation and testing, the emperor saw this crown prince too different in many respects from himself and decided to change his dicision. He deposed the prince and even put him under house arrest. However, after a whole year's effort, the emperor still had not found a satisfactory successor. The emperor was then well over 50 and once again appointed Prince Yin Reng his successor, only to depost the prince a second time three years later for incompetence. Deeply disappointed, Emperor Kang Xi gave up the idea of having a crown prince for the time being.

When Emperor Kang Xi was 69, he decided to go hunting in the Nanyuan deer field, south of Beijing one winter day. Shortly before he was to set out, the emperor fell suddenly sick and was escorted to recuperate in Chang Chun garden palace. But the emperor felt his days were numbered. With a sense of urgency, Kang Xi could no longer delay the appointment of a successor and wrote this imperial edict: The fourteenth son, Yin Ti, is to be crown prince and my successor to the throne.

Crown Prince Yin Ti was a highly qualified successor, having had many times led armies to fight heroically in defence of the frontier and become a favourite of his royal father, who had 30 sons.

The fourth son, Yin Zhen, was different, indulging in an extravagant and loose life. He was also ambitious and hunger for power. When he learnt the emperor was seriously ill, he foresaw a fierce power struggle and plotted secretly to usurp the throne.

First, he rallied round himself a gang skillful in martial arts as his palace guards. Next, he fabricated all manner of pretexts to prevent his brothers from getting close to the dying emperor. Most important was to change the name of the successor in the imperial edict. He bribed a eunuch to steal the imperial edict from the emperor's deathbed and changed the word fourteenth to fourth so that Yin Zhen, rather than Yin Ti should become the successor.

But Emperor Kang Xi regained consciousness and suspected the fourth son of tampering with the imperial edict. The emperor wanted to call in his most trusted son, but Yin Ti was not at hand. Enraged, the emperor threw his pillow at the fourth son but missed. Then he threw his pendant at him. Yin Zhen took it and put on around his own neck. Burning with anger, Emperor Kang Xi fainted away and soon died.

As soon as the emperor died, Prince Yin Zhen, wearing the emperor's pendant, emerged from the royal chamber with the imperial edict. The royal family, courtiers and high officials had no inkling of what Yin Zhen had done and loyally supported him as heir to the throne. He became the third emperor after the Manchus conquered the central plains of China, declaring himself Emperor Yong Zheng.

According to some tales, the prince's plot of changing the successor in the imperial edict was instigated by a Han general named Nian Gaoyao who had engaged in an illicit affair with Prince Yin Zhen's mother before she entered the court as empress. She gave birth to Prince Yin Zhen eight months after becoming empress.

After Prince Yin Zhen succeeded in usurping the throne General Nian Gaoyao became a powerful minister, gaining so in power that even Emperor Yong Zheng felt threatened.

After three years Emperor Yong Zheng framed the general and had him imprisoned. The emperor ordered him to commit suicide and killed his whole family in order to stamp out the source of possible further trouble.

Power Struggles Between Princes

Having succeeded in usurping the power, Emperor Yong Zheng still felt insecure on the throne. Some of his own brothers were his bitter rivals. In order to remove this threat, he took every possible step to wipe out all political rivalry.

First he ordered his brothers to change their names so as to cut family connections with him. Then he called Prince Yin Ti back from the northwest frontier where he was in command of an army and enjoyed high prestige among his officers and men. Upon returning to the capital, the prince was placed under house arrest. The 8th and 9th princes had expressed their intention of taking over the throne. They were on good terms and kept in touch.

Once the 9th prince, Yin Tang, asked Emperor Yong Zheng to appoint one of his close friends to fill a provincial vacancy in southern China. The emperor took this opportunity to accuse the two princes of building up their won forces into a secret clique to usurp the throne. The emperor expelled them from the royal clan and forced them to change their names. Prince Yin Yi was called Dog and Yin Tang Pig in Manchu and both were placed under house arrest.

One dark night Yin Tang was reading in his study when he suddenly heard strange sounds outside the window and saw mysterious figures rushing up. Frightened, the prince called his bodyguards for help but no one appeared. Then a man in black robe jumped in through the window. Prince Yin Tang stepped back to the wall in terror, demanding: “Who are you?”

The man replied: “Don’t worry, Your Highness! The emperor sent me to wish you good health.”

Hearing the man was sent by the emperor, Prince Yin Tang felt panic stricken and said: “I’m well. Please report to the emperor that I am innocent of any ambition.”

“The emperor was only concerned about your health and ordered me to bring you some tonic. If Your Highness takes this tonic, you will soon be in good health,” said the man, handing the prince a small vial. Prince Yin Tang sensed danger in the vial, which might contain poison, and refused to take it. Enraged, the man took out a dagger. “Better take it voluntarily or I’ll take the trouble to help you as ordered.” Prince Yin Tang realized that it was in vain to refuse and opened the vial in tears. No sooner had he swallowed the white powder than he died in great pain.

The next noon when the eunuchs heard no sound from the prince’s room they knocked at the door but received no answer and broke into the room. There were bloodstains on the floor.

The royal court announced the death of Prince Yin Tang but provided no details as to its cause. However, Prince Yin Yi knew only too well what had happened.

At about the same time Emperor Yong Zheng sent his men to northwest China to arrest Prince Yin Tang’s entire family.

Years later, news spread that Prince Yin Yi, Yin He, the 10th prince, and Yin Ti, the 14th prince died one after another within a few years. Only the 3rd prince, Yin Xiang, was trusted by Emperor Yong Zheng and so survived in the power struggle among the princes.

Murder Behind Closed Doors

Once upon a time a curious tutor asked his eunuch host to do him the favour of taking him to catch a glimpse of the imperial court. The eunuch agreed and got him a provisional pass and the necessary clothes to disguise the tutor as one of his servants.

Before they went to the imperial court, the eunuch told the tutor some basic rules and information for entering the court. "When we get to Wumen Gate, the guards will shout orders for pass check. Those who've never been to court will be frightened and often seized for interrogation. If found unqualified, he will be severely punished. This will be repeated at every gate, but they will be less fierce. When we reach the inner gate, the guards will presume that since we have passed several checks there should be no problem," the eunuch explained.

The eunuch took the tutor to the imperial court and passed all the gates without any trouble. He then ushered the tutor into a spacious room and whispered to him: "This is the emperor's living room. You can have a look at the exquisite furniture here, but don't loiter. If the emperor comes, you'll be in trouble." No sooner had the eunuch finished saying this than people rushed in announcing the emperor's arrival. Shocked on hearing the news, the eunuch was at a loss as to what to do. In the critical moment he suddenly hit upon a way out. He would hide his tutor under a plank bed.

Escorted by guards fore and aft, Emperor Yong Zheng entered the living room in a rage. He sat cross-legged on the bed ready for an interrogation. Several hefty bodyguards brought in a man who had been beaten black and blue and was forced to kneel down before the emperor. Showing his disdain for the emperor, the man accused: "Since you usurped power, you have framed your own brothers and killed them one after another. You thought in this way you could wipe out witnesses to your usurption and exterminate your rivals. But you were wrong. The more cruel you are, the faster you will tumble from the throne."

Flying into a rage, Emperor Yong Zheng jumped off the bed and slapped the man's face. The emperor ordered the guards to bind him hand and foot and poured a small vial of white powder into his mouth. The man soon fell to the ground dripping with blood and died in great pain. The guards cut the man's body into pieces which they put into a large vat outside the gate.

After that, silence prevailed in the living room, with only the occasional sounds of the emperor drinking his tea or smoking his water pipe. Soon the emperor ordered the guards to throw the big vat into a sewer, cursing as he spoke: "You bastard even dared to provoke me. That's your end." With that the emperor strode out of the room.

The terrified eunuch pulled the almost paralized tutor out from under the bed and asked: "Did you see what happened today?"

The tutor, trembling stammered out a few words. "Yeh, Yeh, I saw it."

"No. You should say you saw nothing. One slip of your tongue and both of us will be doomed to die. I'm on duty today. And you'd better go home right now."

The tutor returned home in terror and worried the whole night about what might happen. On second thought he decided to write down in detail what had happened in the court. He sewed the account into his cotton padded jacket. The next day the eunuch returned from court in panic and told the tutor of impending disaster.

"What's the matter?" asked the tutor.

"The emperor didn't ask me about anything the whole day when I was on duty. I presumed that he had probably no idea about you in the living room. But in the evening the emperor suddenly summoned me and inquired: 'Who was the person hiding under the bed this morning? You are extremely bold to bring a stranger into my living room.' I knelt down in terror, asking him for mercy. I told him you were a relative of mine and went to the court simply out of curiosity. The emperor refused to listen to any excuses but ordered your execution at once. I am now in no position to save you. The only thing I can do is to help send your coffin to your native place and give a helping hand to your family. You'd better get ready. The palace guards will be here soon."

Almost paralized with fear, the tutor said in tears: "I'm doomed to die since you can't save me. But I hope you'll be kind enough to take care of my family."

Several guards soon arrived and gave the tutor a vial of white powder, the same as he had seen in the imperial living room the day before. In despair, the tutor gulped down the powder and died on the spot in great pain.

The host eunuch helped send the tutor's coffin to his native place and told his family that the tutor had died of an accident. Months later, when the tutor's wife was sorting out clothing left behind by her deceased husband, she found the account written by him shortly before his death. It disclosed all the secrets of her husband's death, but she dared not say anything about the murder behind the closed doors in the court for fear of further brutality.

Rise and Fall of a Poor Scholar

Before he ascended the throne, Emperor Yong Zheng was a dissipated young dandy prince who indulged in drinking and sword fighting. In order to deceive his royal father Emperor Kang Xi, Prince Yin Zhen would disguise himself in plain clothes and go to seek pleasure outside the Forbidden City.

Once he went as far as Hangzhou--a city well-known for its beautiful scenery in eastern China--to take a boat trip on the picturesque West Lake with his friends. On their way to the West Lake, they met a middle-aged man hawking his calligraphy outside Hangzhou's Yongjingmen gate. The scholar claimed that he was skilful in eight different styles of calligraphy.

Prince Yin Zhen loved stirring up trouble and trying to outshine others. He ordered the man to write an antithetical couplet in several styles of calligraphy to prove his skill on the spot. The scholar wrote the scrolls and the prince was surprised by the vigor and beauty of the calligraphy. The prince asked: "You are a learned man, why don't you take the imperial examinations and win promotion instead of hawking calligraphy on the street?"

The scholar said he had attended some lower level examinations, but couldn't afford the imperial examination in the capital because he was short of money. He was now so poverty-stricken that he had to sell his calligraphy to feed his family; attending the imperial examination was completely out of the question.

Touched by the scholar's frustration, Prince Yin Zhen took pity on him and gave him the money to take the imperial examination. He said: "I could use this money for my own profit, but I prefer to support your academic career. If you succeed in the exam and win promotion, don't forget me!"

The scholar expressed deep gratitude to the prince for his kindness. With the money, the scholar was able to pursue his academic career and a few years later he passed the imperial examination. He was later appointed as a member of the Imperial Academy.

Years later, Prince Yin Zhen ascended the throne as Emperor Yong Zheng. Once when he was checking the names of the newly appointed members of the Imperial Academy, he found a name which reminded him of the poor scholar selling his calligraphy in Hangzhou. The emperor called in the scholar and asked about his background. He told the emperor that he had relied purely on his own talent and diligence to become an academic official, and had received no one else's support.

Soon afterwards, Emperor Yong Zheng sent an edict to the governor of Zhejiang province ordering that the newly appointed member of the Imperial Academy from his region should be made to return to Hangzhou and sell his calligraphy for three years before being allowed to return to his post. Only then did the scholar realize that the young man who had given him money for his imperial examination was none other than the present emperor. He now regretted having told lies to the emperor; but he had only himself to blame for lack of gratitude.

Appointing a Successor by Sealed Edict

In view of his own experience in usurping the throne, Emperor Yong Zheng knew only too well the importance of ensuring successor to the throne. He himself took power by making secret changes in the imperial edict announcing a successor, but he did not want his princes to follow suit. As he was growing old, the emperor spent much time thinking about a way to guarantee the power transition but he failed to come up with anything for years. After reigning for 12 years, at the age of 56 the emperor held a court session in the Qian Qing Hall, asking his ministers and generals to give him advice on the matter. The emperor said: "It's an extremely important task appointing an heir to the throne. The former emperor entrusted me with the reign and I've dedicated my life to the nation. However, I'm growing old and I'd better appoint a successor while I'm strong and clear-minded. I've decided to name the heir to the throne in a sealed edict. After my death you courtiers can simply take out the imperial edict and you'll have your new emperor. What do you think of that?"

"His Majesty is the wisest emperor we have ever had. We'll certainly act upon your orders," all the high officials chorused.

"I think this most important edict should be hidden in a conspicuous but safe place so that everyone can keep an eye on it but nobody can steal it."

The courtiers and high officials all looked at each

other with a blank expression feeling it hard to find such a place. Then an old minister laughed heartily as if he had a solution to the problem.

"Do you have any idea?" the emperor asked.

"Your Majesty, I would suggest that the edict be put behind the signboard over the gate of the Qian Qing Hall with the Chinese characters 'open and above-board, just and honourable' on it. It is a place all of us could keep an eye on and no one could hardly have a chance to steal it."

Emperor Yong Zheng and his ministers all agreed with this suggestion. The emperor highly praised the old minister's wisdom. Greatly encouraged, the old minister went on to explain that the words written by the former emperor on the board had profound meaning which should be carried out with regard to appointing a successor to the throne. These remarks however caused Yong Zheng a feeling of guilt, like a thief caught red-handed. Still, the minister had not pointed a finger directly at him.

After the court session, Emperor Yong Zheng ordered the minister in charge of imperial household affairs to carry out the mission. The emperor wrote the name of the successor to the throne in an imperial edict and ordered the minister to put the sealed edict behind the board over the gate of the Qian Qing Hall.

The following year Emperor Yong Zheng fell ill and died suddenly. The courtiers, acting on the orders of the late emperor, removed the sealed imperial edict and read as follows: "The fourth prince Aisin Gioro Hong Li is the heir to the throne."

In this way Prince Hong Li ascended the throne and became Emperor Qian Long, the fourth emperor of the Qing Dynasty. Later, Emperor Qian Long and his successor Emperor Jia Qing also used the same method in naming an heir to the throne.

A Secret Assassin

Hangzhou is the capital city of Zhejiang province in east China. The city's fame rests mainly on its picturesque West Lake. Once Emperor Yong Zheng took a trip to Hangzhou and was especially fascinated with the scenery at West Lake.

For security reasons the emperor did not live in the city but ordered to have a temporary dwelling place built on the lake. Fishermen's boats were requisitioned by the local officials for building such a water palace. As a result many fishermen lost their source of income and the inhabitants along the lake were deprived of the freedom to move about. The surrounding water area of the emperor's dwelling place became a forbidden zone with heavy guards and patrol boats. All the security measures evoked the local people's grievances and indignation.

Traditionally July 15 in the Chinese lunar calendar was a Buddhist festival. On that night as Emperor Yong Zheng took a boat trip on West Lake, he saw thousands of people gathered for the lantern boat celebration, which lighted up the night sky. Sitting in his specially built colourful dragon boat, the emperor enjoyed himself in dining, wining, music and dancing with his charming concubines. Suddenly someone pointed south and shouted: "Your Majesty, please look!"

The emperor looked at the direction with his half drunken eyes and saw two large fire balls flying over toward the dragon boat. In panic, the emperor's bodyguards hurried to throw spears, shooting arrows at the balls. Patrol boats were ordered to fetch the objects shot down, which turned out to be two gauze lanterns with some words written on each. One read: "Leave in three days or you'll be doomed to die." The other read: "Borrow your lantern tonight, but it will be returned tomorrow." The emperor flew into a rage. Just then a eunuch rushed in and reported: "Your Majesty, the red gauze lantern hung on the dragon boat is missing!"

Hearing the shocking news, Emperor Yong Zheng sank into the dragon chair, shouting: "What audacious gangsters! You even dare to steal my lanterns and threaten to take my life!" The emperor then turned on his attendants: "You fools, I'll lose my head sooner or later with you stupid guards. You must arrest the assassin tomorrow, or none of you can escape the most severe punishment." The emperor retired to his chamber in indignation.

After this incident the imperial dragon boat was under heavier guard with more patrol boats keeping a close watch on the assassins. The emperor however was still sleepless, fearing an attempted assassination.

The following day the local soldiers and guards were ordered to search for assassins throughout the city. The picturesque city turned overnight into a battlefield, with an atmosphere of terror. In order to prepare for the worst, the emperor sat up in full battle array against any further attack. At midnight, a light suddenly rose in the southeast part of West Lake followed by a thunderous sound. A big ball of fire flew towards the emperor's dragon boat. The imperial guards at once shot arrows and spears at the fire ball, which soon fell into the water. While people were busy fetching the fire ball, Emperor Yong Zheng felt a sudden push on his back and he dropped into the water.

In panic the guards hurried to pull the emperor out of the lake, but he had already swallowed a lot of water. As officials and guards were helping the emperor to calm down, they found the red gauze lantern that had disappeared the night before again at the same place. There was also a sheet of paper with several lines on it: "You self-indulgent ruler, squandering money and manpower only for your own pleasure. Get out of Hangzhou now, or you'll be a dead emperor before dawn."

Emperor Yong Zheng in his rage kicked the lantern into the water. The emperor ordered the would-be assassin arrested at once and before the case was cleared up, the incident should be kept secret. Anyone who dared to leak the news should be punished by death.

However the assassin was nowhere to be found. The emperor and his high officials were seized with fear that he might appear again at any time. Taking no further risks, Emperor Yong Zheng decided to leave Hangzhou for the capital without delay. As for who the assassin was, history has never revealed the secret.

Palace Maid Yan'er

Prince Hong Li was the fourth son of Emperor Yong Zheng. Clever and hard-working, he had been a favourite of his royal parents since childhood. A young prince of 15, one day he was playing alone in the exquisite Yuan Ming Yuan Palace. Catching sight of the palace maid Yan'er, who was sitting by the lake combing her beautiful long hair, the prince took a fancy to her. Her charming figure, white arms and long black hair were so attractive, it was as if she were a fairy coming down from heaven.

Prince Hong Li tiptoed up to the charming girl and playfully covered her eyes with his hands. Yan'er thought it was one of her playmates playing a trick on her, and scolded: "You naughty girl. Get off your hand!"

But the prince just held on even tighter. To beat off her tormentor, Yan'er struck out with her comb, hitting on the prince on the right of his forehead. The prince promptly withdrew his hands in pain. Yan'er turned round to discover that the person who had been teasing her was none other than the prince himself, now with a cut on his forehead. Panic-stricken Yan'er knelt down at once to beg for his mercy.

Prince Hong Li was not angry with her, knowing she had done it unintentionally. Instead he soothed: "Don't worry, Yan'er. I don't blame you and I won't tell anyone about the matter. It wasn't your fault." Then the prince helped her to her feet and left.

At lunch, the empress dowager noticed the cut on

the prince's forehead and asked how he had got it. Hesitating, the prince said that he had tumbled over the roots of a tree and hurt himself. But when the empress dowager checked the cut, she discovered that it could not have been caused by a tumble, for there were comb marks there too. Pressed further by his shrewd mother, the prince had to tell the truth, but he insisted that it was due to his own mischief and not Yan'er's fault. She had hit out just for joke. He begged the empress dowager not to punish Yan'er but the royal mother just waved him away without saying a word.

After lunch, the prince went to his study and the empress dowager called in the palace maid, Yan'er. Yan'er was indeed very attractive, but her beauty upset the empress dowager even more as she thought her lovely son had been ensnared by the girl. Even though he was hurt, he had still spoken in her defence. If he later married her, the empress dowager would no longer control the prince. To prevent such a disaster, the empress dowager decided to get rid of the palace maid as soon as possible.

Having made up her mind, the vicious empress dowager immediately ordered that Yan'er be given a rope to commit suicide. The charming young girl was thus killed by the despotic empress dowager.

On hearing that Yan'er had been called before the empress dowager, Prince Hong Li hurried to see what had happened to the palace maid. But when the prince entered the room, he found Yan'er already lying dead on the ground.

The prince was deeply grieved over the sudden death of the innocent girl. Crying bitterly over her body, he felt responsible for her cruel fate. After all he had provoked the incident in the first place.

Yan'er had died, but the prince's heart was still

hers. Whenever he had the time, the prince would go to the lakeside where he had met the charming girl, and stare blankly at the lake, as if in search of a fond memory.... Or maybe he was repenting the mischief which had caused an innocent girl's death.

A Monk Outwits Qian Long

In the Jingci Temple by the Nanping Mountain of Hangzhou in Zhejiang province, there lived a monk reputed to be eminent for his high character, wide learning and rare eloquence. He often scoffed at the wrong doings of government authorities and thus acquired the sobriquet "Defiant Monk." The general public had such faith in him that they came to regard him as their apostle against misrule and call him "earthly immortal." Even in the capital the tales of his deeds were on everyone's lips, and something was added to these tales each time they were retold.

This monk's fame was such that it even came to the attention of Emperor Qian Long. Being always mindful of his common subjects' affairs and feelings, he decided to meet the monk face to face. As had been his habit, he would protect himself by incognito. Disguised as a scholar, he came to the Jingci Temple and asked to see the "Defiant Monk" in particular.

Impressed by the visitor's elegant attire and proud bearing, the monk judged him to be a dignitary of some sort.

"Holy man, you are the Defiant Monk, aren't you?" asked the emperor at the first sight.

"Sir, I admire your discerning eyes," remarked the monk. "Indeed I am none other than the Defiant Monk."

"You took the Buddhist vows early in life or later in life, may I ask?"

"It might be said that I turned monk halfway

through life," said the monk in a stiff tone. "Why the question, sir?"

The emperor was far from pleased at the monk's somewhat overbearing manner. Then pointing at the crazy robe the monk was wearing, he asked derisively: "Eminent as you are, why is your robe made up of so many small pieces fitted together? Is it wise to cut into pieces what was originally whole dress material?"

Smiling, the monk said: "It is true my clothes are all patchwork, but I have a heart good and pure. On the other hand, many high officials are only too evil-hearted in spite of the finest silk clothes they have on."

These remarks came like a slap on the royal face. His Majesty was determined to induce the monk to commit errors, so that he could teach him a lesson or two.

Later they took a stroll together and came up to a man who was busy weaving a bamboo basket. Picking up a bamboo strip and pointing at its green side, the emperor asked with a cunning intent: "Holy man, what do you call this?"

"Bamboo skin."

Then touching the other side of a yellow color, the emperor again asked a loaded question: "What do you call this?"

"Bamboo flesh."

As it was, the emperor had secretly hoped the monk would customarily call the green side "*mie qing*," referring to the outer cuticle of a bamboo, and the yellow side "*mie huang*," meaning the inner skin of a bamboo. Through homophonic punning, *mie qing* might be interpreted to mean the destruction of the House of Qing, and *mie huang*, to mean the destruction of a sovereign. If the monk had called a spade a spade, he could be accused of committing a serious offense as suggested by the interpretation of the homophonic puns. But the monk was clever enough to have put himself on guared against such an eventuality and thus foiled the emperor's scheme.

"You have indeed used curious terms in calling the green and yellow sides of a bamboo," commented the emperor showing a tint of embarrassment.

"As moral beliefs are fast changing, so everything else cannot remain unchanged. Or we'll be deceived by people with ulterior designs."

The emperor seemed to feel a whip on his back. But in the circumstances he had to refrain from showing his displeasure. Then as they passed by the temple kitchen, they saw a puppy pissing to a basket full of bean sprouts. The emperor again asked the monk: "Are these bean sprouts clean?"

"Bean sprouts are clean beyond compare," replied the monk, "because they germinate and grow in clean water."

"But how can you call them clean if puppy urine has showered down on them?"

"You are wrong there, sir," retorted the monk. "As the saying goes, what the eye sees not is clean, what the ear hears not true. The thing is, some people have eyes but cannot see the common people are suffering from cold and hunger. And they have ears but cannot hear what all the world are saying against them. They are forever singing the praise of the imperial grace and of a world seemingly in peace and prosperity."

Much enraged as he was by these remarks, the emperor still forced himself to appear calm so as not to expose his own identity. Just then a peddler was loudly hawking his hot boiled eggs. The emperor was secretly delighted at a new opportunity to drive the monk into a corner.

"Holy man, are you keeping a vegetarian diet?"

"Of course, I am. A non-vegetarian diet is strictly forbidden to a Buddhist."

"You are right there," concurred the emperor.

Then His Majesty bought a couple of eggs from the peddler and handed them to the monk, saying: "Holy man, please eat these eggs. They are products of your own temple."

In the emperor's mind, eggs could be regarded as vegetarian, because of their lack of flesh and blood; and they could also be supposed to be non-vegetarian, because of their hatching nature. If the monk refused to eat the eggs, he could be accused of allowing the sale of something non-vegetarian in a place of Buddhist worship. If he accepted the invitation to eat them, he could also be charged with the sin of eating non-vegetarian things in breach of Buddhist discipline. Thus in either case the monk would be committing an offense against the law, Buddhist or imperial.

But without any hesitation the monk crammed the eggs down his throat. Before the emperor had time to pass a remark the monk uttered these lines:

Whatever is inside a shell,
It shows no signs of real life.
As I break it from evil spell,
Of no use is the butcher's knife.

Then the monk roared with laughter. And as the legend says, two full-fledged chickens flew out of his wide open mouth up into the blue sky. Emperor Qian Long began to realise he was no match for the Defiant Monk and left the temple without further ado.

Emperor's Own Choice of Candidate

According to the imperial examination system of the Qing Dynasty, each year 360 candidates would be selected as the best scholars in the highest level examination. Of these, the top three scholars were called Zhuang Yuan (No.1 scholar), Bang Yan (No.2 scholar) and Tan Hua (No.3 scholar).

As a rule, the number one scholar in the imperial examination would be chosen by the emperor himself. After the examination, the chief examiner would present the emperor with a list of the top ten scholars, and leave the final decision up to him.

During the exam period, candidates from different parts of the country would come to Beijing, and the hotels would change their names to solicit the special customers. Most of them would call themselves Zhuang Yuan Hotels (No.1 scholar hotels), just to meet the psychological needs of the candidates.

One year, Emperor Qian Long decided to make inspections incognito to get firsthand information about the candidates' attitudes towards the exam. One evening, the emperor came to a small inn and asked: "Are there any candidates staying here?"

"We have one," answered the owner.

"Only one?" asked the emperor, incredulously. However, he could guess why the candidates didn't want to stay here. Since the hotel was called the Bang Yan Hotel (No.2 scholar hotel) and every candidate aimed at the title of number one scholar, it wasn't likely that the hotel would draw much custom from the candidates. But the inn keeper said the name had actually been picked by his customer, who was a candidate himself.

His curiosity pricked, the emperor dropped in to see what kind of a person the candidate would be. The young candidate was studying hard under a lamp and on hearing his visitor's step, he got up to welcome him.

Emperor Qian Long asked him his name and then what he thought his chance of winning a title in the exam would be. The scholar was called Cheng Gong. Like other candidates, he was also eager to come top in the exam. However, he was perhaps not as ambitious as most, and would be quite satisfied with the title of No.2 scholar.

The emperor appreciated the young man's frank and practical attitude but wondered how the candidate could be sure of winning the number two title.

"To tell you the truth, I am not even sure of winning that. By setting myself that goal, I'm only trying to cheer up my own spirits," said the young man.

"You seem to know your own limits. But do you mind my having a look at your papers?"

"Sure, here you are. Please give me your advice and instruction," pleaded the scholar.

"Well written!" praised the emperor. "Are the papers all written by yourself?"

"Of course. If you have any doubts, I can write something to show you right now," pledged the young man.

"Good!" said Emperor Qian Long, who was himself a learned man. He decided to test the candidate on the spot. He pointed at the opposite window in which a young lady was dressing and making up in front of a mirror, and produced the first line of a verse: "One girl dressing and making up in front of two mirrors on the wall, produces three different pictures."

It was an excellent verse, but not easy to make a matching line, similar both in form and content. Cheng Gong bowed to the visitor to show his respect for the eloquent line. The emperor made a bow in return. Seeing the shadows of their bowing to each other on the wall, Cheng Gong was enlightened and composed a matching line on the spot: "One lamp lighting up two people's bows projects four shadows on both sides of the wall."

Emperor Qian Long gasped in admiration and assured the young man of his victory in winning the second title in the exam.

After the imperial examination, the chief examiner presented a list of the top ten scholars for the emperor's perusal. The emperor found Cheng Gong's name in tenth position. However remembering that he had already promised the young man the second title, the emperor moved his name up to the second place.

The chief examiner thought the emperor might have made a mistake and eagerly reminded him of the correct name list. The emperor ignored his advice and ordered him to announce the list as it stood.

Cheng Gong was overwhelmed with joy and exclaimed in admiration that the strange visitor who had comc to his hotel room to talk with him, was really foresighted.

Emperor and a Donkey Driver

Emperor Qian Long once decided to make an incognito inspection of Tongxian county in the outer suburbs of Beijing. The emperor disguised himself as a merchant pretending to go to the county for some fermented bean curd. To make the trip he hired a donkey at the Qihemen Gate, east of the city. The donkey driver was a man in his 50s who loved boasting and talking nonsense. On their way to Tongxian county, the driver kept praising the Emperor Qian Long. He said that the emperor was a great ruler with tremendous civil and military accomplishments.

"May I ask who you are?" asked the donkey driver.

"I am Gao Tianci, a merchant. And you?" replied the emperor.

"My name is Wang Da."

"Where are you living?"

"Outside the Qihemen Gate."

"How do you like your job?"

"My job is serving people. I'm no better than a servant."

"Then why don't you find any other job?"

"As a matter of fact, it wouldn't be difficult for me to get a better job: I have a rich and influential relative who would be only too glad to offer me a good job, if I went to ask him for help. However, I am a man of upright character and don't like to curry favour with others."

"Who is your rich relative, may I ask?"

"The number one person under the sun, Emperor

Qian Long himself. We have been close friends since childhood."

The emperor felt both a mixture of surprise and annoyance but took care not to reveal his true feelings. Having arrived in Tongxian county, Emperor Qian Long first went to make his investigation of official affairs. Only shortly before leaving the county, did the emperor buy the fermented bean curd to cover his real purpose. He then rode the same donkey on his way back home.

The emperor found the donkey fast and strong and wanted to keep it for himself. When they approached the Qihemen Gate, the donkey driver asked Emperor Qian Long to dismount. But the emperor said: "I live not far from the Forbidden City. If you escort me back home, you will receive twice as much."

Driver Wang was of course delighted to earn the extra money. When they got to the Donghuamen Gate of the Forbidden City, an officer standing on the remparts of the city wall cried: "His Majesty has come back!" A group of palace guards and high ranking officials marched out to welcome the emperor on their knees along the approach to the gate.

By now, Driver Wang was completely panic-stricken. "Heavens!" he murmured to himself. "This fellow was none other than the emperor himself. I'll be in real trouble now for all the nonsense I was saying earlier." Trembling with fear, he couldn't utter a word. He stood there staring blankly, while the emperor was escorted by high officials into the Forbidden City on the back of his donkey.

As a result, the poor driver not only received no pay for the trip, he also lost his donkey. How could he make a living without the donkey? What a stroke of bad luck! He was about to trudge home with a heavy heart, when a eunuch appeared to call him to the palace.

As soon as he saw the emperor, Driver Wang promptly knelt down to plead for mercy: "Your Majesty, I didn't know you were the emperor. I did not mean to ridicule you with any nonsense, but I still deserve a punishment. You shouldn't pay me for the trip and if you like, you can also keep my donkey."

Emperor Qian Long laughed: "We are close friends, aren't we? You are innocent because you didn't know who I was. As for the donkey, how much do you want for it? Offer a price and I will pay you."

"If you like it, you can have it as a gift," said the driver.

"Then what should I give you in return?"

"I can no longer be a donkey driver without the animal. But I could make a living as a cart driver if I had a cart."

Emperor Qian Long ordered that Wang Da be given 50 carts to start a cart company. Later, Wang hired many people to help him pull the carts, and thus was the first rickshaw company in Beijing formed, according to certain tales.

Betting on Chess Playing

Duoduo, who held the title of Prince Yu, was the 15th son of Nuerhachi and one of the founders of the Qing Dynasty. He was also given the appellation of "Iron Hat Prince," meaning that his princeship was hereditary and that his successors also enjoyed the privilege of dispensing with the ritual of kneeling to the emperor on any occasion. By the time of Emperor Qian Long the title of Prince Yu had passed down to the fourth generation. The young Prince Yu and Emperor Qian Long were both chess addicts and tolerably skilled in playing the game. They often saw each other and seldom parted without measuring their strength at the game.

Once Prince Yu suggested a betting on a match with Emperor Qian Long.

"I like that," said the emperor with enthusiasm. "What are the conditions of the betting?"

"If I lose a game, you can have a stud on my gate pulled out as a trophy. In case you lose, you must grant me a promotion to a higher rank and a corresponding increase in my official salary."

With full confidence to win out in the match, the emperor generously agreed to these conditions and at once had the chessboard set between them.

At the beginning stage of the first game, the emperor was in full control of the situation, with his chief chessmen, called chariots, horsemen and cannons, taking up advantageous positions in a swift offensive. On the other hand, Prince Yu assumed the defensive, making each move carefully with a view to launching a counter-attack at an opportune moment. Thus the prince felt uncertain in making his moves, so that he failed to hold in check the emperor's all-out assault and went down to defeat.

"Well, what have you to say of this game?" asked the emperor in elation.

"You win a stud from my gate, of course."

In the second game, Prince Yu found that the emperor, still flushed with his success in the first game, appeared to be overly self-confident. So he thought it wiser to switch to the offensive. First he got rid of one of the emperor's overreaching chariots at the expense of one of his own. Then with cannon fire he bombarded off the chessboard his rival's defensive pieces. Finally he drove forward with the full power of one chriot and one horseman. The emperor had to concede defeat when his defenses broke down.

Immediately the prince spread out a sheet of paper before the emperor and asked him to write out an edict promoting him to a higher rank. As a betting was a betting, the emperor kept his word. And the match went on until well after midnight at the end of the 10th game when tiredness overcame them.

"The final count is five wins for each," said Prince Yu. "So you are at liberty to take away five gate studs to show your triumphs. But you must also promote me five grades up with corresponding salary rise."

The emperor had overrated his own ability in chess playing. The outcome was indeed something hurting his pride as a chess player.

"Five gate studs in exchange for a promotion five grades up," muttered the emperor, "it's unfair!"

But an emperor's word was law. His Majesty could not go back on his word and only regretted having made a disadvantageous betting.

The prince was quick to nail the emperor down to his agreement on the betting, saying: "A gentleman is always faithful to his word. Honour is at stake."

"Of course, I'll do as I say," the emperor assured the prince.

Back in his inner chambers, the emperor felt upset for what had happened. He had a mind to avenge his defeat on the prince in some way. But this was out of the question, for the prince enjoyed immunity to any punishment, a practice followed since the time of Duoduo, the first Prince Yu. After much head-racking, the emperor came up with an idea to win what might be called a spiritual victory. He issued an order to increase the height of the walls surrounding Prince Yu's mansion, so that these walls would resemble those of a prison. The idea lay in a symbolic imprisonment of the prince for life.

Thinking the idea to be comic, the prince said: "I feel all the more secure, as no thief can climb over such high walls."

An Unbeatable Scholar

Ji Xiaolan, the chief compiler of the great anthology *The Complete Collection of Ancient and Modern Books*, was a remarkable scholar, quick-witted, eloquent, and humorous. Emperor Qian Long, also a learned man and fond of outwitting others, often designed tricky questions to baffle this scholar under his patronage.

Once the emperor took Ji Xiaolan with him on a visit to Hangzhou. When the royal party came before a grocery His Majesty suddenly pointed to the signboard over the door of the store and asked the scholar: "What is that?"

Ji looked up to find the signboard bearing four characters: "yellow poplar wood combs." He was at once aware of the emperor's intention to test his wits. If he said what it really was, he reasoned, the emperor would surely take it as an insult to his royal intelligence, for only a moron, certainly not an emperor who was the master of the land, would fail to recognize a signboard when he saw one. So he came up with an unexpected answer: "That's a couplet."

Puzzled at the reply, the emperor queried its truth: "How can a single line make a couplet?"

But the scholar said: "Your Majesty may know that Hangzhou is a cultural city which must be viewed in its entirety. One line of a couplet may be found at one place, and the other line at another." Then pointing to a signboard over the door of a store some way off, he continued: "Please look, there is the other line of the couplet." It happened that this signboard bore also four characters: "white lotus root starch."

The emperor saw it was a clear case of sophistry on the part of Ji Xiaolan. But the characters on both signboards did make a perfect couplet. And what Ji had said was too plausible to pick fault with. So the emperor was obliged to give him credit for it.

Later when they stopped before a picture-mounting shop, they found the signboard bearing the words: "Mounting fine artistic works of Tang, Song, Yuan, Ming dynasties." Here came another opportunity for the emperor to do his scholar down as he asked: "Is this also one of the lines of a couplet?" With this question the emperor was setting a trap for Ji. The trick was this. If Ji said yes, he would have a hard time finding the other matching line. If he answered no, he would be accused of having said an untruth to his emperor at the earlier time.

But Ji said with a nod of his head: "Yes, it certainly is. The other line is there by the door of the drug-store across the street." The emperor looked and saw on a board these clearly written words: "Gathering quality medicinal herbs from Sichuan, Guangdong, Yunnan, Guizhou provinces." Again a perfect couplet there was.

As it was, Emperor Qian Long felt a secret admiration for the scholar's quick wits. But to satisfy his royal ego he still tried to subdue Ji intellectually with even more catchy questions. When boating on the Miluo River, into which the great ancient poet Qu Yuan had jumped to end his own life, the emperor asked Ji: "If a sovereign wants a subject of his to die, how must the subject act?"

"He must not refuse to die," came the reply.

"Do you believe it to be true that a loyal subject is

not afraid of death?"

"Of course, I do."

"Well, you are a loyal subject of mine, aren't you?"

"By consulting my conscience, I feel I am absolutely loyal to Your Majesty. I would never hesitate a moment to go through fire and water for you."

"Well, then, I order you now to throw youself into the Miluo River to end your life."

"Your imperial order shall be obeyed."

Making a deep bow to the emperor, Ji ran toward the end of the boat and assumed a jumping attitude. But he stopped short and a few moments later returned to the royal side.

"Why, you are refusing to carry out my order?" demanded the emperor.

"I was certainly willing to follow your imperial order," said the scholar calmly. "But I was on the point of plunging into the river when I heard the voice of Qu Yuan. He took me to task as he said: 'Over 2,000 years ago the King of Chu State ruled his people with a heavy hand, favouring the treacherous but persecuting the loyal. In the end he ruined himself as well as his country. I ended my life in the Miluo River in angry protest against the injustice of the time. But today you are serving a benevolent sovereign in an age of peace and prosperity. What's the reason for you to throw yourself into the river? If you jump into the water to end your life, what would people say of your emperor?' His criticism of me made me see the light. Now I realize I must not injure your fair name with my death. So I am back here."

The emperor said in admiration: "What a rare talent he is!"

Ji Xiaolan was also an easygoing man, unmindful of conventions. In the heat of summer he would be stripped to the waist while working. Once he was in such an undressed state when it was announced that the emperor was coming to his office. To avoid an affront on His Majesty, the scholar hastily hid himself under a table. Pretending not to have seen the act, the emperor sat quietly in a chair by the table. After a long while, getting uncomfortable in the cramped space under the table, Ji signed to an attendant by pointing a middle finger upward as he asked: "Has the old man gone yet?"

At once displeased and amused, the emperor exclaimed with pretended sternness: "Get out of there, you rude man!"

Crawling out from under the table, Ji Xiaolan knelt before the emperor and begged his pardon.

"I'll pardon you," promised the emperor, "if you can give a good reason for calling me 'old man'."

In the Chinese language, the term "old man" is literally expressed in three words: "*Lao Tou Zi* (old head son)." Thus Ji Xiaolan was able to give a clever reason.

"The fact is," he said, "Your Majesty is generally addressed as 'Ten Thousand Years' and hence 'old'. A sovereign is always regarded as the head of all people and hence 'head'. And Your Majesty is by nature a 'son of Heaven' and hence 'son'. With these ideas put together, Your Majesty is most properly addressed as 'old head son'."

"But why did you point up a middle finger of yours?"

"Well, it refers to you as a sovereign," Ji explained. "In a family shrine there is usually a board inscribed with the words: heaven, earth, sovereign, parents and teacher, and as the word sovereign is placed in the middle, it can be signified with a middle finger. Am I right?"

Thus time and again Ji Xiaolan was able to resort to sophistry to perfectly explain away his answers to questions meant to baffle him by Emperor Qian Long. In the end His Majesty thought no more of beating such a genius of a scholar.

A Dish of Phoenix Eggs

Li Diaoyuan was a versatile playwright with great knowledge and a large circle of friends. He was also a favourite of Emperor Qian Long, who would sometimes summon him to the palace to recite poems and sing operas at imperial feasts.

Once Emperor Qian Long ordered an official to summon Li to the palace, but he was nowhere to be found. When the official was told that the writer often frequented theatres, he went to one and found the playwright acting in a play on the stage. On the emperor's order, the writer was snatched to the palace even before he could change his costume.

The emperor rebuked: "As an official scholar, you are not allowed to mingle with actors and actresses, let alone act in a play on the stage. Aren't you afraid of losing your post?"

"Your Majesty, if I were removed from the post, I could find some other work to do," replied Li Diaoyuan.

"As a man of letters you could do neither farming nor weaving. How would you make a living?"

"I could work as a playwright or an actor."

"What if I ban your plays?"

"Then I could open a restaurant. I am a good cook."

The emperor was surprised to know the scholar was also a good cook and asked doubtfully: "Really?"

"I dare not deceive Your Majesty."

"Good. On Spring Festival Day I will give a grand

banquet for my ministers and generals and you can present a most delicious dish for the occasion."

"Please give your order."

"A dish of phoenix eggs," said the emperor.

The phoenix is a legendary bird from ancient times and nobody has ever seen one, let alone obtain its eggs. How could he present such a dish? The playwright knew the emperor was deliberately putting him in a difficult position. However, the resourceful playwright thought since nobody had ever seen a phoenix, he could cook a dish at will.

At the Spring Festival banquet, the emperor and high officials were expecting to have a taste of the never known dish of phoenix eggs, when the playwright presented to the first table a big plate of fragrant shining eggs. The scholar and cook carved the eggs into slices and presented a slice of egg first to the emperor.

Wondering what it was made of, the emperor hesitated but could not resist the savoury smell. He tasted it and pronounced it delicious. After the emperor had a taste, the ministers and generals all followed suit and devoured it all. "The phoenix egg is the most delicious dish we have ever had," flattered the officials to the emperor. The resourceful scholar had defeated the emperor in a battle of wits.

Imperial Lady Xiang Fei Dies for Loyalty

Emperor Qian Long happened to learn that a Uighur Chieftain in Xinjiang, northwest China, had a very charming wife nicknamed Xiang Fei (Lady Fragrance). The emperor wanted to take this rare beauty from the chieftain to become one of his imperial concubines.

When General Zhao Hui was appointed to take command of Xinjiang, Emperor Qian Long asked the general to bring him the lady. As soon as he arrived in Xinjiang, the general began great efforts to fulfil the emperor's special mission.

Before long the general succeeded in kidnapping Lady Xiang Fei and immediately reported the good news to the emperor. Overjoyed, Emperor Qian Long ordered the local officials along the way from Xinjiang to Beijing to send troops to escort Lady Xiang Fei from one city to another and see to it that the lady should not be tired, fall ill or commit suicide on the way. If anything happened to the lady, the officials concerned should bear the whole responsibility.

Emperor Qian Long specially prepared a building in Zhong Nanhai Palace for Lady Xiang Fei and decided to make her an honourable imperial lady. But Lady Xiang Fei resolutely refused and stayed aloof from the emperor, no matter how sincere the emperor showed his good intention. Terribly homesick, Lady Xiang Fei would stare blankly towards the northwest with tears running down her cheeks. She sometimes even thought of committing suicide to end her miserable life. In order to prevent any such accident, the emperor sent heavy guards to keep watch day and night for her security.

To please the lady, Emperor Qian Long ordered a mosque built in the Hui nationality area, opposite to Zhong Nanhai Palace with similar architecture to that in the lady's hometown. Whenever she felt homesick, she would mount the second floor of the mosque, accompanied by a group of palace maids of Hui nationality to view the Hui people in the busy market. Only at such moments did Lady Xiang Fei feel relieved, as if she were in her own hometown. In time this building became known as the Lady's Gazing Tower.

Although she was treated as royally as an empress, Lady Xiang Fei did not change her love for her husband and hometown. She was distressed all day long for she knew the emperor would not let her go. On the other hand, the emperor was also depressed at not winning the charming lady. He even lost interest in handling state affairs.

The emperor's mother was very worried about the matter. She persuaded her son to give up the lady, but in vain. The emperor insisted in winning over Lady Xiang Fei.

Once when Emperor Qian Long left the palace to worship the gods, the empress dowager seized the opportunity to talk to the lady privately. "The emperor sincerely loves you. What makes you so indifferent as to refuse him?" asked the empress dowager.

"I am married and should be faithful to my husband. No matter how sincere His Majesty loves me, I will not change my mind," replied Lady Xiang Fei.

"If the emperor insists, what can you do?"

"I'd better die, or first kill the emperor, then die."

Greatly shocked and worried about the emperor's safety, the empress dowager pondered for a while and asked: "What if I let you die for your loyalty?" Satisfied but weeping bitterly, the lady thanked the empress dowager for her sympathy. With tears running down her cheeks, the empress dowager sadly ordered a guard to give the lady a piece of white silk to hang herself in a side room.

When Emperor Qian Long learnt the news, he hurried to the Ci Ning Gong Hall in which the lady had committed suicide, but could not enter the locked room. The emperor cried bitterly, striking on the door. When the door was opened, came out the empress dowager looking sad.

Emperor Qian Long rushed into the room and found Lady Xiang Fei lying dead on the bed. Mournfully the emperor almost cried his heart out, but the deceased could not be revived. With a sense of guilt Emperor Qian Long ordered a great funeral ceremony for the lady as compensation.

A Miniature Golden Dragon Boat

Once upon a time there was a restaurant with the special Mongolian flavour of boiled mutton in Niujie Street (Ox Street) in south Beijing. Its owner was a Hui national by the name of Bai Shuyu. Dressing as a commoner, Emperor Qian Long often frequented the restaurant for its specialty and became acquainted with the owner. Once the emperor invited the shop owner to his home to show him how to cook mutton. The shop owner agreed.

The following day Bai Shuyu arrived at the west gate of the Forbidden City according to the address left by the emperor. However the imperial guards did not allow him to enter until he showed them the imperial address. Then Bai Shuyu was politely ushered into the inner palace. After a while a man appeared accompanying a group of people. Taking a close look, Bai recognized the person in the middle was none other than his frequent customer, the one who had offered to teach him how to cook mutton.

When the shop owner heard people calling the man His Majesty, he knew his long-time customer was none other than the emperor. He promptly knelt down asking for mercy.

"You are innocent and a very good cook," said the emperor.

"Your Majesty, please excuse me, if I have unintentionally offended you one way or another. I really didn't know you were the emperor."

Emperor Qian Long waved his hand and motioned

for him to start cooking his special dish. Thereafter the shop owner was quite often summoned to serve the emperor in the palace.

As the Dragon Boat Festival was approaching, Emperor Qian Long remembered the boating tradition and ordered a miniature golden dragon boat built in celebration of the festival. Upon the order, the chief official in charge of imperial household affairs went to Qianmen market in the south of the Forbidden City in search of a highly skilled goldsmith to make a golden dragon boat within only a few days.

Before long the golden dragon boat was sent to the palace, but before presenting it to the emperor, the head eunuch ordered a craftsman to make a copy of the miniature with silver and gold plating and kept the one made of real gold for himself.

The next day the miniature golden dragon boat was presented to the emperor who was pleased with its exquisite design. However at a close look, he found it was not made entirely of gold. Having ordered an official to check up, the emperor was told that the boat was made of gold-plated silver. As the forgery was brought to light, the eunuch responsible for the manufacture made a false charge against the goldsmith, saying: "Your Majesty, the goldsmith must have wanted the gold for himself and tried to deceive you with a boat made of silver."

Enraged, the emperor ordered the goldsmith and his whole family punished by death.

The goldsmith was panic-stricken at the unexpected disaster and at a loss what to do. He had crafted the boat of real gold with his own hands. How could it become silver? He was innocent and hoped some influential person would plead his case. Then he was introduced to the shop owner Bai Shuyu, who happened to know the emperor personally. However Bai was reluctant to involve himself in the dispute, for he had no evidence to prove the goldsmith innocent. If he pleaded for a culprit, he himself would be punished. But the goldsmith vowed that he had been wrongly treated and begged the shop owner to help him.

Bai Shuyu in sympathy agreed to take a hand in the matter. He presumed that if the goldsmith were innocent, someone might have played an underhand game in switching the boat. In view of such possible wrongdoing, how could he sit idle and refuse to help the innocent goldsmith? But he realized the case might be very complicated and should be handled in a very careful way. Otherwise not only the goldsmith could not be saved but he himself would be in trouble.

One night Bai Shuyu happened to be called into the palace to play chess with the emperor. During the game Bai Shuyu took a chance to express his anxiety and sighed sadly.

"What's wrong with you?" inquired the emperor.

"I'm upset by a horrible story," answered the shop owner.

"What story?"

"I dare not tell."

"Speak out. I won't blame you."

"I heard the goldsmith would be severely punished for making a dragon boat with silver instead of gold. Is that true?" asked Bai.

"True. He would be punished by death," replied the emperor.

"Your Majesty, but I was told the goldsmith is innocent."

"How do you know?"

'It's said the dragon boat was only a model. If you were satisfied with it, he would make a gold dragon boat after the model."

Surprised, the emperor said that no one had ever told him about the matter. But the shop owner assured him that it was true.

"In such case, the goldsmith should not be punished, but he should quickly make a dragon boat of real gold," demanded the emperor. For the survival of the whole family, the goldsmith had to borrow a lot of money to make another gold dragon boat for the emperor. The incident almost ruined the goldsmith's family if not for the help of the shop owner.

In order to express his gratitude after the shop owner died, the goldsmith collected money to build a pagoda in honour of the shop owner in east Beijing.

Gaining Favour by Flattery

One fine day in the late spring of 1750, Emperor Qian Long made a sightseeing trip to the Yuan Ming Yuan Palace. By midday, the emperor felt a bit hot and asked for a sunshade, but the attendants had not prepared one in advance. The emperor was very angry and rebuked the attendants: "Who is in charge of this trip?"

Looking at each other in blank dismay, nobody in the entourage dared answer. Eventually, someone replied: "Your humble servant is to blame."

Emperor Qian Long looked at the young man and asked: "Who are you?"

"My name is He Sheng, formerly a Manchu cadet, now appointed to attend Your Majesty."

When Emperor Qian Long took a close look at the young attendant, he was suddenly reminded of a similar figure, the late young palace maid, Yan'er, who had been forced to die because of his unintentional mischief. Consequently, the emperor had a special feeling towards the young attendant. On his return from the sight-seeing trip, the emperor appointed He Sheng to the post of overseer of the palace guard, and also put him in charge of some imperial household affairs, such as organizing the emperor's food, clothing and leisure time activities. He Sheng did his best to watch the emperor's every mood and anticipate his every desire. Before long he was the emperor's trusted right hand man: later still, he even rose to the post of prime minister.

Emperor Qian Long's tenth daughter was his favourite often dressing herself like a man, and accompanying him on his trips outside the capital. He Sheng also seized every opportunity to flatter the princess in order to win her royal father's favour.

Once, whilst accompanying her father on a trip, the princess caught sight of a red garment in a shop and murmured to herself: "What a beautiful dress!" Without delay, He Sheng bought the garment at a high price and presented it to the princess as a gift. The emperor teased: "You should thank your would-be father-in-law!" However, years later, the words said in jest came true: when the princess grew up, she married the son of Prime Minister He Sheng.

Prime Minister He Sheng then became a relative of the royal family. With his great power and influence, he terrified most of the officials to such a degree that they were even more frightened of him than of the emperor. Many of them went to seek his patronage, presenting him gold, silver and all kinds of treasures for flattery and bribery. In order to keep these possessions, He Sheng built himself four big treasuries and chose the eight most trusted and intelligent girls of his own clan as the keepers. The treasuries were heavily guarded with 16 wolfhounds and outsiders were not allowed to approach under any circumstances.

According to some statistics, during the reign of Emperor Qian Long the annual national revenue was about 70 million taels of silver; but He Sheng alone accumulated 700 million taels of silver during his 20 years in power!

A Rare Treasure

One summer afternoon, Emperor Qian Long arrived at Yuan Ming Yuan Palace for a short rest. The trees and flowers all looked fresh and new after the rain. On the journey to Yuan Ming Yuan, the emperor had caught sight of something like a red ball in the center of the lake; the ball had sent out bright rays in all directions, but gradually the rays had diminished, and in the end, faded away altogether. However, the next day he saw the spectacle repeated in exactly the same place. Puzzled, the emperor called in a group of high officials to discuss the matter.

In the discussion, some officials suspected that the phenomenon might be a heavenly fire; others thought it was a kind of earthly light; the rest assumed the rays must be reflections of light from a long way off. But an old man with white hair and a long beard disagreed: "It must be the radiation of some precious treasure in the lake."

"Whatever it is, I want people sent to look carefully in the lake," the emperor ordered.

The following day, a group of boatmen and palace guards jumped into the lake to search for the so-called treasure. Hours later they had found nothing more special than a huge clam, which was brought to the palace, eunuchs and high officials all gathered to see the rare treasure. The white-haired old man assumed that the red rays must be reflections of the pearls in the huge clam.

Some people said that if there were pearls in the clam it would be a good omen for the emperor. It would mean the heavenly god was sending His Majesty a blessing.

Emperor Qian Long was overjoyed and ordered the clam cracked open, and a big pearl sending out golden rays was found inside. The emperor put the pearl in his palm and gasped with admiration. But what should this pearl be used for? Some officials suggested putting it on the board above the front door of the court; others argued it should be on display in the palace museum.

"But I'd prefer putting it on my crown as a decoration," the emperor said. Everyone present flattered him that this was a superb idea.

However, when the emperor put on the crown with the big pearl on it, he felt himself being lifted like a feather. Bewildered, the emperor called in some high officials for an explanation.

One senior official said: "The pearl was formed with a heavenly spirit inside it. If we bore a hole in it, the pearl will let the spirit go. That way Your Majesty would no longer feel as though he was being lifted."

The emperor took the official's advice and ordered a skilful craftsman to make an air hole in th huge pearl. As a result, the emperor indeed no longer felt as though he was being lifted like a feather when he put on the crown but at the same time, the pearl stopped emitting golden rays.

By putting the pearl on his crown, Emperor Qian Long unwittingly set an example for his vain officials to follow. They also started using pearls to decorate their official hats; later still, the pearls even used as a sign of official rank, with different sizes of pearls being used for the different ranks of officials in the Qing Dynasty.

Dining in a Beggar's Home

Once Emperor Qian Long disguised himself in plain clothes to make a private trip with the state ministers He Sheng and Liu Yong. They left Yuan Ming Yuan Palace for the mountainous areas to the west of Beijing.

Yuan Ming Yuan Palace was as exquisite as a fairyland; outside the garden, there was beautiful countryside, with paddy fields, running rivers, huts, laboring people, dogs, pigs and chickens. Liu Yong was a learned official with a humorous touch, and hence a popular member of the emperor's entourage.

Throughout the journey, Liu Yong explained the local traditions and customs and told folk stories to delight the group of trippers. So enthralled by his stories and jokes, the group even forgot to eat lunch. Late in the afternoon, they were all hungry but found themselves in a desolate place far from villages or restaurants.

They climbed a hill and saw several tumbledown huts clustered together in the distance. Feeling considerably happier, they headed for the place, which turned out to be a village of beggars. All the inhabitants were beggars, and the village head was called "Beggar Wang".

The emperor and his high officials were so hungry that, ignoring all conventions, they condescended to ask for food from the beggars. Poor as they were, the beggars still advocated brotherhood. As Beggar Wang heard people coming to ask for food, he took out two ox bones and struck them against each other, giving the signal to prepare for the entertainment of guests. Responding to the signal, the village beggars brought forth their food and dishes and set out a big table of food in Beggar Wang's home.

The emperor had dainties of every kind in the palace and had never eaten such a coarse meal.

However, in his state of hunger, Emperor Qian Long thought the meal quite delicious.

"I am sorry," said Beggar Wang. "We poor people can only offer you a very coarse meal."

"How can you call yourself poor with so much delicious food? You are quite rich," said the emperor, who even ordered that the name "Beggars Village" be changed. He asked the village head to give him a pen and some paper so that he could write down a new name for the village.

Amusingly, the beggars said they had not had things like pen and paper in their homes for many generations. Emperor Qian Long nodded in silence. But soon after the trip, the emperor sent a stone tablet inscribed with three big characters in his own handwriting: "Most Prosperous Village". The name has been preserved ever since, and it now really is a prosperous village in the west suburb of Beijing!

A Base for Firing Weapons

A firing weapons base was one of the military units for training troops in the Qing Dynasty. Originally it was called blue dragon navy base built in the reign of Emperor Kang Xi and located near the summer villa at Rehe, Hebei province. Most of the 10,000 strong soldiers were recruited from coastal areas, such as Guangdong and Fujian provinces. They were able to fight both on land and water.

In the reign of Emperor Qian Long General Ni Mashan was the commander of the navy base. Under his strict training, the navy became a force with strong fight capacity. However the general was displeased by the powerful Prime Minister He Sheng for his strictness.

On one of Emperor Qian Long's reviews of the navy, the prime minister seized the opportunity to make a charge against the general. He Sheng deliberately asked the emperor to cancel the review, saying: "Your Majesty, I suggest that you should not review the navy."

"Why not?" asked the emperor.

"The commander of the navy base is reported to have long harboured rebellious ambitions. Your Majesty's security would be a problem, for the general is not trustworthy." However the prime minister couldn't produce any evidence to prove his views. Emperor Qian Long reproved: "You are too suspicious." The emperor did not believe He Sheng's story, but He Sheng would not give up his plan to remove his political rival.

Before Emperor Qian Long came to review the navy, He Sheng secretly sent men to fire three shots into the wall of the reviewing hall.

As General Ni Mashan issued the order, the review began with warships sailing out midst the din of gongs and drums, sailors strong and grand gathering at the rally. It was a foggy day making the review a bit mysterious. When the shooting exercises started, the whole lake seemed on fire, to the great delight of the emperor. At that moment He Sheng rushed in and knelt before the emperor, reporting: "Your Majesty, bad news!"

"What?" inquired the emperor.

"Attempted assassination!"

Shocked, the emperor asked: "Where is the assassin?"

"He must be in the navy, and shot at the reviewing hall during the firing exercise."

"Any evidence?" asked the emperor.

"Please look here, Your Majesty." He Sheng pointed at the wall of the reviewing hall.

The emperor indeed saw three bullet holes in the wall. Burning with anger the emperor ordered the exercise stopped at once. The whole navy was forced to return to their barracks and wait for a thorough examination.

General Ni Mashan was summoned to report to the emperor with regard to the incident. But before the general could finish his explanation, he was bound up by palace guards.

The general cried for mercy, but the emperor waved his hand, ordering: "Push him out and behead him."

After the death of General Ni Mashan, He Sheng

sent away thousands of the general's men home in order to prevent them from a rebellion. Thus the once victorious navy was destroyed in a twinkling, leaving only the reviewing hall as a historical relic.

Later, He Sheng instigated Emperor Qian Long to build an army base in a place where several thousand *mu* of fertile land would be requisitioned causing tens of thousands of farmers to lose their means of livelihood. In order to boycott the plan, the farmers lined up along the roadside to petition the emperor on his way to the Fragrant Hills, west of Beijing. The farmers knelt down, crying out their grievances over the plan. The emperor however made high-flown remarks, like: "It is important to build the army base from the viewpoint of national defence. How could such a strategic plan be changed just because of occupying some of your land? Don't make a fuss but go away."

The farmers implored the emperor in tearful voice for mercy, but Emperor Qian Long remained firm in his attitude. Then a white-haired old man came up and knelt before the throne presenting his case: "It's very important to build an army base. What we farmers are petitioning for is not our land, but because the location is improper for building an army base in view of geomancy."

"What's wrong with the location?" inquired the emperor.

"The dragon is the symbol of Eight Banner Armies which took over power under the forefather's leadership. Dragons love water, so the army base should be built in a place near water. However, the present site is far away from water and the would-be army base would suffer from drought, an omen harmful to the nation."

Emperor Qian Long believed in geomantic omens,

so he had the patience to listen to the old man's story. The white-haired old man went on saying: "In my opinion the base should be built in a place near Qingshuihe River in the district of Landiancan. The river rises from Jade Fountain Hill which has springs all year round."

Convinced by the geomantic omen, the emperor agreed to change the site and decided to build the army base by Qingshuihe River in the district of Landiancan.

The white-haired old man used his talents to save the farmers from a disaster. After his death, the local people collected money to build him a tombstone in honour of his wisdom and contribution.

Saving a Temple Pillar by Wisdom

In the western suburbs of Beijing, there was an old temple called Dajue Temple. It was built on a mountain with green trees and clear waters, and was an ideal scenic spot for monks to cultivate their minds. Emperor Qian Long had stayed as a monk in the temple, before ascending the throne.

Once Emperor Qian Long revisited the temple accompanied by Prime Minister He Sheng and State Minister Liu Yong. Leading a group of monks, the abbot welcomed the emperor at the gate and acted as a guide showing the emperor and his group the three main halls.

The emperor was deeply impressed by the temple's Ming Dynasty architecture and was fascinated with one of the long and thick nanmu wood pillar in the Tianwang Hall. It was a rare specimen, and its like was seldom seen elsewhere.

The return visit brought back fond memories for the emperor and so he decided to stay overnight in the temple. As he sat down to dinner, the emperor once again gasped with admiration at the nanmu wood pillar.

As soon as the emperor and his entourage left the temple the next morning, the abbot ordered a monk to send for a black-smith to make three big iron hoops for fastening the nanmu wood pillar in the Tianwang Hall. Other monks couldn't figure out what the abbot meant by fastening the well preserved pillar with iron hoops. The abbot said he was only acting in accordance with the Buddha's order.

As a matter of fact, when the abbot saw the emperor's admiration for the nanmu pillar, he feared that he might lose the rare wood. It was in order to guard against any possible requisitioning of the pillar, that the abbot ordered the pillar fastened with iron hoops.

One morning, shortly after the monks had finished their breakfast, they heard a sharp voice: "Come to receive the imperial edict!"

Remaining calm, the old abbot led a group of responsible monks to kneel at the gate of the temple and receive the edict.

A eunuch read in a solemn voice: "The royal court needs top quality wood to repair the Qian Qing Hall in the palace. It is reported that the nanmu pillar in the Tianwang Hall of Dajue Temple is suitable material for the repair. We hereby order the abbot to send the pillar to the palace immediately."

It was actually a scheme thought up by the powerful Prime Minister He Sheng to seize the nanmu pillar and use it for flattering the emperor. He Sheng was good at reading the emperor's mind. When he saw the emperor's admiration for the nanmu pillar, he guessed the emperor's real intention. On returning to the palace, He Sheng suggested that the nanmu pillar in the Dajue Temple would be ideal material for repairing the Qian Qing Hall.

The emperor was naturally pleased with the suggestion and promptly issued the edict to requisition the material.

The monks were at a loss as what to do. If refused to offer the pillar, they would annoy the emperor; if they went ahead and offered it, they would offened the gods. In their awkward position, they could only put their palms together, and murmur to the Budddha for help, "Glory to Amitabha!"

However, the old abbot calmly replied: "Honoured Sir, it would indeed be a great honour for this humble temple to offer its nanmu pillar for the mending of the Qian Qing Hall. But I am afraid this pillar would be of no use, as it has been cracked too badly after hundred years in the temple."

"How is that so?" asked the eunuch incredulously.

"I would not dare lie. Please check it yourself."

The eunuch entered the Tianwang Hall to take a closer look at the pillar and found the pillar being fastened with three iron hoops. Seeing the pillar's condition, the eunuch could only return and report to the emperor.

Emperor Qian Long couldn't even believe his ears when he heard the report. He hadn't seen any cracks or iron hoops in the pillar on his visit to the temple the other day. The emperor turned to minister Liu Yong, who was famous for his good memory and asked him whether he had seen any cracks in the pillar.

As Liu Yong opposed the requisition of the nanmu pillar for mending the hall, he gave an affirmative answer: "Yes, I do remember seeing some crackings in the pillar."

"Then why didn't you tell me?"

"Rich and powerful as you are, Your Majesty, I didn't think you would care for that old wood."

The emperor was ridiculed by his minister but he controlled his temper and turned to flare up at the chief instigator Prime Minister He Sheng: "What a fool you are!"

Building a Wall to Change Geomancy

Xiacun Village (meaning the lowest place) was originally called Xinglongcun Village (meaning rising of a dragon), and was situated on the east bank of Qingshuihe River in the west suburb of Beijing. If people took a walk on the west bank of the river, an inverted reflection of the dragon-like village could be seen in the clear water. The young people of the village were very fond of learning martial arts. They invited some monk martial art experts to teach them Shaolin cudgel, a well-known martial art that had handed down generation after generation from the monks in the Shaolin Temple. The villagers even set up a martial arts association called the Shaolin Association of the Five Tigers.

Emperor Qian Long was also fond of martial arts. When he learnt that the members of the Shaolin Association of the Five Tigers were almost unmatched in martial arts, he decided to see with his own eyes how powerful they were.

The emperor selected ten strong officers and men from the palace guards, all of whom were sons of the Eight Banner Army and highly skilled in martial arts, to hold a competition with ten members of the Shaolin Association of the Five Tigers.

An open space outside the village served as the matching ground. Emperor Qian Long sat in a chair on the high platform with Prime Minister He Sheng and other high officials standing on either side.

From the start, it was obvious that the officers and

men of the Eight Banner Army were no match for the members of the Shaolin Association of the Five Tigers. The former only knew a stylized form of martial arts which was no match against the fierce attacks of the villager's who could employ varied tactics in either single, double and group fights. As a result, the officers and men were defeated in each round of the competition. Emperor Qian Long realized that he had underestimated the tough villagers and their fierce martial arts made a deep impression on him.

Seething with jealousy and hostility Prime Minister He Sheng hatched a plot to attack the villagers. He deliberately asked the emperor: "Your Majesty, why were you so pleased when the villagers won the matches?"

"I was pleased to see that the peasants were so skilful in martial arts."

"I'm just worried at the hidden danger."

Surprised, Emperor Qian Long urged him to elaborate. He Sheng put it secretly: "I received a report about a possible rebellion in this Xinglongcun Village shortly before we came here, but I couldn't believe it, for I had not seen any evidence. Today I have seen with my own eyes something unusual here. For instance, when we entered the village, I found the villagers were conceited and arrogant in word and manner. They didn't even pay due attention to Your Majesty."

Glancing at his master's thoughtful face, He Sheng continued: "It was reported that the local people believed they could one day produce a king of their own." Emperor Qian Long was shocked at the news, but He Sheng had something even more thrilling up his sleeve. He said: "Shortly before the competition started, a geomancer came to tell me a secret. This village is quite exceptional in terms of geomancy and its name has a special meaning. As you know, Xinglong literally means the rise of a dragon, a symbol of the throne. Moreover, this village is situated near to the Qingshuihe River. One day, when a dragon jumps into the water, a new king will emerge in this village."

At this point, Emperor Qian Long became very nervous, for he was very superstitious and believed in geomancy. The emperor asked He Sheng what to do with regard to this hidden danger.

He Sheng replied: "According to the geomancer, we can do something to change the village's geomancy."

"How?"

"Just cut the connections between the village and the river by building a wall standing in between the two. This will separate the dragon from the water and cast a shadow to cover the dragon-like village reflected in the water. The dragon will die without water, and then the village will no longer constitute a threat at all."

Greatly relieved, Emperor Qian Long at once ordered a wall built, using the pretext it was being built in honour of the martial arts competition. The emperor personally signed an inscription: "Shadow Casting Wall" and ordered the village's name changed to Xiacun Village (the lowest place) to prevent the village from ever producing a king.

Earning a Garden by Providing a Chamber Pot

He Sheng rose to the high post of prime minister not because he was talented or made any great contributions to the nation, but because he was very good at flattery. As prime minister, all his efforts were directed to using every means to please the emperor and win his favour. Over the years his efforts succeeded and he became a most powerful and wealthy official.

Ever since he was a small eunuch, He Sheng was adept at currying favour. Once he even earned a big garden by providing Emperor Qian Long with a small chamber pot in his moment of need.

One day, Emperor Qian Long went to the Yuan Ming Yuan Palace for sightseeing. On his way to the palace, the emperor ordered the entourage to stop at a small town half way, by kicking at his chair in the carriage. As soon as the carriage was laid down on the ground, the high officials all knelt down to await the emperor's order. As the emperor didn't utter a word for a few moments, an old eunuch came to lift the curtain to see what had happened to the emperor, who was looking annoyed and embarrassed. Completely puzzled, the entourage didn't know what to do.

At the critical moment, the young eunuch He Sheng ran up with a small chamber pot in his hands and presented it to the emperor. After a moment, He Sheng took back the pot which the emperor had filled. Meanwhile the other stupid officials were still kneeling down and waiting for their orders.

As soon as the emperor arrived at Yuan Ming Yuan Palace, a sumptuous feast was prepared in his honour. At the banquet, Emperor Qian Long gave an account of what he thought on the trip. He pointed out: "The emperor and his trusted high officials should be close friends, because they knew each other very well. But I felt disappointed on my way here this morning. When I ordered that the carriage stop at a small town on the way, all you high officials did was kneel down and wait for my orders; not one of you came to ask what I needed. If I were to die of constipation, what would you do?"

Cheerfully wining and dining, the high officials suddenly lowered their heads in silence on hearing the emperor's dressing down. The emperor then praised eunuch He Sheng highly, saying: "Only he knew what I wanted and gave me help. As a reward for his loyalty, I grant him the garden in the southern part of the palace."

He Sheng promptly knelt down and kowtowed to the emperor for his generous gift. He Sheng had received many gifts from the emperor because of his flattery, but never such a generous gift as a whole garden. He was pleased but by no means totally satisfied with just a garden. His real ambition was to seize the throne when an opportunity arose.

As He Sheng was dreaming of becoming an emperor himself, his patron Emperor Qian Long grew tired of the rule, and handed down to his son, Prince Yong Yan, who later became Emperor Jia Qing. In the reign of Emperor Jia Qing, Prime Minister He Sheng was accused of scheming to usurp the emperor's supreme power. His private imperial garden was an evidence of his ambition, and so in the end he was severely punished.

To Suffer From One's Own Attack

Prime Minister He Sheng and Minister of State Liu Yong were the two most influential high officials during the reign of Emperor Qian Long. However they were quite different in behaviour, the prime minister greedy and power-hungry, Liu Yong learned and upright. In terms of knowledge and moral character, if He Sheng were compared to a chicken, Liu Yong could be an eagle flying high in the sky. However, He Sheng saw Minister Liu Yong as a thorn in his flesh and tried to seize every opportunity to frame him up in order to clear the way for his political ambition.

One day, the two ministers attended Emperor Qian Long's grand banquet. He Sheng tried to attack Liu Yong in the presence of the emperor by provoking him to accuse the emperor of wrongdoing. Synically He Sheng said: "Minister Liu, you are well-known as a strictly principled official who dares to handle any case impartially. Is that true?"

"No doubt about it," replied Liu Yong calmly.

"But it seems to me you also bully the weak and fear the strong, because you dared not handle case involving a very powerful person," He Sheng pushed a step further.

"It's not true."

"Are you sure?"

"Sure, but I don't know which case you are referring to." At this point, Liu Yong already sensed his words implied more than they said.

He Sheng pointed at the man sitting in the center

at the first table and said: "If you dare to handle the case involving His Majesty and accuse him, I would admire your courage and justice by kowtowing to you in public."

The high officials present were all shocked to hear such provoking remarks. Liu Yong thought to himself: "The scoundrel wants to make use of the emperor to kill me." In the feudal society anyone who dared to point out errors of an emperor in public was doomed. However Liu Yong was resourceful enough to take up the challenge. In order to defeat the sinister prime minister, Liu Yong walked over to expostulate with the emperor.

Emperor Qian Long was enjoying a piece of meat when Liu Yong said: "Your Majesty, please allow me to make a report to you."

"What's so urgent?" retorted the emperor.

"Your Majesty, I am now facing a difficult problem which involves law and order, power and dignity, and I don't know how to deal with it."

"What's the matter?"

"If I had evidence to prove a person guilty, but he happened to be very powerful, what should I do?"

"Punish him."

"What kind of punishment should be given to a grave robber?"

"According to Qing Dynasty law, a grave robber should be punished by death."

"Does the law apply to everyone, even top officials?"

"Of course, emperor and commoners are all equal before the law."

"Your Majesty, do you remember the so-called work of repairing the Ming Tombs?"

Emperor Qian Long now came to understand minister Liu was beating about the bush to point a finger at him. However the emperor remained calm and argued: "The Ming Tombs were at that time dilapidated with the passage of time and in need of urgent repair. The purpose of repair was to protect historical relics."

"Your Majesty, excuse me for my outspoken opinions. As was well-known to all, it was only a pretext to repair the Ming Tombs. Its real aim was to replace the superb wood of the tombs with inferior materials so that the better wood could be used for building your own tomb. We officials in charge of the repair work knew this only too well, but nobody dared to speak out. And I was now in an awkward position as whether I should uphold the law or protect the throne."

Confronted with this stubborn and fearless official, Emperor Qian Long felt he had a tough nut to deal with. He then tried to threaten: "Do you think you have the right to punish me?"

"Your Majesty, just now you pointed out that emperor and common people are equal before the law. I hope Your Majesty will keep your word."

In order to show his justice, the emperor said: "You win. I should plead guilty and be punished. But the punishment will be only nominal. Next year I will go out for inspection of some parts of the country, which can be considered a kind of banishment."

"It is the wisest way, Your Majesty!" approved Minister Liu Yong who at last succeeded in his battle with Prime Minister He Sheng, for he proved himself to have the courage to accuse the emperor for his wrongdoing.

Free from the dilemma, Emperor Qian Long then turned to make a charge against Liu Yong: "You even dared to accuse me in public. According to Qing Dynasty law, you committed the crime of humiliating the throne."

"If it was against the law, I deserve punishment."

"You deserve the death penalty for that crime," threatened the emperor.

"Your Majesty, but I'll follow your example of just taking nominal punishment. I ask to be removed from my post and return to my hometown as a commoner," replied Liu Yong. He took off his official hat, presented it before the emperor, and left.

Prime Minister He Sheng was pleased to see the downfall of his political rival. But in the bet, he was the loser who had to bow to Liu Yong in public, hence was humiliated in the presence of other high officials.

The following day Liu Yong went to say goodbye to the emperor before leaving the capital for his hometown. Emperor Qian Long was reluctant to see such a talented high official leave, and sighed: "Liu Yong, according to your knowledge and ability, you could have been appointed prime minister if you had behaved yourself."

On hearing this, Liu Yong promptly knelt down to thank the emperor.

Surprised, the emperor asked: "Thank me for what?"

"Your Majesty, I thank you for your new appointment as prime minister," replied Liu Yong.

Emperor Qian Long was not annoyed at such a joke and indeed allowed him to resume his title. Deeply disappointed, the sinister He Sheng suffered not only humiliation in public but a heavier blow in his political struggle.

Emperor Qian Long's Adopted Daughter

For his misappropriation of beams and pillars from the Ming Tombs, Emperor Qian Long punished himself by a symbolic exile: an investigation tour outside the capital. One day on his way to a county, the emperor stopped at a small village for a rest. He was accompanied by two of his ministers, He Sheng and Liu Yong. Tired and hungry after a day's trip, they decided to stay overnight at a peasant's home.

Hearing their knocking at the door, an old man and his daughter of about 15 came to answer it. The peasant had three rooms in the thatched house, so he agreed to put them up for the night. On orders of her father, the young girl soon got ready a supper for the guests, with steamed sweet potato, pickles and noodles in soup. The emperor and his ministers wolfed down the meal, which they thought the most delicious they had ever had. Their ridiculous manner amused the peasant and his daughter, who was very charming even though dressed shabbily.

The next morning the host prepared a big breakfast for them as a farewell. Deeply touched, the emperor wanted to do something in return and asked: "Old brother, I thank you for your warm hospitality, but I can't give you anything valuable in return right now. But would you mind if I adopt your daughter as my own so that I can take care of you as relatives in the future?"

The peasant thought his own days were numbered but his daughter was too young to lead an independent life. If his daughter had an adoptive father to take care of her, he would feel relieved. The peasant accepted the emperor's offer and ordered the young girl to kneel before him. The emperor gave her one tael of silver and a yellow hankerchief which would be recognized should she go to ask him for help whenever she met with difficulties. The emperor said: "Just come to the Forbidden City and show the guards this yellow handkerchief. You will be taken good care of."

Years later, a serious natural disaster landed the peasant and his daughter in a state of dire poverty. Suffering from hunger and cold, the old peasant and his daughter decided to go to the capital in search of help from her adoptive father. They arrived at the Forbidden City but forgot to bring the yellow handkerchief, so they were not allowed to enter. Helpless and penniless, the father and daughter had to make a living by begging in the street. The old peasant fell ill and the girl was put into a hopeless position. One day when the girl was wandering about beside the city moat, she thought of ending her miserable life by drowning herself, but she was reluctant to leave her sick old father alone. In despair, the girl cried loudly at the moat. Just then Minister Liu Yong passed by and recognized the girl as the emperor's adopted daughter. The girl, overjoyed to meet the minister, told him her sad story.

Minister Liu Yong took the old man and his daughter to the palace and told the guards the two were none other than relatives of the emperor himself.

The next day Minister Liu Yong led the old peasant and his daughter to call on the emperor. Emperor Qian Long had completely forgot about his adopted daughter and refused to recognize them. But Liu Yong argued that the emperor should keep his word and take care of the old man and his daughter as relatives. The emperor reluctantly agreed to help settle the father and daughter in the guest house.

The old peasant and his daughter now had ample food and clothing but had no friends nor freedom. It was like living in prison. Moreover, they were looked down upon by the palace royalty, who regarded them with freezing irony and burning satire. Suffering both from illness and mental depression, the old peasant soon died. Alone and deeply grieved over her father's death, the girl also fell ill. With a heavy heart, the girl wished to die in her own native place.

One day she begged for an audience with Minister Liu Yong pleading in tearful voice: "Your Honour, after my death, please do us the favour of burying both my father and me in our native place." Her voice was so feeble that the minister could hardly hear her. He nodded in agreement, sympathizing with the girl, who was seriously ill.

The poor girl died the following day and Emperor Qian Long ordered the burial of the peasant and his daughter in a public cemetery. But Minister Liu Yong argued that the girl was the emperor's adopted daughter, who should be accorded a funeral ceremony like that of a princess, otherwise people would say the emperor was not as benevolent and humane as befit him. Confronted with this upright minister, the emperor had to agree to accord the girl a princess's funeral ceremony but bury the two in their hometown.

A Battle of Wits

Minister Liu Yong was a man of letters, resourceful and full of humour. His talent and learning gave a deep impression on Emperor Qian Long, who however disliked his upright character and took the chance to ridicule him whenever possible.

One moon festival Emperor Qian Long went to Yuan Ming Yuan Palace for a taste of the seasonal lotus seed in the garden lake, accompanied by high officials He Sheng and Liu Yong. After eating a lotus seed the emperor composed a line on the spot: "Bitter is the core of lotus seeds." He then asked his high officials to compose a matching line.

Prime Minister He Sheng was excellent at flattery. In order to please the emperor, he promptly offered the matching line: "Stink is the belly of a sow." Emperor Qian Long frowned and retorted: "It is moon festival today. You should not present such dirty words." He Sheng had intented to show off his poetic talent and flatter the emperor, but instead he suffered humiliation.

Emperor Qian Long then turned to Minister Liu Yong, asking him to give a matching line. Catching sight of a pear tree on the road side, Liu Yong chanted: "Sour is the taste of a pear-pit." The emperor nodded with satisfaction.

After a while the emperor casually picked an unripe green persimmon and presented it to Liu Yong, saying: "My dear lord, just now you composed a good line, so I reward you with a persimmon." Liu Yong expressed his gratitude to the emperor for the fruit and cut it into small pieces to share with his fellow nobles, who had to bear the astringent taste.

Emperor Qian Long felt annoyed and reproached Liu Yong: "I gave that persimmon especially to you. Why did you share it with others?"

"Your Majesty, I dare not enjoy the fruit by myself alone. His Majesty's grants should be shared by all my fellows so that all of us can be grateful to the throne." Liu Yong's reply was reasonable, so the emperor had to control his temper even though he was angry.

As the group was strolling along the lake, they came to a pear tree. The emperor ordered a eunuch to pick a pear and he gave it to Liu Yong to see how he would act. When Liu Yong received the pear, he devoured it himself at once. This time the emperor seized on the minister's action and asked: "Liu Yong, why didn't you share the pear with the others?"

"Your Majesty, today is moon festival and everyone would like to see reunion and unity. Nobody would like to be apart on this occasion. While His Majesty and ministers are celebrating a happy gathering, if I shared the pear (the Chinese for pear is *Li*, meaning separation), I would be blamed for evoking a bad omen."

"You outwit and cripple Liu Yong!" mocked the emperor.

Once in order to celebrate Emperor Qian Long's birthday, courtiers, ministers and generals all except Liu Yong vied in presenting rare treasures to the throne. As the emperor did not see a gift from Liu Yong, he was angry and muttered to himself: "You villain, you always gained extra benefits from me but openly despise me on my birthday. I'll teach you a lesson sooner or later."

At the emperor's birthday party, high officials all presented their gifts, including Liu Yong, who limped into the palace with a red silk box. Emperor Qian Long was a bit surprised to see Liu Yong's gift, which turned out to be a toy, a clay tumbler. Displeased, the emperor shut the box and demanded Liu Yong's explanation of sending such a gift.

Liu Yong replied: "So far as Your Majesty is concerned, the most precious thing in the world is to keep the nation in peace and prosperity under your stable reign. Therefore I presented this gift to wish your reign be as stable as this never falling tumbler."

On hearing this Emperor Qian Long at once turned from anger to joy, saying: "You are really thoughtful. You sent a gift costing little but most significant."

On another occasion when Emperor Qian Long made an investigation tour south of the Yangtse River, the local people were ordered to present the emperor with their native products. One was Chinese dates. In order to show his benevolance, the emperor shared the dates with his ministers and local officials. Having eaten the dates, Emperor Qian Long ordered everyone to count how many date pits each person had left and declared that each pit would cost them one tael of silver. The money would be collected for the peasants to grow more date trees. But Liu Yong reported that he had not left a single pit.

Emperor Qian Long rebuked: "Liu Yong, I saw you eating quite a few dates. How could you leave no pits?"

"Your Majesty, your humble servant has swallowed all the date pits," replied the quick-minded minister sarcastically.

A Family of High Officials

Minister He Sheng once made a report to Emperor Qian Long, accusing Minister Liu Yong of wild ambition. He pointed out that Liu Yong went in for large-scale construction of a garden for himself as big and fine as the imperial garden in his hometown, Jinan city in Shandong province. In order to clarify the point at issue, the emperor decided to make a personal investigation of the matter.

In the city of Jinan, Emperor Qian Long indeed saw a large building situated in a scenic spot with green trees and clear water. On the front door of the building there was an antithetical couplet with two lines written on each of the plaques. One read: "Serve the Qing Dynasty whole heartedly whether you are from the Liu or Zhang family;" the other: "Contribute to the great country selflessly whether you are of Han or Manchu nationality." A horizontal plague on top of the door reads: "The First Family under Heaven."

Emperor Qian Long thought the couplet had a good meaning, but the words on the horizontal scroll were too much. The first family under heaven could only refer to the imperial family. How could an ordinary family make this claim?

When the emperor entered the courtyard of the building he met an old man and asked: "Excuse me, but may I ask what you mean by calling your home 'The First Family under Heaven'?"

"I'm sorry, but you'd better go and ask my father that question," answered the old man indicating the inner room.

Entering the next room, the emperor asked a white-haired old man, who motioned him to go into a third room for the answer. "Go and ask my father directly," he said.

Emperor Qian Long entered the third room and saw a grand old man, certainly over 100, supporting himself with a stick with dragon head design. The emperor knew the old man must be a national hero, for only those who had made great contributions to the nation were granted such a stick by his grandfather Emperor Kang Xi. The walking stick with a design of dragon head was a symbol of power and position which bestowed the holder the right to impeach even the emperor, if he were found guilty. The emperor paid respects to the old man, who bowed to welcome the arrival of the emperor. The grand old man then gave the word to call the whole family to pay respects to the emperor. This brought more than a hundred people, old and young, male and female into the courtyard. What a big family, thought Emperor Qian Long, "The First Family under Heaven"might mean the large number of people in the family.

Having granted an audience with the big family, the emperor asked again about the real meaning of the words on the plaque. With a faint smile, the grand old man replied: "Your Majesty, your humble servant dared not to claim ourselves in this way. It is a title bestowed by the late Emperor Kang Xi." He then produced a scroll of yellow silk and opened it to show the emperor in the handwriting of the late Emperor Kang Xi "The First Family under Heaven" with the imperial seal on it.

But the emperor still couldn't fully understand its real meaning. The grand old man said it had a long story. He said: "Since the Qin Dynasty about 2,000 years ago, ours was a big family whose members have been high officials generation after generation. There have been 12 prime ministers, more than 80 first class scholars and 100 courtiers, ministers and generals in the line of our family. And now we have five generations totalling 108 members living under the same roof. Hence the late emperor granted us this honourable title."

"I see. But is this garden house built by Liu Yong?"

"No, Liu Yong is my great grandson. He had no money to build such a large house. It was handed down from our ancestors."

Having finished the investigation, Emperor Qian Long came to know He Sheng's accusation was a slander intended to discredit the upright minister Liu Yong. Thereafter the emperor took He Sheng's words with a grain of salt.

A Suzhou Nun Becomes an Imperial Lady

During his trip to the picturesque city of Suzhou in east China, Emperor Qian Long one day disguised himself as a pilgrim to pay homage to Buddhists in an old temple outside the city. As the emperor and his bodyguards were worshipping the Buddhists by burning incense and candles, they saw a very charming young nun adding oil to the lamps at the niche. "What a pretty girl! She looks like an angel from the fairyland of heaven." The emperor gasped in admiration, fixing his eyes on the nun, almost out of sorts. One of the bodyguards tugged at the emperor's sleeve to remind him to keep his mind on Buddhas. But the emperor was no longer in the mood to pay homage to the Buddha moulded in clay. He was fascinated with the charming nun.

Soon the emperor decided to issue an imperial edict to summon the young nun to the palace as his concubine. But imperial rule did not allow him to call to the palace a Buddhist nun who had seen through its worldly affairs, so the emperor had to give up his idea, though very reluctantly. Disappointed, the emperor returned to the capital before scheduled.

Upon returning home, the emperor ordered a monastery and imperial temporary palace built side by side in a scenic spot west of Beijing. It was called Quan Zhong (Wellspring) Convent. The emperor sent one of his trusted ministers to bring the charming nun from Suzhou to live in the convent. On the pretext of worshipping Buddha, Emperor Qian Long frequented the convent to meet the young nun.

People began to gossip about the emperor's romance with the nun. They ridiculed him, saying,"With the companion of a charming nun, the monastery is far better than the imperial palace."

Despite the luxurious life, the young nun became bored and felt homesick. The emperor comforted her by promising to take her back to her hometown, Suzhou.

Six months later the emperor told the nun to get ready for the return trip. Overjoyed with the good news, she could scarcely believe it and asked: "Is it really true?"

"Sure, I won't cheat you," answered the emperor.

The nun dressed up and set out in a cart following behind the emperor in great fanfare with a bevy of attendants on hand. After about an hour's drive, someone came up to report: "Your honourable lady, here we are in Suzhou!"

Greatly surprised, the young nun could not believe her ears. Usually it took months to get to Suzhou from Beijing. "How is it possible to arrive in Suzhou so soon?" she asked.

"There is no doubt about it," was the answer. As she lifted the curtain, the nun saw small boats sailing in rivers across the streets, shops selling southern special products and pedestrians speaking the typical Suzhou dialect. Seeing the familiar native sights, the nun was delighted though still puzzled.

What was the real story? It was in fact a man-made Suzhou city which the emperor ordered especially to please his nun concubine. The merchants and wares were all transported from Suzhou for the purpose.

Indulging herself in the luxury of palace life and

the lovely scenery, the young nun's belief in the Buddha gradually faded and she became an imperial lady.

Liu Yong Floors Royal Questions

Courtier Liu Yong had won favor with Emperor Qian Long for his quick wits and resourcefulness. But His Majesty often tried to derive pleasure from baffling him with catch questions.

On the night of one Lantern Festival, which falls on the 15th day of the first month by the Chinese lunar calendar, a sea of jubilant people were milling about on the grounds of Beijing's Zhengyangmen Gate, where a myriad of colourful lanterns were brightly shining. In the company of his imperial ladies and palace maids and courtiers, the emperor was revelling in the tower on top of the Zhengyangmen Gate in the spirit of celebrating the festival with the common people.

Now in a joyous mood His Majesty had a mind to make fun of Liu Yong. As everyone's wine cup was being filled and refilled, the emperor put a question to his courtier: "My dear Liu, clever as you are reputed to be, can you tell me how many persons are moving about down there?"

After a moment of reflection the courtier replied: "Two."

"Two?" the emperor exclaimed with evident displeasure. "So you are trying to fool me, aren't you?"

Liu Yong at once went down on his knees and said: "Let me explain, Your Majesty. I say two because all the people down there are of two kinds: the fame-seeking and the fortune-seeking."

Chuckling over the explanation, the emperor remarked: "What a clever head you have!"

Just then there happened a curious thing. In the distance a band was playing up ahead of a funeral procession while another group of musicians were leading a traditional bridal parade, with the bride carried in a sedan chair. The emperor was thus inspired to make up a new question for Liu Yong, saying: "My dear Liu, I wish to ask you another question. If you are able to give the right answer, I'll promote you two grades up and allow you a salary rise of 2,000 taels of silver a year. But if you give the wrong answer, I'll reduce you to a man of no rank."

"I am ready for the question, Your Majesty," said Liu with confidence.

"In our great land of Qing, each year how many children are born and how many persons die?"

"Only one child is born and 12 people die," came the reply.

The emperor expressed disbelief: "Ours is a country of hundreds of millions of people. Who will believe that only one child is born and only 12 people die each year?"

"But Your Majesty may think that each year no matter how many children may be born in this big country of ours, their year of birth is symbolized by only one of the 12 animals designated by tradition. Hence I say only one child is born in a single year. On the other hand, one may have a particular symbolic animal to indicate one's year of birth, and so all the people in the land cannot have more than 12 such animals for personal identification of age or year of birth. All the people that die in a year can and must be identified by one or the other of the 12 symbolic animals. Hence I say only 12 persons die in a single year."

The emperor was delighted at Liu's wits. "You are really living up to your reputation as a clever soul," said His Majesty in earnest. "You have won my admiration."

A Courtier with Quick Wits

Emperor Qian Long had an attendant-courtier by the name of Zhang Yushu, who was noted for his learning and wit and humour. One year, he went with the emperor on an inspection tour to his native place Zhengjiang in Jiangsu province. It was on the night of the Moon Festival, which falls on the 15th day of the eighth lunar month, that the royal party were boating on the Yangtse River under a bright moon. The emperor was in such a joyful mood that he ordered wine for all in the boat. As his spirits rose with drinking, he composed one line of a couplet:

Dragon King at dinner, having moon for candle, stars for lamps, mountains for foods, seas for wines, served on a plate as large as the earth.

Then he asked Zhang Yushu to supply the antithetic line. Zhang found this line was all imaginary, calling for an equally imaginative matching line. He racked his head as he set his cup slowly to his lips. No sooner had he drunk down a full cup of wine than he came up with the line:

Jade Emperor in war, taking thunder as drum, clouds as flags, winds as swords, rains as arrows, fought in a battlefield as vast as the sky.

This second line, for its even greater imaginative power, was so much appreciated by the emperor that he called out again and again: "What a perfect couplet!"

After this, the emperor still wanted to baffle his courtier with another quiz. Pointing to a cargo boat on the river, he asked Zhang: "What do you think the boat is laden with?"

As it was in the night, it was indeed impossible to ascertain the cargo covered with tarpaulin. But Zhang was not to be easily beaten. He seemed to be unthinking when he made the answer: "The boat is laden with 'east-west'."

In the Chinese language, the term "thing" or "things" is literally expressed as *Dongxi* (east-west). The emperor was not satisfied with such an answer and told Zhang to explain.

"The Yangtse River is flowing eastward to the sea," said Zhang in a calm tone. "A boat going upstream is laden with goods from the east, and a boat going downstream is laden with goods from the west. Hence I say it is laden with 'east-west'."

When the emperor came to think of the answer, he found Zhang had made a fitting generalization about the goods carried in vessels sailing the Yangtse River. So he considered that his courtier had passed the test.

During the visit to Zhengjiang, Zhang Yushu came to know that the local officials were always fleecing the people. The rice grown in the Zhengjiang area was usually of a red variety with a high content of vegetable oil much favoured by southern people. But the local authorities often demanded the removal of the outer layer of red rice before it was collected for government granaries in the form of white rice. Thus greater labor as well as a larger amount of the grain would be involved for the purpose. This gave rise to a general complaint against the local authorities. Zhang thought of a way out for the folks of his hometown. He instructed them to mix red rice with white rice and sit in the street separating the two varieties grain by grain on the day the emperor was expected to come to town.

When the emperor came accompanied by Zhang Yushu, he witnessed a disorderly scene of the townspeople at work. These people, men and women, old and young, were ceaselessly quarrelling or picking fault with one another over the speed or quality of the work. They dinned so much noise into the royal ears that His Majesty became annoyed. Then he asked Zhang what was going on. Zhang reported to him the whole truth about the unreasonable demand on the part of the local officials, and added: "The people here all think it is Your Majesty's order for them to hand in only white rice. But the fact is, the rice collected here will never go to the capital."

"To save trouble," declared the emperor, "rice of any color, white or red, will do for the imperial granaries from now on.'

On the request of Zhang Yushu the emperor wrote out an edict to put a stop to the practice of collecting only white rice. This won the acclaim of the people in Zhengjiang and elsewhere.

Assassination Attempt on Archery Ground

After many years on the throne, Emperor Qian Long still clung to the good old customs passed down by his forefathers from their nomadic days. Every year when he returned from a hunting excursion to Chengde, where the Summer Villa was located, he would hold a pompous celebration, complete with horse race, wrestling tournament, martial sport and archery match. One year, such a celebration was especially jubilant, because he was so happy to have been able to bring from Xinjiang to Beijing his beloved Xiang Fei, a Uighur lady who meant much more to him than all the precious game he had ever bagged on the hunting grounds.

On the day for the archery match, after a sumptuous banquet Emperor Qian Long came on the grand stand in the company of his civil officials and military officers. The contestants, carrying bows in their left hands and arrows in their right, came before the stand kneeling one by one to the emperor to show their respects. At a wave of the royal hand, these archers mounted their horses that neighed loud and long as they galloped away kicking up clouds of dust.

In a moment arrows whistled through the air to their targets amid outbursts of cheering from the audience. In a particularly joyful mood, the emperor was generous in rewarding the participants. On his orders, whoever scored a single hit would receive a prize, and no one would be penalized for missing all the marks. Thus encouraged, these bowmen did their utmost in displaying their wonderful shooting skills, arousing the spectators to wild excitement.

Three regular rounds of shooting had just been completed when a young man in Uighur attire stepped out from the ranks of a contesting team of the Hui nationality, and made a request to the team leader: "Sir, the competition today is easy enough. Will you please let me win one more prize for our team?"

Bringing the young Uighur to the presence of the emperor, the team leader, who was also a Uighur chieftain, asked for special permission for the young man to show his excellent archery. Impressed by his good looks and soldierly bearing, the emperor was pleased, asking: "Where is he from?"

"From the homeland of Lady Xiang Fei," an imperial attendant stepped forward to reply. "He is here to offer native products as tributes to Your Majesty."

A person from the native land of Lady Xiang Fei meant a great pleasure to the emperor. He allowed this young Uighur to shoot three arrows, saying: "If you give a good account of yourself, I'll favour you with ample reward."

At once a spirited horse was led before the young man for the shooting performance. But he expressed wish to ride on his own camel instead. The emperor graciously nodded agreement. Swiftly the young man mounted the animal kneeling on the ground, which, at a lift of the rein, rose to its feet and ran to the target area. Drawing his bow in full, he let fly the first arrow which whistled through the air and hit the bull's eye. Immediately loud cheers went up from the audience. The camel ran past the target again and the second arrow found the same mark. There was another round of rousing cheers. Then the young Uighur drew his bow to the full for the third time, and took careful aim at the target which was 40 or 50 steps from the grand stand. All of a sudden, he turned about on his camel and let go the third arrow that flew straight toward the emperor. But with a subconscious alertness, His Majesty dodged in time, and the arrow missing its mark went through the painted silk screen behind the royal seat. All present were stupefied with terror and for a moment thrown into a state of inaction. Taking advantage of this, the would-be assassin pressed hard the camel between his legs and rode swiftly toward the northeast. But soon he found a high wall in his way as the imperial guards were closing in from behind. At this critical moment he kept his wits about him. Giving the camel a few furious lashes, he reined it up and leaped over the wall to safety.

It was for avenging his father's death that this Uighur had attempted Emperor Qian Long's life. Ten years earlier his father had stated grievances to the authorities in behalf of the Uighur people, but was falsely accused of committing a high crime of "rebellion." Without bothering to ascertain the truth about the charge, the emperor ordered his death by dismemberment. The son was compelled to flee his native place. In the course of his wandering, he learned the martial arts from various masters, vowing to avenge himself on the killer of his father. It happened that he made the acquaintance of a Uighur chieftain from Yili and became his attendant. When this chieftain went to Chengde for the celebration held by Emperor Qian Long, he brought along the young avenger as well as native products for Lady Xiang Fei. This afforded a fair chance for the young man to fulfil his vows. But as luck would have it, the assassination attempt on the archery ground failed.

After the escape of the young Uighur, Emperor

Qian Long was in violent rage. He gave orders to put to death the chief of the imperial guards as well as those guarding the gates. But when it was reported to him that the unsuccessful assassin had escaped not through the gates but over the wall, His Majesty was in such blind fury that he ordered the death of the wall. And when one prince boldly reminded him of the impossibility to put the wall to death, he exclaimed: "Then put the wall in prison!"

Of course, these imperial orders must be obeyed, especially at a time when His Majesty was in a state of anger. But how to imprison a wall was a real problem.

Later on, one old courtier came up with a brilliant idea: "As only a section of the wall was guilty of failure to keep the assassin from escape, another wall to surround that section will serve the purpose of imprisoning it." Thus another wall was built as suggested, and it came to be known as "Big Belly Wall."

The Lake of Drowning Emperor

In summer one year, Emperor Qian Long went to his palace at Baiyangdian Lake in order to see the fish diving in and out of the water there. He waited for several days but not one fish appeared.

Frustrated, he went to the court eunuch who served him and angrily asked why the diving fish did not surface. No one could truly answer this question so one of the more-experienced eunuchs invented a reason: "Your Majesty is the genuine dragon coming down to the mundane and travelling by a dragon boat. Humble creatures like fish and shrimp should step aside and follow far behind. How can they be seen?"

"In that case, if I dress in plain clothes and travel in a plain boat, fish and shrimp will not be evading from me," said the emperor.

The eunuch dared not elaborate on his flattery so he agreed with the emperor's reasoning: "Then they will not be hiding from Your Majesty."

However, the eunuch knew that even if the emperor changed his clothes and boat, the rare diving fish may not appear. And he did not want to be found guilty of deceiving the emperor. In order to free himself from this predicament, he said, "Your Majesty, Baiyangdian Lake has another interesting sight—red carp. Why not go for a look?"

Emperor Qian Long was always game for a sightseeing advanture that would give him some amusement. Thus the emperor said, "All right. Be ready quickly!"

The eunuch went to get the boat. Learning that they would go to look for the red carp, all the boatmen balked. No one wanted to go since it was very dangerous to drive in the deep, surging water. After the eunuch promised to give them more money, however, they agreed.

Emperor Qian Long and the eunuch dressed as tourists, and as the boat reached its destination, they saw red carp sporting in the water, as expected. As soon as the boat anchored, fish swarmed around the boat, their shimmering bodies radiating in every direction. What a beautiful view!

The emperor was so excited he tried to grab a fish. Forgetting his sea legs, he bent too far overboard, and the boat tipped. His Majesty fell out and into the water with a flop.

The eunuch was terrified and cried out, "Help him!"

Nonetheless, the boatmen were indifferent. So the eunuch, too frantic to keep the secret, shouted, "Oh heavens! He is the emperor!"

The boatmen stood gaping for a moment and then dived into the water. By the time the emperor was hoisted back on board, he had already drunk a lot of water because he did not know how to swim, and his eyes were tightly shut.

In tears, the eunuch pleaded, "Oh heavens, think of a way to revive him."

One of the boatmen wiped the water from his face and laid a bamboo pole across the boat. Taking the emperor's waterlogged body in his arms, he hung it belly-down over the pole. After a while, the water stopped trickling from the emperor's mouth. Slowly he cracked open his eyes, mumbling, "Where am I?"

The boatman, forgetting the emperor's true identity, said humorously, "In the Palace of Hell!"

"What?" queried the emperor.

The quick-witted eunuch spoke up, "Your Majesty, he said you are on the Lake of the Drowning Emperor." (The pronunciations of the two phrases "Palace of Hell" and "Lake of the Drowning Emperor" are the same in Chinese)

The emperor murmured weakly to himself, "Since this place has such an unlucky name, no wonder I fell into the water!"

Dream of Shacun Village

In spring one year, Emperor Qian Long schemed up a new trick to amuse himself: Like a well-armed general, he led a large group of soldiers and guards on an imaginary military expedition. They left the capital and marched southward.

One day, they arrived at a forest so dense that no sunlight could pierce its forbidding darkness. Not a whisper of human habitation could be detected, only the wilds and a path leading onward. As they approached ever nearer, the emperor sensed the tension and terror in his group, the bated breath and haltered steps.

"Where are we?" he asked.

"Your Majesty, it is the Shacun Village," the head eunuch answered.

"Shacun Village!" the emperor looked nervous. He had heard that forest outlaws appeared and disappeared unexpectedly in this area. He had also read many reports about the governmental revenue being robbed or about the routing of his troops here.

It was a long road back, and he feared that such a retreat would brand him as a coward. The only way was to force himself to march forward. It seemed that the road was endless, and Emperor Qian Long shook with anxiety and fear. Finally, they saw daylight on the other side. By that time, the emperor's heart was in his throat and his clothes were wet with sweat.

Soon after they emerged from the forest, the emperor rode at great haste to his palace, located in the south. Night had cast its shroud by the time he arrived, but the emperor was still badly shaken. Even in the safety of his own bed, thoughts of Shacun Village still pursued him. At last, fear gave way to weariness, and he dozed off.

The ensuing nightmare was much more horrifying than the day's experience. In it the emperor envisioned a group of masked outlaws welling up from all directions. With gleaming eyes as big as lanterns, the bandits were brandishing a knife in each hand. His armed escort was in utter chaos, but they fought with all their might and at last the fiends withdrew.

Qian Long was relieved; but when he looked up, he saw a masked outlaw towering over him. While holding a huge blade as keen and bright as a shaft of light in hand, he bellowed, "Where is the bastard emperor?"

"He is running northwards," answered the emperor. Then, the big fellow sent his men, like hounds, in pursuit.

The emperor seized this moment to shout, "Help!"

The eunuch waiting outside the doors of the royal bedchamber heard the emperor cry out in his sleep and called to him,"Wake up, Your Majesty."

But the emperor did not wake up, and the angry ogre in his dream returned. He scolded the emperor for his deception and motioned to kill him. The sharp knife came within a hair's breadth from the emperor's nose.

At this critical moment, a man dressed like a scholar stopped the big fellow and said to him: "Though the emperor gossips and leads a pretty raunchy life, he has done some good things in the past. I hope you will reconsider and let him live. If he learns a lesson from this experience, he may continue to do well with his deserving subjects by befriending them and getting rid of the scoundrels."

The threatening figure withdrew his knife and said to the scholar, "For your sake, I will spare him this time."

In humble gratitude, Emperor Qian Long cupped his hands before his chest, a gesture that jolted him from his sleep. Opening his eyes, he found himself in bed and saw the panic on the stunned eunuch's face.

"Go get a pen and some ink."

After dressing, he came to the table and wrote on the paper "Virtuous Admiration." He studied the words for a while and said, "This is what I have gained from this trip."

The eunuch now understood what the emperor meant. So, the servant carved the two words on a nanmu board and tacked it on the palace gate. Since that time, Shacun Village was called "The Village of Virtuous Admiration."

Emperor Qian Long and the Empress

Emperor Qian Long's decades of reign were crowned with glory in civil and military affairs. Then tributes of admiration, often elaborate to obsequiousness, were forever charming his ears. Resting on his laurels, the emperor began to turn his mind to sensual diversions. But palace rules long established by his forefathers kept him from unbridled indulgence. So his favorite eunuchs were quick to advise him to pursue pleasures incognito.

At the time there lived in the capital a courtesan called Third Lady. It was well known that she was on intimate terms with the high and noble in court circles. Many fame or fortune seekers frequently crossed her threshold to curry favour with her, trying to achieve their ends through her influential connections.

It happened that a certain garrison commander of the imperial city had borne a grudge against the world's oldest profession. All in the business were once ordered by him to clear out of the city within a day on pain of punishment. Only Third Lady was found to be totally disregarding the order. This enraged the commander so much that he decided to arrest the lady himself. At midnight he and his men broke into her house boisterously. Just outside an inner apartment he heard the lady leisurely leaving the bed and throwing words through the window:

"What's all that noise about out there? Who can take the responsibility for disturbing the very important person here?"

Immediately her maids came out making an effort to quiet the disturbance. The commander was still giving loud orders to his men when he heard the lady shouting to him:

"What's all your yelling for? Here is a slip for you to take good look at. I hope you won't regret for what you are doing."

By lamplight the commander read the characters written in red ink on the slip: "You may go now. You will hear more tomorrow at court. This is my imperial order." The commander was absolutely stunned and hastely withdrew with his men.

The story of such royal misconduct gradually found its way into the ears of Empress Nala. This first lady in the imperial palace was reputed to be as shrewd as she was resourceful. Even Emperor Qian Long was somewhat in awe of her. At first, she would offer a good word of advice during his pleasure, especially in bed. To keep the skeleton in the cupboard, the emperor was obliged to listen and bear it. But then, as such advice was more frequently given, His Majesty became more angry than annoyed. It so happened that the garrison commander that had once attempted to arrest Third Lady was the empress' uncle. The emperor suspected the empress to be behind it all. His dislike of her began to grow, so much so that he even tried to exclude her from his party on one of his inspection tours to south China. It was through the intercession of the empress dowager, who was also in the party and claimed to need her daughter-in-law's company, the empress was allowed to make the trip.

When the royal party arrived in Jinan of Shandong province, the eunuchs obliged the emperor's desire for pleasure and gaiety by staging on the Dragon Boat singing and dacing perfermances by groups of southern maidens of rare beauty. The emperor was so charmed by their rhythmic movement and gay tunes that he should fail to see whether he was now in heaven or on earth. The performances over, he had some of the best-looking performers remain on board to keep him company.

This made Empress Nala too emotionally upset to go to sleep in the night. Then true to her duty as empress, she composed by the lamp light an admonitory memorial, which she brought herself to the emperor's boat before daybreak. At the moment the emperor was still in sound sleep, with one of the dancing girls in his arms. Another girl was awake when the empress made her appearance. Much impressed by the elegant attire and dignified manner of the unexpected visitor, the girl sensed who it was and made an attempt to shy away from the scene. Just then the emperor woke to find the empress standing motionless at the bedside with something in her hand. He was surprised, then said in anger: "What are you here for?"

At once the empress knelt down and said: "There is something very important for Your Majesty to consider."

The emperor raised his voice: "Is this the hour for you to intrude? Any matter can be brought to me through the eunuchs on duty, you know. Now you are here without my permission, you must be plotting something sinister against me."

Looking earnest, the empress pleaded: "It is by the grace of Your Majesty that I have been made your empress. It ought to have been my duty to wait upon you personally, especially on a long journey such as this. I have just learned of a kind of impropriety on the part of Your Majesty, which compels me to venture into your presence to offer a word of advice. My intrusion may be incurring your displeasure, but my duty dictates no otherwise. What should be brought to your attention is that those with you here are nothing but tramps in the street, too lowly for your touch. Should the health of Your Majesty be impaired, who could take all the responsibility?"

At this, the emperor flew into a rage, shouting at the top of his voice: "Hold your glib tongue! You will suffer for this. Come, guards! Throw her out!"

Remaining on her knees, the empress went on: "For the sake of our long union as man and wife, Your Majesty should pause and ponder on my words, even at a moment of anger. And I would smile to die for your good."

Waving away the dancing girls who had by now put on their clothes, the emperor stared at his empress with wide eyes. She had more to say:

"I mean well in what I say. I have never intended to offend. Now I have aroused your anger and suspicion, how can I possibly remain in charge of the inner palaces? I am willing to give up my place as empress to some one more worthy of the role. But before I withdraw from your presence Your Majesty may very well read my memorial which I have composed with all my heart and soul."

With reluctance the emperor began reading the memorial. It was indeed a piece of writing full of earnest and effusive expressions, quoting from wide sources and dwelling on the evils of lascivious pleasure. Before he could read it through the emperor turned furious and rose to slap the empress in the face, crying out loud:

"Who do you take me to be? A libertine like Emperor Yang of the Sui Dynasty, eh? You have been my empress for so many years, and yet you allow yourself to talk such nonsense. How can this be tolerated!"

Throwing down the memorial, he ordered the eunuchs to drag her out. Then the empress cried injustice, appealing to heaven and earth and the imperial ancestors for succour. But the emperor declared: "She is out of her mind, no longer fit to be an empress. She ought to be shut up."

Still in her kneeling position, the empress allowed no one to come near her. Getting into his clothes, the emperor declared he was to see the empress dowager aboard another ship. Catching hold of his legs, the empress begged him to finish reading her memorial. His Majesty was now in violent anger and kicked her aside. Falling on her face, the empress began crying bitterly.

When on board his mother's ship, Emperor Qian Long gave his full account of what had passed between him and his wife. But he failed to mention anything about his affairs with the dancing girls.

The empress dowager knew her daughter-in-law to be always honest and outspoken. But she decided something proper should be done about it. Then she called the empress before her presence and said:

"At your age you ought to have known better. It seems you are now unable to make a change in your temper. If you go on rowing with the emperor, things between you will grow worse. For your own good, I suggest you stay behind and do some Buddhist meditation in a quiet and peaceful place around here. Don't you believe this to be a better way out?"

Now Empress Nala began to see that her mother-in-law was clearly siding with the emperor. In the circumstances, she had no choice but to express her willingness to follow the empress dowager's suggestions, as she had lost too much face to return to the imperial palace. Subsequently, on orders of the empress dowager Nala was taken by eunuchs to a nunnery nearby.

Long after the event no news came to Nala that she would be called back to the palace. With a sigh of hurt feeling she said to herself: "Now I see the empress dowager had meant me to turn nun as a retribution for my uncalled-for act. It is only wishful thinking that I might regain His Majesty's love. I would do well to live the rest of my life here on this tract of pure sacred ground." Then she had her head shaved and took the Buddhist vows.

On his following trips to south China Emperor Qian Long also went by way of Jinan, but he never made mention of the empress' existence there. Years later, on a trumped-up charge by an imperial concubine, Nala was taken back to the capital for trial. Curiously enough, it was through a good word from Third Lady in her behalf that she was acquitted of the charge. But the emperor had her sent to a nunnery in Yangzhou of Jiangsu province to embrace the Buddhist cause to the end of her life. The end came soon afterwards.

A court censor, Adang'a by name, submitted to the emperor a petition for her burial as an empress. What the emperor had to say was this: "How can a woman without hair on her head be accorded the dignity of an empress? Let the matter drop here."

The Abdication of Emperor Qian Long

When Qian Long was crowned emperor, he invoked the blessing of Heaven for a reign of 60 years, and he vowed to abdicate in favour of one of his sons at the end of the period, not to break the record of his grandfather Emperor Kang Xi ruling the country for 61 years. In the end his wish came true. After 60 years on the throne he was still hale and hearty. But he was resolved to fulfil his vows. In fact, he had already made all preparations for his eventual retirement. For comfort and pleasure in his remaining years, he had erected the palace of Peace and Longevity, embracing beautiful gardens and splendid halls of all descriptions.

At the time Emperor Qian Long was already an octogenarian. At a meeting of princes, lords and high court officials, the emperor made known his desire to step down from the throne. Most present voiced no particular personal opinions. But to Prime Minister He Sheng the imperial wish came like a bolt from the blue. He felt as if the ground was sinking under his feet. Sensing the urgency of the matter, he stepped forward to give the emperor his counsel:

"Your Majesty is blessed with all heavenly and earthly vigor. As you are still enjoying excellent health, adbication seems to be out of the question."

Then he went so far as to say: "Your Majesty would do well to reflect for a moment on the example of Emperor Xuan Zong in the Tang Dynasty. What became of him after he gave up his throne to his son

Emperor Su Zong? Didn't he get the cold treatment as a result?"

As it was, Emperor Qian Long was not without his misgivings. But it was below his dignity as emperor to unsay what had been said. With a wave of his hand, he told He Sheng: "My mind is made up. You need say no more of it." Bowing his obedience, He Sheng withdrew with a woebegone look on his face.

Subsequently, the emperor had a secret imperial edict taken out from behind a high-hanging horizontal board bearing the inscription "Justice and Honour." When a piece of yellow satin covering the edict was removed, there were seen red-inked characters written in the emperor's own handwriting: "My 15th son Yong Yan shall be heir to the throne. He shall be conferred on the title of Prince Jia Qing. When he succeeds to the crown, he shall change the title of reign to Jia Qing."

Yet Emperor Qian Long was far from willing to be entirely dispossessed of power in state affairs after his abdication. He would still hold the highest-ranking title of Grand Emperor traditionally reserved for the living father of an emperor. In the abdication pronouncement drafted by the chief privy councillor under his order, there were provisions upholding his supreme powers and sanctity. Here are some examples. On an imperial edict the seal of the Grand Emperor must be affixed before that of the emperor. The special word *zheng* usually exclusively used by an emperor to refer to himself could be likewise used by the Grand Emperor. In court documents, the title of the Grand Emperor, when referred to, must be written in a more prominent space than that of the emperor. At state banquets attended by both the Grand Emperor and the emperor, the former was seated while the latter had to stand to show filial respect. And in the selection of the emperor's wife, the decision rested with the Grand Emperor.

On the other hand, Emperor Jia Qing himself was neither weak-spirited nor mediocre. Once on the throne, he took most state matters in his own hands and often defied the authority of the Grand Emperor. His long-cherished ill feelings against He Sheng were getting more and more intense. The Grand Emperor knew the prime minister would suffer a fatal end at the hands of his son, but could only do feebly to shield him. To avoid serious unpleasantness with his son, the Grand Emperor turned much cooler in his attitude towards his once favorite courtier.

Once He Sheng reported confidentially to the Grand Emperor that General Hailancha, who had just returned to the capital after putting down a rebellion, had possessed himself of much war booty including valuable furs. But the Grand Emperor showed displeasure at He Sheng for the accusation, saying: "What's wrong about that? Considering the large number of rebels the general killed, it is nothing for him to keep some furs against the cold. On your part, you have never killed a single rebel, but have you ever refused to take a gift?" At this, He Sheng withdrew shamefaced.

Then, too, the Grand Emperor would not hesitate to take the shine out of He Sheng, if need be. Here is a case in point. As was the usual practice, all court communications to local authorities must be appended with the names of the two co-prime ministers. In the second year of Jia Qing's reign, one of these ministers, Agui, died. Then at a meeting of privy councillors called by Grand Emperor Qian Long at the Longevity Hill, he said to He Sheng in a serious tone: "Agui was a venerable courtier with much to his credit. When he was still alive, it was all right for your name to be associated with his. Now he is dead, it is not proper to append your name alone to a court communication. The local authorities that are unaware of the real situation at court might take it for granted that you are in charge of all court directives. What do you think of this?" Thenceforward no name of a prime minister was appended to a court communication.

Now Qian Long, as the Grand Emperor, had much less duty of a ruler on his shoulders and more time to cast backward glances. What had been most unbearable to him concerned the miserable death of the palace maid Yan'er. In connection with Yan'er he thought of He Sheng whose fate he had come to be worried about. One day he held at the Palace of Peace and Longevity a "Banquet for a Thousand Elders," which He Sheng and other higher courtiers attended. After the banquet, he told He Sheng to stay for a private conversation.

"Dear He Sheng," said the Grand Emperor in earnest, "it is perhaps destiny at work that I have showered favours on you and have even tolerated your wrong doings. In doing this, I feel, I am repaying my debts to some one in the nether world. But you don't seem to understand what is deep in my mind. With your far from pardonable behaviour, you have made too many enemies. After I leave this world, I am afraid, you will reap the whirlwind.'

This brought a flood of tears to He Sheng's eyes. Going down on his knees, he said sobbingly: "May Heaven bless our Grand Emperor a long, long life! How I wish to live under your aegis forever!"

"Well, as the saying goes, man proposes, God disposes. What's the use saying all this?"

With that, the Grand Emperor closed his eyes to rest his mind, and giving a wave of his hand, said no more. He Sheng knocked his forehead on the floor thuddingly several times before he withdrew.

The Fate of a Powerful Courtier

Emperor Jia Qing's ascension to the throne abdicated by his father Qian Long was somewhat of a weight on the mind of Prime Minister He Sheng. But still feeling secure under the aegis of Grand Emperor Qian Long, He Sheng clung to his habitual arrogant and domineering ways. At all times he congratulated himself on having a part in helping the new emperor to the throne and prided himself on remaining in the confidence of the Grand Emperor. It was on these accounts that he could sometimes be so bold as to act presumingly even before the young emperor.

All this, of course, did not escape the eyes of the emperor. But in view of his present position as the new sovereign, he knew he had not yet built up sufficient strength to take issue against the prime minister long entrenched in power. He also knew he must avoid doing anything to embarrass the Grand Emperor who still patronized He Sheng. So without revealing what was really in his mind, he appeared to be kind to He Sheng. To indignant opinions directed against He Sheng, the emperor even said: "I rely on the prime minister to rule the empire. He must be treated with all proper respect."

He Sheng was so satisfied with his circumstances that he felt as if treading on air. Now he had something unsavory up his sleeve. It was his recommendation to the emperor of his own old tutor for secretarial service. Beneath the cover of attending to literary matters in court, the purpose was for the man to spy on the emperor. But the emperor was not blind to the truth. He appeared to be unsuspicious, often taking the man as a congenial companion in composing poems or lyric songs. As it was, the emperor was biding his time.

In the late winter of the third year of Jia Qing's reign, while all the garden trees were trembling in the cold winds, from the Hall of Peaceful Mind came the word that the Grand Emperor had fallen ill. Now at the age of 88, he was too weak to be responsive to all medical efforts. Finally on the third day of the first month by the lunar calendar the following year, the Grand Emperor died.

After the death of the Grand Emperor, Emperor Jia Qing found himself suddenly in possession of increased power, enjoying a freedom hitherto unknown to him. He was ready now to remove the thorn in his side. Surely he lost no time in ordering the arrest of He Sheng who had held the reins of power for over 20 years.

He Sheng was holding a sumptuous banquet in celebration of the birthday of his wife when the bearers of the imperial edict invaded his house. At the loud cry "His Majesty's edict is here!" He Sheng put down his chopsticks, elbowed aside the concubines near him and went down on his knees. Immediately striking his ears was this: "Prime Minister He Sheng shall be forthwith dismissed from his post and arrested to stand trial by the Ministry of Justice for his high crimes of forming cliques to usurp power and conspiring against the throne."

The once high and mighty prime minister was now paralysed with fright. Two imperial runners stepped forward to pick him up from the floor and had him handcuffed. Manacles were also put on all other members of the house with the exception of the tenth princess, who was He Sheng's daughter-in-law and Emperor Jia Qing's sister. All at once the prime minister's magnificent mansion was a scene of disorder and confusion. Wine, women and song had given way to wails of despair, cries for mercy and abusive shouts.

In the pandemonium only tenth princess remained calmer than the rest of the distressed lot. Though looking somewhat ruffled, she seemed to be the only straw to clutch at. All in the house, old and young, high and low, knelt before her, imploring her to appeal to the emperor for pardon.

Accompanied by a couple of personal maids, the princess went at once to the imperial palace to see the emperor and tearfully made a plea for leniency. The emperor, recalling how the princess had encouraged the He Sheng family in their evil deeds, got more angry. With a wave of his hand, he returned to his inner chambers, leaving the princess standing there in great dejection.

Two days later, in an imperial edict He Sheng was indicted on 20 charges. The once all-powerful courtier was allowed to take his own life. All in his house holding any official ranks were reduced to commoners. The princess and her husband were removed to another place, where they would live apart from court life. All of He Sheng's property was confiscated and added to the imperial treasury. At the time a popular saying ran: "The downfall of He Sheng is the fortune of Jia Qing."

He Sheng seemed to have had a premonition of his eventual fatal end. After his death, on his body was found a slip of paper on which was penned the poem:

The long illusion is now all real,

With me leaving the gay world behind.
When I lie on my back in perfect peace,
Another life to me may be more kind.

Jia Qing's Aversion for the *Ruyi*

Ruyi is an ornamental object generally regarded as a symbol of good luck. Usually made of bamboo, jade, bone, or metal, it has a slightly curved handle, the larger end of which is shaped like a glossy ganoderma or a patch of cloud.

In keeping with time-honoured customes of the Manchus, at each Spring Festival princes, lords, high officials, or provincial governors would present to the court the *ruyi* as a tribute of respect or blessing. But after Jia Qing came to the throne, he ordered a stop to the practice, saying in a special edict: "You all think the *ruyi* brings you good luck. But I think there is no such luck to speak of."

This made the courtiers puzzled. They wondered why the emperor was making a mountain out of a molehill. The *ruyi* was after all a small object having no vital bearing on state affairs.

Yet in the emperor's mind, he had at least two reasons for his aversion for the *ruyi*. One reason had something to do with his dislike of He Sheng, the prime minister in the early years of his reign. Long before Jia Qing succeeded to the crown, his father Emperor Qian Long had decided on the heir to the throne in great secrecy. It happened that He Sheng was the only person taken into Qian Long's confidence. To curry favour with the chosen crown prince, He Sheng gave Jia Qing an inkling of the secret by presenting him alone of all the princes a *ruyi* meaning to wish him good luck in a royal future. It eventually turned out to be true that

Jia Qing was declared heir to the throne. Then Jia Qing came to disrelish the idea of He Sheng knowing the secret. Should the fact of his reception of the *ruyi* from He Sheng found its way into the court history, he felt he himself would be held up to ridicule by the whole world. So he determined to have the *ruyi* forbidden as a tribute to the court. Thus no official historian would dare write about the *ruyi* in connection with the dark secret.

The other reason concerned an event that bore anything but good luck as signified by the *ruyi*. One year, on his return trip from the Summer Villa of Chengde, Emperor Jia Qing made a stopover at the royal country residence at Baijian. Most of the court officials had to go there for the purpose of escorting the emperor back to Beijing. This left the capital carelessly guarded. A band of rebellious peasants led by Lin Qing of Hebei, taking advantage of the situation, made an attempt to invade the Forbidden City. With the assistance of some sympathetic eunuchs, over 100 of these rebels broke into the palace through the Xihuamen Gate on the west, and some 30 of them fought their way in through the Donghuamen Gate on the east. They would have succeeded in taking the inner palaces if more than 1,000 imperial guards equipped with fire arms had not rushed over from the Longzongmen Gate to engage them in a fierce battle lasting a day and half. Being greatly outnumbered, the rebels went down to defeat.

When the news of the uprising came to the Baijian residence, Emperor Jia Qing first trembled with fear and then flew into a rage. Bringing his palm down on the table with a thud, he cried out loud: "Those defenders of the city are nothing but nincompoops! How could they have let the rebels break free into the palace?

What a shame to the Great Qing Empire!" Immediately he ordered two of his able generals, Prince Lawangdaoer and Lord Suonuomuduo, to speed back to the capital to regain control of the situation.

"Sweep each and every rebel into the net of justice!" the emperor roared.

On reaching Beijing, the generals dispatched large numbers of troops to patrol around the Forbidden City and in areas inside and outside of the Chaoyangmen Gate. All efforts were made to ferret out rebels that had gone underground. Emperor Jia Qing was back in his imperial palace two days later when security was assured.

From the Qian Qing Palace, where he usually conducted state affairs, the emperor gave orders for removing from their posts and putting on trial the two city garrison commanders Ji Lun and Yu Ling. He also amply rewarded those giving a good account of themselves in the defence of the city, including his second son Mian Ning. At the same time he issued an edict to blame himself for what had happened. In this edict of self-criticism he said: "In face of this untoward incident resulting from deplorable errors and lack of high virtues on my part, I have no choice but to reproach myself." On the other hand, he sternly rebuked his courtiers:

"The greatest evil today lies in your procrastination and dereliction. In admonishing you, I have often talked myself hoarse, and yet you have failed to take in the meaning of what I say. The recent events, as a result, have been something unparalleled in times past."

Thus reproved, the courtiers kneeling on the floor all had their hearts in their mouths, seeming to feel the approach of a disaster.

It would be the emperor's birthday in a few days. On such an occasion a jubilant celebration was always in order. But on account of the peasant uprising the emperor felt no enthusiasm for it. To the courtiers eager for the celebration, he voiced his displeasure:

"On my birthday in other years it was a happy thing to see the *ruyi* that signifies your loyalty to me and my grace to you. As there is anything but good luck this year, so you can dispense with it. As symbol of good luck, it could only add to my troubles. I am truly in no mood for the celebration of my own birthday."

A Cook Attempts the Life of Jia Qing

Once Emperor Jia Qing was taking a stroll in the Yuan Ming Yuan Palace when a man near him suddenly thrust a dagger at him. Before the weapon could strike home the man's hand was stayed by a quick-eyed, nimble imperial bodyguard. Then the would-be assassin was overpowered by other guards rushing on him.

That the assassin had been caught under his nose aroused the emperor's displeasure at, and even suspicion on, his high courtiers. To make clear what might be behind the crime, he ordered a grand trial to be conducted by government ministers and other important high officials. But repeated interrogations failed to reveal any plot suspected by the emperor.

The assassin, Cheng De by name, was found to be a cook of the imperial household. When asked why he should attempt the life of the emperor, he said something very curious:

"I have always envied the emperor his riches and glory. There is a world of difference between his life and mine. If I could finish him off, wouldn't a lowly cook like myself have the pleasure of sitting on the throne, too?"

The confession was reported as it was to the emperor. Seeing that no bigger fish could be caught in the case, Jia Qing decided to hush up the matter. Only Cheng De and his two sons were to be put to death.

On the day set for the death punishment, Cheng

De, with his hands bound behind him, was escorted by a group of guards to the execution ground at Caishikou in the south of the city. Tied to a wooden stake, he saw his two sons, aged only 16 and 14, dragged before him. Still pupils in a private school, the good-looking boys kowtowed to him to show their filial devotion before they met their death. Cheng De shut his eyes in extreme grief, with tears streaming down his cheeks.

Then it was Cheng De's turn to meet his end. The end came but slowly. First his ears were cut off, then his nose, his nipples. Next, mincing work started from his left arm, then extended to his chest, to his back. At first there was blood flowing out, but soon only a kind of yellow fluid oozed from the wounds. When the work on his upper body was done, he suddenly opened his eyes wide and shouted in a sharp tone: "You blood suckers, make it quick!"

"It's His Majesty's wish to make you suffer longer," said the chief of the executioners coldly.

Cheng De shut his eyes again, and uttered not a single word or a cry of pain to the end of the slow torture.

Emperor Jia Qing's suspicion was far from cleared with the death of Cheng De. Extensive investigations failed to throw any light on the case. The person or persons who were supposed to have aided and abetted Cheng De in the crime remained unknown. It was not until 10 years later when the peasant uprising led by Lin Qing made a vain attempt to invade the imperial palace that the whole truth had come out. In the course of trying the case of the captured Lin Qing, a local official of Shangdong, Wu Jie, found out that on the day before the attempted assassination of the emperor, Cheng De had spent a night with one of Lin Qing's men, Cui Shijun. Then Wu Jie came to the conclusion that Cheng De was a member of a particular sect of the then organized peasant movement. But Wu Jie did not report to the emperor what he believed to be true, for he felt that with the death of Cheng De the case had long since been closed.

To his dying day Emperor Jia Qing was still ignorant of the true identity of the man who had almost taken his life.

Tales of Emperor Dao Guang

Emperor Dao Guang was the second son of Emperor Jia Qing. When a prince, he went by the name Mian Ning. During his 30 years on the throne, he was decadent in domestic affairs and capitulationist in foreign relations, leaving little or nothing for the world to remember him by except loss of sovereign rights and shame to the country. But many a tale has been told about his life. As it was, though not endowed with great wisdom, he was clever in small matters.

Once, as a boy of 10, Mian Ning gave a good account of himself before his grandfather Emperor Qian Long on the Weixungeer hunting grounds. With a single arrow he killed a deer, a feat that won the gift of a coat decorated with peacock plumes from his delighted grandfather, who even composed a poem to celebrate the event:

Old age is no hitch to ride and fight;
Plumes to my son's lad a dead deer brings.
With glad event coming two years sooner,
From my heart a fitting verse springs.

The words "two years sooner" in the poem refer to the fact that Qian Long hunted down a bear at the age of 12, but Mian Ning shot an arrow into a deer at the age of 10. Qian Long was so very glad that his grandson had done better than himself. From then on Mian Ning was the apple of everyone's eye.

At the time that a band of rebels led by Lin Qing invaded the imperial palace during the absence of Emperor Jia Qing from the capital, Mian Ning and other princes were studying at the Qian Qing Palace. When word came that the rebels were pressing toward the inner palaces, Mian Ning was seized with fear, but soon kept his wits about him.

"How many rebels are coming?" he asked the court official on duty.

"Your humble old slave is too dim-sighted to have made good count," replied the official. "There might be 100."

Presently Mian Ning gave orders to lock the Longzong Gate and the Jingyun Gate, then returned to the Hall of Peaceful Mind. From a spot under the eaves of the hall he caught sight of some men, with the tops of their heads wrapped in something white, moving some way off. With a fowling piece brought him by a eunuch, he took aim and pulled the trigger. But nothing happened. The he found the shotgun was not loaded. In the emergency he made use of his wits. Off his coat he ripped two silver buttons for pellets, which immediately felled a couple of rebles and scared the others away.

When Emperor Jia Qing was back in the imperial palace from the Summer Villa of Chengde, he amply rewarded Mian Ning and conferred on him the title of Prince of Wisdom. Thus two silver buttons won him great glory and paved his way to the position of heir to the throne.

In the year Dao Guang succeeded to the throne, an inventory was once made of the palace storage overstocked with heaps of silk fabrics, chinaware and other things. In a report to the emperor the imperial housekeepers suggested transferring elsewhere the portions that were beyond palace consumption. But the emperor issued an edict to distribute these portions among government ministers and other high officials in amounts varying with their ranks. Even the official historiographes received their shares. As a result, this imperial grace earned the acclaim of the whole court.

Of all the Qing emperors, Dao Guang was the most frugal-minded. He often had his trousers, worn out at the knees, patched up for longer wearing. The courtiers all followed suit. Some even put knee patches on new trousers. One day, seeing such patches on the trousers the chief privy councillor was wearing, the emperor asked:

"You wear patched trousers, too?"

"Yes, I do, Your Majesty," replied the chief.

"How much silver do you pay for one of your patches?"

The chief was puzzled for a few moments before he managed to say: "About one-third of a tael."

"That's cheap enough," commented the emperor. "Here in the palace each patch costs five taels of silver."

His Majesty again asked: "How much do you spend on eggs at home?"

The chief was at once tongue-tied for an answer. He was then obliged to make up a story to cover up his embarrassment.

"As a child, I suffered from a kind of malady allergic to eggs," he explained. "As I have never eaten an egg since childhood, so I am ignorant of its price."

Emperor Dao Guang always had a high regard for filial piety. When he ascended the throne his mother was still living. Once on the occasion of the empress dowager's birthday, "Old Laizi Amuses His Parents," one of the 24 traditional stories on deeds of filial devotion, was performed in the palace, with the emperor playing the leading role of Old Laizi. In a vari-coloured constume and wearing a false white beard, he beat a toy drum and sang and danced like a child, evoking ripples of mirth from the empress dowager and all others present.

Here are two lines passing judgment on Emperor Dao Guang:

Many tell tales of him in mirth;
Few bless him with a good name.

A Princess versus Her Housekeeper

In the Qing Dynasty, princesses often suffered serious mistreatment by their housekeepers, especially after marriage. It was not uncommon for princesses to be humiliated and bullied to death at their hands.

According to a long-established palace rule, a princess and her husband, called *fuma*, would live in a house bestowed on them by the emperor. When the princess' parents-in-law came for a visit, they had to go through the ritual of kowtowing to their daughter-in-law as if they were having an audience with the emperor himself.

More curiously, the *fuma* usually lived separate from the princess in another room. Unless invited, he could not spend a night in the same bed with his own wife. And the princess' invitations must be extended through the housekeeper, who could withhold the communication as she pleased. More often than not bribery of the housekeeper was a necessity for realizing a night union between husband and wife. There were times when the bribery might not be heavy enough to please the housekeeper. In such case the princess would find herself waiting in vain for the nocturnal appearance of her *fuma* in her room. And a feudal sense of shame would inhibit her from making an inquiry about the matter. Even if she could bring herself to inquire, the housekeeper might read her a lesson on the high virtues expected of a princess. So even to her own loyal parents a princess seldom had the courage to disclose what was on her mind.

Thus in the Qing times few princesses had the opportunities to bear children. What children the *fuma* might have were often borne him by concubines. Most princesses, it is true, died lovesick. After the death of the princess the *fuma* was not supposed to continue living in the emperor-bestowed house. The house as well as what was left in it must revert to the palace. But it was customary for the housekeeper to keep for herself of the things except the house. No wonder the housekeeper was wont to mentally ill-treat the princess so as to hasten her death.

But there was a case of princess and *fuma* living a happy life and raising many children. This concerned Emperor Dao Guang's eldest daughter and her husband Fu Zhen. At first the couple suffered such fate at the hands of their housekeeper that for a year after marriage they had not been able to share the same bed for once. The princess came to find such a state of affairs so unbearable that she decided to dispel all sense of womanly shame and complain to her imperial parents against the housekeeper.

Kneeling before the emperor, the princess asked: "Dear father, whom on earth have you married me to?"

Much surprised, the father answered with a question: "Isn't your husband Fu Zhen, the *fuma*?"

The princess began to sob. "Who is Fu Zhen? What is he like? After a year of marriage I haven't seen him once."

"Why don't you see each other?"

"The housekeeper won't let us."

"How can the housekeeper meddle in affairs between you husband and wife?" remarked the emperor wonderingly. "You can make your own decisions, can't you?"

Thus encouraged by the imperial assurance, the

princess returned home and gave her housekeeper a hearty scolding. Then with unprecedented boldness she openly invited her *fuma* to live in the same room with her. Their love for each other soon grew deep. As a result, in the following years the princess gave birth to eight children, holding the highest record in the number of offsprings for a princess in the history of the Qing Dynasty.

As shown by this story, the Qing emperors could be really ignorant of the circumstances in which a princess was separated from her husband by the hidden hand of a housekeeper. The root cause for the housekeeper's audacity to act in the way she generally did probably lies in the feudal idea regarding intercourse between man and woman as a thing of shame. It was indeed something deplorable and ridiculous. Emperor Dao Guang's eldest daughter must have been the bravest of all princesses.

Decision on Heir to the Throne

Once 69-year-old Emperor Dao Guang fell ill. But it did not keep him from making earnest efforts to attend to state affairs until he felt his health was giving way early in the following year. A meeting of important court officials was then called to discuss his decision to choose his fourth son as heir to the throne. This prince would be vested with the imperial power to read memorials to the throne and receive high officials in audience.

Somehow the emperor was unable to fully assure himself that he had made the right decision. Weighing the choice in his mind, he felt he must not count out his sixth son who kept emerging in his vision. Then with a deathbed effort he declared he would give both sons an oral test before coming to a final decision.

For the test both brothers made preparations as best they could. Each turned to his own tutor for counsel. The younger prince was advised by his tutor to show prowess in talent to rule the country. Whatever questions the emperor might ask must be answered in full and intelligently.

On the other hand, the elder prince's tutor, who was named Du Shoutian and holding the position of chief privy councillor, told his pupil to take a different course.

"As the matter stands," he pointed out, "you are no match for your brother in the realm of state affairs. There is only one way for you to come out of the test the winner."

"What is it?" asked the elder prince eagerly.

"His Majesty might mention something about his illness and old age which would not allow him on the throne any longer. In that case you must immediately fall prone on the floor, saying not a word but shedding abundant tears to show your filial piety."

Both of the heirs apparent duly followed their tutor's instructions. After the test Emperor Dao Guang decided in favour of his fourth son on the grounds that this prince was full of filial devotion, a virtue regarded by ancient sages as most admirable in the rulers of an empire.

Soon afterwards Emperor Dao Guang died. His fourth son succeeded to the crown as Emperor Xian Feng, who was perhaps the most decadent and inept ruler in the history of the Qing Dynasty.

An Emperor Misbehaves

During the 11-year reign of Xian Feng, countless unsavory stories had stemmed from him as a libertine of ruler.

When the Taiping Revolution (1851--1864) was in full swing, the rebellious peasant troops once took the city of Hangzhou, killing the local governor in battle. An imperial meeting was held to decide on the successor to the governorship. Governor He Guiqing, who had jurisdiction over the Huaihe River and the lower Yangtse River areas, submitted to the throne a memorial recommending Wang Youling, a high administrator in Jiangsu province, for the post. On the memorial Emperor Xian Feng just scribbled in red ink the name "Wang Yongling" three times over, without making any specific indication of his approval or disapproval. This only left the court officials all puzzled. In a second memorial He Guiqing again recommended Wang Youling. This time the emperor wrote on the memorial a single line of comment: "All you know is Wang Youling!" In his third memorial He Guiqing asserted he would be willing and ready to accept punishment if Wang Youling should prove to be unequal to the office. Finally the emperor said yes, but much time had been wasted for no purpose.

Ond day in the 8th year of Xian Feng's reign, a eunuch passed an imperial message to Su Shun and six other cabinet ministers, ordering them to go to the Yuan Ming Yuan Palace as soon as the court meeting was over. Inside these gardens they would await the arrival of the emperor at a scenic spot called High Hills and Long Streams.

The emperor soon came in a boat. After landing he mounted a horse and told the seven courtiers to take off their coats and follow him on foot. After a long while of random riding, now slow and now fast, he found them puffing and panting from exhaustion. Then in a pavilion at the place called Lion's Wood he entertained them to a hearty meal. A large bowl of noodles as appetizer was followed with dish after dish of delicacy prepared by artists from the imperial kitchen. Having eaten their fill, these ministers habitually knelt down and acknowledged their thanks for the imperial grace. But it was not all. His Majesty again favoured his loyal subjects already full up to the throat with generous quantities of tasty rice gruel, which it was out of the question to decline. Seeing no other way out, they were obliged to agonize their stomachs. All this over, the emperor once more rode here and there on horseback, closely followed by his ministers, who were not allowed to go home until His Majesty dismounted at the Tower of Light by nightfall. Quite a few days later these men were still smarting from this royal mischief.

Emperor Xian Feng frequently went boating in the Yuan Ming Yuan Palace. Each time he would have troops of palace maids lining the lakeshore to cheer him with a "Pleasant crossing!" At the moment the oars began to be pulled, the maid at the head of the line started the cheering, which was continued in turn by another and still another all the way along the line. These joyfull shouts reverberated in the air and lingered till the royal pleasure-boat reached the other shore. A baby prince in the emperor's arms soon learned the cheers, able to parrot the palace maids crying out: "Pleasant crossing!"

Emperor Xian Feng was also notorious for his indulgence in wine and women. Still feeling insatiate with his many imperial concubines, he often went for clandestine love affairs outside the palace. Once he was infatuated with a saucy young widow named Cao, who had delicate feet measuring barely over three inches long and wore shoes with fragrant insoles and pearls on the tips. Throwing aside all royal decorum, the enamored emperor went so far as to take her into the palace to grace his bed. Thus for a time she was popularly known as "Palace Widow Cao."

Even at a time the edifice of his empire was tottering to a fall, Xian Feng still could hardly refrain from lascivious pleasures. There was then a young actress called Zhu Lianfen. A rare beauty, she had talents for poetry and calligraphy and was gifted with a melodious voice for singing arias from Kunqu operas. Very frequently she was called into the palace to keep the emperor company. Meanwhile, a court censor, Lu by name, also had intimate relations with the versatile actress. Lu was resentful that on account of the emperor he had few opportunities to see her. For purposes of his own, he submitted a long admonitory memorial to the throne, dwelling on the virtues of decent conduct with arguments supported by quotations from wide sources. He concluded that it was beneath the dignity of an emperor to have illicit relations with a lowly actress.

After reading the masterpiece of the censor, the emperor broke into a loud laugh and exclaimed: "Our honourable Lu is being jealous!" Then he casually wrote in red ink a brief note on the memorial: "Isn't it true that a dog always resents its being deprived of a bone it is gnawing at? This is my imperial comment."

His Majesty also made remarks to the effect that it was improper for a subject to be jealous of his emperor. Being of a tolerant nature, he reminded his subjects, he had no desire to mete out punishment to the censor.

A Girl Defies the Emperor

Early in 1853, the third year of Xian Feng's reign, the Taiping Revolutionary forces swept eastward along the Yangtse River, taking Jiujiang, Anqing, Anning and other places. Meanwhile, part of these forces marched north into Hebei province, posing a threat to Beijing and Tianjin. Like an old boat tossing in rapids, the Qing court was on the point of sinking. But fresh on the throne, Emperor Xian Feng was blind to the situation. He even issued an edict to gather the cream of young womanhood from the provinces for his pleasure in the palace. For a time local officials were bestirring themselves in seeking out beautiful maidens and sending them to Beijing.

On the list of the selected was the daughter of an imperial army officer. Well-educated and skilled in embroidery, she often helped in the support of the family with scanty earnings from teaching neighborhood children to read and write. With no other way out, she could only bid a tearful farewell to her parents before she was taken to the capital with other girls of similar fate.

Outside the Kunning Palace in the Forbidden City, these hapless maidens had to stand in a long line, awaiting the arrival of the emperor who would make the final selection himself. Remaining where they were from early morning till noon, they failed to see anything of His Majesty. Getting thirsty and hungry and awed by the solemn imperial guards, these girls of local stock found their plight unbearable. As the waiting seemed to be endless, many began to heave sighs, murmur complaint, and even give way to cries of despair. Immediately the guards threw to them threatening words:

"Stop crying and wipe your tears! His Majesty will be here in a moment. Try not to anger him if you don't like to get a good whipping or risk your heads."

Fear came over many girls, but not the daughter of the imperial army officer. Pushing her way to the guards, she said in indignation:

"To be here, we have left behind happy homes and our dear parents. Even if we are chosen as palace ladies, what kind of life will be in store for us? We'll live like prisoners for life, to be sure. We have done nothing yet to repay our own parents for all their love and care for us. And yet they must bear the sorrow of lifelong separation from their daughters. Is all this human? I am not even afraid of death, let alone whipping."

With a look of defiance in her eyes, the girl went on to say:

"Now the peasants in the South are rising in rebellion. They will soon be masters of the vast lands along the Yangtse River. At this critical time when half of the country has fallen into their hands, what the emperor should do is to get able generals for the defense of the empire. Yet he thinks of little else but how to satisfy his lustful desire. Clearly he is more interested in forcing people's daughters into the dark world within his palace than in the future of the country. Is it the proper thing for a good emperor to do?"

The guards now looked awestricken. They were trying to shout down the girl when the emperor came on the scene. Immediately they dragged her before His Majesty and tried to compel her to kneel and ask for pardon. But the girl refused to go down on her knees and struggled to shake off the hands pressing down on her shoulders.

"What's all this about?" the emperor demanded.

The girl said over again what had just offended the ears of the guards. The emperor's ears were offended, too; but her words gave him pause. To put up a benevolent appearance, he swallowed the affront.

"What a remarkable girl!" the emperor exclaimed with affected kindness.

It happened that a court official had recently lost his wife. As a royal grace, the girl was married to him. And by an imperial order all other girls were sent back to their homes.

Ci Xi Gains Imperial Favor

Yehe Nala was the maiden name of Ci Xi, the empress dowager who "ruled behind the curtain" in the last decades of the Qing Dynasty.

In ancient times, when the Manchu chieftain Nuerhachi resorted to force to unite the various tribal clans in Northeast China, the Yehe clan suffered frightful slaughter at his hands, with hardly a male member able to escape with his life. Just before his death the Yehe chief Buyang vowed in indignation: "Even if only a woman is left of my people, she will have the mission to avenge us on the Manchu butchers." This caused the Manchu rulers to make a specific rule that no Yehe woman would be allowed in the palace for any purpose. But Ci Xi, who was of Yehe descent, proved to be an exception to the rule.

Brought up by her father who was a local official at Wuhu in Anhui province, Ci Xi grew into a young lady with charming looks peculiar to southern maidens and a talent for singing a wide range of popular southern tunes. It was on these accounts that she managed to find her way into the palace, won favour with the lustful Emperor Xian Feng, ruled the country for several decades, and finally in a way fulfilled her forefather's vows against the Manchus when she brought the Qing court to the brink of ruin.

Early in the reign of Xian Feng, Ci Xi was chosen as a palace maid for service in the Yuan Ming Yuan Palace. She was settled in a garden house called Parasol Trees Retreat, where, besides passing her time in singing, she often pondered over ways to raise herself to greater heights. When she was back home with her father, the fame of her beauty and talent was such that many eligible young men had sent go-betweens to ask her hand in marriage. All these offers she had refused, for she had high aims of her own.

One day, Emperor Xian Feng in company of his palace ladies passed by the Parasol Trees Retreat and was surprised to hear sweet southern songs issuing from the midst of the trees. He felt so enchanted by the singing that he began to imagine the singer must be as charming as the melodies. With so many attendants around at the moment, he hesitated to seek out the singer right away. But on the following day, accompanied by only two close eunuchs and some bodyguards, he returned to the place and again heard tunes sung in the same enchanting voice. Without the slightest hesitation this time, he went into the house and sat cross-legged on the *kang*, a kind of earthern bed, which now served as a temporary royal seat.

"Who is there singing?" the emperor asked eagerly.

"It is Laner, a palace maid," answered the eunuchs.

Laner was the pet name of Ci Xi. When she was brought in to his presence, the emperor was at once carried away by her amorous looks. Before many words were exchanged he invited her to sit at his side and sing what he had just heard. Clever enough to see what was likely to happen, the attendants made themselves scarce from the scene. A while later, His Majesty said he was thirsty, then Laner was quick to pour a cup of tea for him. But instead of holding out his hands for the tea cup, he pressed his fingers on her tender white wrists. Flushed with seeming shyness, she bowed her head, with her silky dark hair coming under the tip of his nose. Taking advantage of this, he put his lips to her hair and admiringly gazed at her for a long while. In the end he brought her with him back to his private chambers in the imperial palace.

Doing the best she knew how with her feminine charms, Ci Xi was able to keep Emperor Xian Feng absolutely bewitched. A year later she gave birth to a child, who was named Zai Chun and the only son of Xian Feng. For this His Majesty conferred on her the title of High Imperial Lady. From then on Ci Xi was a different person. Discarding her mantle of a sweet and gentle soul, she began to hold her head high as if she was already the mistress of the inner palaces. As it was, even Empress Ci An would not mean much in her eyes.

A Ruse to Finish off Eight Regents

When Zai Chun succeeded to the throne left by his father Xian Feng, this child emperor's own mother was honoured with the title of "Holy Queen Mother," who also acquired the name "Ci Xi" so that she could rank herself in position with the empress dowager who had the name "Ci An," for both names were prefixed with the character "ci," meaning benevolence. Gradually Ci Xi came to be known as the West Empress Dowager, and Ci An, the East Empress Dowager. But Ci Xi was far from content with a mere high-sounding title. Her aim was to "hold supreme state power."

From a careful analysis of the situation at the time Ci Xi realized what stood in her way to power was a gang of eight high court officials, especially Sushun, the most crafty of them all. These officials had been made regents by Emperor Xian Feng in a deathbed will. Aware of their strength, Ci Xi decided to resort to wits rather than force to win out in the struggle for power.

The first step Ci Xi took was to league with Xian Feng's younger brother Yi Xin who held the title of Prince Gong and also regarded Sushun as his political enemy. As she saw it, Yi Xin, with the advantage of being brother to the emperor who had just departed this life, could more easily win the sympathy and support of the imperial house. But since she was far away at the Summer Villa of Chengde, how could she possibly get in touch with Prince Gong remaining in the capital? Clearly, Sushun was now in full control of communications between Beijing and Chengde. There's the rub. She must find a clever way out, and she did succeed after racking her brains.

One morning Ci Xi's favourite eunuch An Dehai should be so flagrant as to take liberties with one of empress dowager Ci An's personal maids. When informed of this, Ci Xi had the man brought before her and exclaimed in terrible anger: "You scoundrel! How dare you commit such an offense even in the empress dowager's quarters!" Then pointing a finger at the offender, she said to the head eunuch she had just called in: "Give him a good thrashing! Then send him back to the Office of Imperial Household Affairs for reassignment. I can't allow this kind of man in my service any more."

Being a favourite of Ci Xi, An Dehai had often played the bully among fellow palace attendants. Now he was to pay more than he owed. His buttocks were so badly lacerated from the flogging that he could hardly move. Immediately afterwards, he was taken back to Beijing for reassignment as ordered by Ci Xi. But once back in the capital, he lost no time in seeking out Prince Gong and presented to him a secret edict from empress dowagers Ci An and Ci Xi, asking him to go to Chengde at once.

The sudden appearance of Prince Gong at the Summer Villa was a great surprise to Sushun. But emboldened by the now dead Emperor Xian Feng's special edict in his hands, he did not take the matter seriously as he should. He thought it was only natural for a younger brother to come mourning over the death of his elder brother. Then Ci Xi and Yi Xin were closeted together and decided on their course of action. On the way of escorting Xian Feng's hearse back to the capital Sushun was to see the end of his power and of himself.

Prince Gong left Chengde for Beijing earlier than the party escorting the royal hearse. In company of seven of the eight regents and many other civil and military personnel, the child emperor and empress dowagers Ci An and Ci Xi started the journey home ahead of the party, with Sushun and a few others bringing up the rear. The royal members travelled as fast as their vehicles could carry them. They had been back in the capital two days when Sushun and others escorting the hearse just came within the county limits of Huairou. In a long narrow valley, a detachment of soldiers suddenly emerged from behind a huge rock and blocked the way. They claimed they were local troops and wanted to pay their respects before the hearse. This happened at a moment when Sushun was completely off his guard. Before he could react he heard a shout: "Seize Sushun!" In no time he was unhorsed and bound up hand and foot by the "respects-paying" men. Furiously trying to break himself loose, he cried out loud: "How can you be so lawless and lay your hands on me, a regent appointed by imperial order?"

At that moment, Xian Feng's another younger brother Yi Xuan who held the title of Prince Chun appeared before Sushun. Fishing out from his pocket a roll of yellow paper, he declared in a loud voice: "Here is the imperial edict!"

At once all quieted down, with their eyes fixed on the yellow paper roll. Unrolling the paper, Yi Xuan read aloud:

"When my father, the preceding emperor, was dying, he personally ordered Zai Yuan, Sushun and others to establish me as crown prince, but he never said anything about their right to assume power as regents. Sushun and others shall be dismissed from their posts and arrested forthwith for their crime of falsifying the imperial edict."

On the same day of Sushun's arrest, when Emperor Tong Zhi received court officials in audience, Ci Xi and Prince Gong made a surprise announcement that all the regents were to be arrested and thrown into prison for their crime of "falsifying" the imperial edict.

Five days later Sushun was beheaded at the Caishikou execution ground. Of the seven other regents, Zai Yuan and Duan Hua were granted the permission to take their own lives, and the rest were banished or exiled to distant frontiers.

With the downfall of the eight regents, Ci Xi changed the new emperor's title of reign "Qi Xiang," meaning auspiciousness, to "Tong Zhi," meaning "co-ruling" by mother and son.

The Burning of an Imperial Edict

On account of too much wine and sex Emperor Xian Feng fell seriously ill at the age of less than 30. Fully assured of her son's position as heir to the throne, Ci Xi felt the more satisfied with herself. Now the emperor meant so little to her that she only showed him a smack of obedience. In fact, she would rather he died sooner than later, so that she could carry her child son onto the throne and let herself "rule behind the curtain."

Some loyal eunuchs found Ci Xi's designs repugnant, then went to the sick emperor and informed against her. The emperor had had a mind to dispose of her, but he had not the heart to do so until his last moments of life when he began to see the red light. Calling Empress Ci An to his bedside, he put in her keeping a secret edict written in red ink to the effect that if Ci Xi should take advantage of her position as mother to the heir to the throne and act wrongfully, Ci An must deal with her in conformity with rules laid down by the imperial ancestors.

The emperor also had this to say to Ci An: "On account of her son Ci Xi would have to be honoured as queen mother by convention. But she is far from trustworthy. You must make decisions on your own. If Ci Xi behaves herself, you may treat her with courtesy. In case she oversteps her authority, you must make known to important court officials my secret edict and demand her death to preclude troubles."

With her son's ascension to the throne, Ci Xi had

hoped that her dream to "rule behind the curtain" as queen mother would soon come true. But soon, too, she found herself standing all alone. Empress dowager Ci An seemed to be her own mistress and hold aloof from her. Seeing the going was hard, Ci Xi bent her mind to making a breakthrough in her fight for power.

Some time later, in a casual talk with Ci Xi the tactless Ci An hinted about Xian Feng's secret edict in her own hands, with the purpose of warning Ci Xi not to overreach herself from the position as queen mother. But the result was to the contrary. Ci Xi now knew how to carry her fight. She must find and attack the weak spot in this woman Ci An before she could remove the greatest obstacle in her way: the secret edict.

After that talk, Ci Xi appeared to be meek before Ci An, often dancing attendance on her to show "gratitude" for her kind "expostulation." At first Ci An was wise enough to keep a safe distance between herself and the schemer. But then an event occurred to throw her off her guard.

Once, Ci An fell ill, feeling no appetite for food. All medicines failed to work a cure. Ci Xi had heard tell of human flesh as a wonder drug. Now came the opportunity, she thought, to win Ci An's favour and trust. Then she bore great pains to have a small piece of flesh carved from her arm. This titbit was carefully prepared as a medicine for Ci An, who soon got better as a result. On a sickbed visit to Ci An, Ci Xi shed tears to show happiness about her recovery. In the course of chatting, Ci Xi let fall a remark: "It has not been in vain for me, your humble servant, to do you some slight service."

Ci An gave Ci Xi an intent look wondering what she was trying to say. Ci Xi seemed to have more to say, but held back words just on her lips.

"For all the medicines I took, I didn't think my illness could have been cured," Ci An commented on her medical treatment. "But this recent does of medicine worked wonders."

With a smile, Ci Xi said in a low voice: "I once heard a story that human flesh could cure even supposedly incurable diseases. I never believed it before, but now it had proved to be true."

Ci An felt stunned with the words "human flesh." "What are you saying?"

Ci Xi slowly rolled up a sleeve and bared a bandaged arm. "Please look, sister."

"What on earth did you do?" asked Ci An with amazement.

Hastening to roll down her sleeve, Ci Xi said with a shake of her head: "There's nothing the matter."

The more Ci Xi hemmed and hawed, the more Ci An pressed for an answer: "What happened? Tell me the truth."

With an uneasy look on her face, Ci Xi said: "Your long illness made me feel so upset that I was hardly able to eat or sleep well. Then I heard about the story of the wonder drug, and so I used a bit of my own flesh as your medicine. I'm so glad it did work wonders on your illness."

Ci An was at once astonished and moved. Holding Ci Xi's hands in hers, she said in a voice trembling with gratitude; "My good sister, it's so very kind of you to have suffered for my sake."

"It's nothing at all," said Ci Xi in seeming earnest. "All I wished for was your speedy recovery. The child on the throne needs your aid and guidance. I am always willing and ready to offer you my heart or liver, let alone a bit of flesh."

Ci Xi's words warmed the heart of good-natured

Ci An. What jealousies between them, along with Xian Feng's deathbed will or edict, were all cast aside. Asking Ci Xi to sit at her bedside, Ci An remarked in gratitude: "My good sister, you have a heart of gold. In the past I was unkind to you; now don't let that upset you any more. From now on we two sisters will work together to help our child emperor rule the country."

At this, Ci Xi shed more tears and even began to weep aloud. Ci An wiped Ci Xi's tears as she said with a smile: "Cheer up! Don't feel bad for me any more. Am I not getting much better now?"

"I'm so happy you have finally come to see my heart laid bare to you. But what still saddens my heart is the emperor's failure to do justice to my loyalty when he was leaving this world for Heaven. Now even all the waters of the Yellow River are not enough to wash off all the shame I am bearing."

Then Ci Xi began crying so heartbreakingly that Ci An decided to do something to comfort her.

"After all, the source of your troubles is this piece of paper, isn't it?" remarked Ci An, holding in her hand the secret edict just taken out of its repository. "If only you have in your loyal heart the destiny of the Great Qing Empire..."

Before Ci An had time to finish what she was saying, Ci Xi went down on her knees and made a vow: "Let me be struck by thunder if I should be in any way disloyal to you or the cause of the House of Qing."

"Don't say such things. Please get up."

But Ci Xi refused to get up on her feet. Ci An finally had to say: "If you cannot rest assured, then I'll have the edict burned."

Immediately Ci Xi rose to her feet, and shedding no more tears, took the edict out of Ci An's hand and threw it into a chacoal burner. Her face was flushed with a joy of liberation as she gazed intently at the red flames suddenly spurting up from the burner. These flames seemed to be lighting up the road to the destination of her ambition.

Now Ci Xi threw a significant look to Ci An. Surprised to find the look different from any other she had ever seen in Ci Xi's eyes, Ci An felt as if a gust of cold wind was cutting her to the bone.

Thereafter Ci Xi went unbridled in her ways, often flying in the face of Ci An whose consent she seldom secured before making decisions. Now Ci An began to see she had fallen into a trap set by a wicked woman. It was already too late to regret.

Soon afterwards, word came out that Ci An was dead. It was said that Ci An died after taking medicines prescribed by doctors under the orders of Ci Xi.

A Prince Turns the Head of Beggars

After her disposal by death or banishment of the eight regents, Ci Xi was satisfied with her prospects of assuming state power. Then she began to think of enjoying herself outside the palace walls.

One day, Ci Xi persuaded Ci An to go boating with her on the Beihai Lake. In a pleasure boat rowed along by eunuchs, they felt boundless delight drinking in the beauty of the lake with its green ripples, its reflections of a white pagoda standing on top of a hill, the trees lining the lakeshore, and specks of clouds floating in the blue sky.

All of a sudden, a man, almost stark naked, started out from beneath a willow tree, plunged into the water, and swam to a point not far from the pleasure boat. Showing absolutely no regard for the presence of the two empress dowagers there, the man began to clean his body as if in a bath. Ci Xi was frightened at the sight of the bathing intruder, taking him to be an assassin sent by remaining confederates of the eight overthrown regents. She urged the eunuchs to double their efforts to row the boat to a landing place on the north side of the Tuancheng, a walled-in round terrace with palatial buildings. Meanwhile orders were given for the arrest of the man in the lake.

Soon after the empress dowagers were safely settled in seats in a hall within the Tuancheng, the man was brought before them. Curiously enough, the man, only in a pair of shorts still dripping with water, turned out to be none other than Yi Cong, who was fifth in line among the late Emperor Xian Feng's brothers and holding the title of Prince Dun.

Yi Cong had meant to purposely anger his two sisters-in-law when he chose to swim at a time they were boating on the lake. He had resented that Ci Xi with power in her hands was not impartial in her treatment of the royal brothers. Yi Xin, the sixth in line, had been conferred on the title of "King of Court Counsel" with power to conduct the privy council, enjoying double official salaries. And Yi Xuan, the seventh in fraternal order, was holding a position as commander-in-chief of all imperial forces. As for Yi Cong himself, apart from being the title holder of Prince Dun, he had not got any new post of importance. So for venting his pent-up discontent on his two sisters-in-law, he had gone swimming or bathing in the manner they had just witnessed.

As she saw the prideful look on Yi Cong's face, Ci Xi knew what was boiling in his mind, but said reproachfully: "Oh, my brother, our late emperor has been in heaven only a short time, with his remains not quite cold, and yet you should have bathed half-naked before your royal sisters-in-law. Don't you know our ancestral rules and the laws of the imperial court?"

Taking advantage of the fact that he was of the same generation with the empress dowagers, which put him on an equal footing with them in the imperial family, Yi Cong posed a counter-query: "If the remains of our late emperor, as you say, are not yet quite cold, how can his wives be so cold-hearted as to throw mourning aside and come here for pleasure? Don't you know the ancestral rules and the laws of the imperial court on your part?"

These questions left Ci Xi tongue-tied for an answer. Knowing she was in the wrong herself, she tried to soften up the matter, saying: "You are saying the right thing, I know." Then she told the imperial bodyguards to help Yi Cong put on his clothes and warned him not to catch cold.

Always revenge-minded, Ci Xi knew what to do next. In an edict issued in the name of the two empress dowagers, Yi Cong, Prince Dun, was conferred on the title of emperial high commissioner assuming command of all beggars in the land. This new title would bring Yi Cong more income, but he would in fact become head of beggars. This bitter pill of insult offered by Ci Xi was something he had no choice but to swallow.

Emperor Tong Zhi Takes a Eunuch's Life

After Tong Zhi's ascension to the throne, in line with conventions established in the Ming Dynasty, his late father Emperor Xian Feng's wife, Ci An, was honoured with the title of "Maternal Empress," and his own mother, Ci Xi, the title of "Holy Queen Mother." To all imperial edicts or memorials to the throne both titles must be appended without distinction. But in relations with most courtiers Ci An stood a notch higher than Ci Xi, because Ci An had been Xian Feng's offical first lady, while Ci Xi had just been a higher imperial lady promoted from a mere palace maid. Although Ci Xi enjoyed a position as mother to the reigning emperor, she had not yet built up a large court following.

Ci Xi made all efforts to put herself on a better footing in palace rivalry. She soon made her influence felt in the inner palaces when she had gathered around her a number of eunuchs to do her bidding. Of these eunuchs, one was called An Dehai who won favour with Ci Xi for his cunningness in intrigues of all sorts. With the queen mother as his patroness, he was frequently throwing his weight about and even meddling in court affairs. When Emperor Tong Zhi grew into a sensible young man, he came to dislike the overbearing An Dehai and often reproved him to his face. But in such events Ci Xi always sided with the eunuch and blamed her son. This only added to the young emperor's aversion for this favourite of his mother's. Then it came to pass that His Majesty often played a game of beheading a clay figurine with a pocket knife. When asked why he played such a game by the eunuchs in his company, the young emperor said in all earnest: "I am practising the killing of An Dehai." Now these eunuchs had no doubt this man would lose his head sooner or later.

In the autumn of the eighth year of Tong Zhi's reign, Ci Xi sent An Dehai on a mission of purchasing imperial robes from makers in southern cities. Tong Zhi showed no objection to this, but after a confidential consultation with Ci An, he sent a secret edict to Governor Ding Baozhen of Shandong province, ordering him to get rid of An Dehai on his way south. The governor in turn ordered Chen Shengwu, a local official of Dongchang prefecture, to have the eunuch arrested. But being a timid man, this official was too fearful of the consequences to make the arrest after tailing the eunuch for three days. Again Governor Ding Baozhen ordered a local commander, Wang Zheng, and his men to do the job. An Dehai was finally arrested at Taian and brought to the governor in Jinan.

"I am on official business under the orders of the queen mother," An Dehai yelled to Ding Baozhen. "Anyone daring to touch a hair of my head must be tired of living!"

Then it dawned on An Dehai that he had fallen into a trap when Ding Baozhen made public the orders straight from the emperor and the empress dowager Ci An.

On hearing about An Dehai's arrest, Ci Xi was stunned with disbelief. Immediately Ci An called a meeting of privy councillors and imperial household officials to discuss the matter. The dicision reached was to act according to long-established palace rule that any eunuch that should venture beyond the limits of the imperial city must be put to death. An Dehai was to be executed where he was. But the announcement of the decision was held up for two days before it was made at the insistence of Yi Xuan, namely, Prince Chun.

After An Dehai met his end at Jinan, for days his dead body was not buried but left on the execution ground to public view, just to show the man was really dead. Somehow people in Shandong said the body might not be his, but could be that of a petty eunuch under him. The purposeful exposure of the dead body only aroused greater suspicion than less.

An Emperor Breaks from Palace Life

When Emperor Tong Zhi was 11 years old, both empress dowagers Ci An and Ci Xi started the process of choosing a queen for him. To the imperial palace came young candidates from noble Mongol and Manchu families. Ci Xi settled on a high court official's daughter called Feng Xiu as the first lady of the emperor. Though a rare beauty, Feng Xiu was skittish in conduct and address, not quite to the liking of Ci An and the emperor himself. Another young lady, also the daughter of a high court official, was slightly younger than Feng Xiu and not as beautiful, but was sedate, poised, and culturally and morally better cultivated. Finally, winning Ci An's approval and Tong Zhi's heart, she was chosen the first lady holding the title of Filial and Wise Empress Yi. At the same time, Feng Xiu was decided on as the second lady with the title of High Imperial Lady Hui.

After marriage Empress Yi was the more loved and respected by the emperor for her gracious manners and gentle disposition. During their leisure time they often sat together commenting on poetic works, ancient and modern. She could even recite fluently the poems that had flowed from the pens of past masters. With their relations built on mutual admiration, they grew fonder and fonder of each other. But jealous-minded Ci Xi resented her son's love and care for her daughter-in-law. She would give her the cold shoulder even when she came to pay her filial respect. The relations between them soon became strained.

Once Ci Xi said to Tong Zhi: "As Lady Hui is always so virtuous and sensible, you should care for her more. In contrast, the empress is still immature and not quite refined; you needn't go to her palace too often. Keep your mind on state affairs, else you'll go wrong."

In the meantime, Ci Xi had her trusted eunuchs watch over the movements of the emperor. As a result, His Majesty was so resentful that he decided to live in the Qian Qing Palace apart from both Empress Yi and Lady Hui.

Now without the company of his dear empress, Tong Zhi came to feel unbearably lonesome. Then his personal eunuchs suggested going incognito for pastimes outside the imperial palace.

At the time there was a scholar from Hunan province living in a house across from the residence of Zeng Guofan, a celebrated and very important person serving the Qing court. The scholar was in the capital for taking the imperial court examination. One day he came in and found a young man looking over his composition papers on the desk and making corrections as he read. The unexpected visitor left the room before the scholar had time to ask who he was. His servant said the young man might be a guest of the venerable Zeng Guofan and had happened to walk in for a look around. Later the scholar went across the street to see Zeng and showed him the papers the young man had corrected. On examining carefully the papers, Zeng was greatly surprised and said with all respect: "Great heavens! It's His Majesty that made the corrections." The scholar was so awed that he felt his hair standing on end. With no more courage to take the court examination, he packed up and went home.

Emperor Tong Zhi often disguised himself in plain clothes and went shopping at the place Liulichang where flourished a variety of bazzars. Once he tried to pay for some fine writing paper with small pieces of gold in the shape of watermelon seeds. But the shopkeeper refused to take them on the ground that they were not money for legal circulation on the market. Then the emperor told him to have a man carry the paper and go with him to his home for silver money. When the shop attendant came before the Noon Gate of the imperial palace, he was afraid to enter it. Immediately he put down the paper and returned to the shop without the money. The next day the emperor sent a petty eunuch to the shop with silver for payment.

While he went roaming, Tong Zhi ran into people of all sorts. Once, he was taking shelter from the rain in a temple when in came a man appearing to be in reduced circumstances.

"What are you doing for a living?" asked the emperor out of curiosity.

"I'm jobless and living by begging," came the reply.

"What kind of work do you think you are best fit to do?"

"A job at the customs house in Guangdong province," said the man without hesitation.

With pen and paper and ink always ready for use by visitors to the temple, the emperor wrote a letter and told the man to take it to the office of an infantry commander. After reading the letter the commander was only too glad to rig him out with new clothes and luggage and give him money for a trip to the customs house in Guangdong. It was before long that the man made a fortune there.

Emperor Tong Zhi was also in the habit of frequenting tea houses and restaurants within the imperial city. Once, a courtier with exuberant spirits was drinking alone on the upper story of a restaurant when he heard singing in the next room. The singing was so melodious that he could not help uttering loud cries of praise. According to customs generally observed in the capital, it was all right to raise such cries when people of the performing trades or women of the streets were singing. But it would amount to an insult to shout applause if the singer happened to belong to the upper society. So on this occasion an attendant of the singer was enraged and shouted at the top of his voice: "Who is howling so rudely?"

In his state of intoxication, the courtier retorted: "I'm a member of the imperial academy. If you have the guts, you can go to my place and settle the matter with me."

Some time later, someone quietly let the courtier know that the man doing the singing that day was none other than the emperor himself. Soon afterwards, to the great surprise of his colleagues, the courtier asked for leave and disappeared from Beijing.

The Death of Emperor Tong Zhi

Under the maternal domination of Empress Dowager Ci Xi, Emperor Tong Zhi found no joy in home life. He could not come too close to his beloved Empress Yi, but was often compelled to be intimate with Lady Hui for whom he conceived little love. Spiritually much depressed, he began to find outlets for his emotions in sensual pleasures outside the imperial palace. To be inconspicuous in his movements, he shied away from the more celebrated brothels, but sought the company of clandestine prostitutes after nightfall, escorted by only a couple of petty eunuchs.

At first, some good people unaware of his true identity would kindly advise him against such indulgence at his immature age. But then when it came to be known that this young libertine was none other than the reigning emperor, they all pretended ignorance and held him up to ridicule behind his back. Soon this young severeign fell a victim to terrible syphilis, with ulcerous skin eruptions quickly spreading to his face and back. Diagnosis made by doctors attending him pointed definitely to a case of venereal disease, and yet these medical professionals had to support Ci Xi's arbitrary assertion that is was a case of smallpox. Consequently, the patient showed no improvement in his condition. When he found out what was going on he roared in fury: "I am not suffering from smallpox. How can you cure me with medicines suited to smallpox?"

"Your humble slaves are acting on orders of the

queen mother," the doctors ventured an excuse with a guilty conscience. "There is nothing we can do, Your Majesty."

His Majesty decided to say no more about the matter, though feeling a world of resentment.

According to a time-honoured palace rule, an emperor might not pass a night with an imperial lady or concubine without first getting the approval of his empress. Such approval was expressed in a written message sent to the lady in question, instructing her to prepare for the reception of the emperor. The lady might decline the visit of the emperor if she received no such message which must also be affixed with the empress' seal.

As Emperor Tong Zhi got a little better, he asked Empress Yi's approval for a night visit to Lady Hui, just to please his mother Ci Xi. When it was refused him, he even went down on his knees before the empress to beg for it. Finally the empress was obliged to satisfy his wish. A night union with Lady Hui worsened his condition so much that the imperial doctors could only heave a sigh of helplessness the following morning.

Seeing his own end nearing, the emperor called in Chief Privy Councillor Li Hongzhang for a confidential deathbed consultation. When Li came to the imperial bedside, he found the empress was also there. He made to withdraw, but was waved to remain by the emperor, who said respectfully: "You needn't go away just because the empress is present. You served under the late emperor and have been my tutor. The empress is but the wife of your pupil. You can advise me on important matters even in her presence."

As the chief privy councillor was kneeling to show his respect as a loyal subject to the empress, the emperor hastened to say: "Please stand up. This is no time for ceremony."

Then holding Li's hands in his, he said sadly: "My dear tutor, I am afraid I have lost all hope of recovery." Casting a glance at the empress, he added: "In case of my death, some one must be chosen as my successor. Who do you think would be the best choice?"

Finally in great secrecy they decided on Prince Zai Shu who was cousin to Emperor Tong Zhi. An edict dictated by His Majesty was put in written form at the bedside by Li Hongzhang. Then the emperor looked over the 1,000-word long decree and nodded his approval before he bade his tutor to go home and rest. Also he wished he could see him again the next day.

Weighing in mind the possible consequences of the matter, Li Hongzhang felt his own life was at stake. Soon after he left his pupil's private chambers, he went direct to the queen mother's quarters and presented her the edict. Ci Xi at once flew into a fury and tore it to shreds.

"Get out of here!" she yelled at Li Hongzhang.

In the meantime, on orders of Ci Xi the dying emperor was given no more medicine, food or drink. After his death, the lower part of his body was found to have festered, giving out a foul smell. In the small of his back there were ulcerated holes through which kidneys could be seen.

The Four Year Old Emperor

On the very afternoon Emperor Tong Zhi died, princes, privy councillors and other court officials were summoned by queen mother Ci Xi to attend an emergency meeting in an inner palace. But it was after a long wait that Ci Xi came swaggering into the meeting hall, wearing informal clothes. Instead of taking a seat she stood by a chair. Stepping forward, the courtiers paid her their respects and inquired after the health of the emperor.

"The emperor is all right," Ci Xi said with a smile, then fell silent for a moment.

Sensing something serious had happened, these nobles and high officials were speechless, their hearts pounding heavily with expectation of what Ci Xi would have to say next. They waited but pricked up their ears.

"The emperor is in very bad health," Ci Xi finally said. "You know he has no son. If worst comes to worst, there must be one to succeed him. Among those in the imperial house, who do you think would be the best for the throne?"

Long in awe of Ci Xi's wilful temper, most present dared not venture a word about such a serious matter. But one man, called Wen Xiang, said in a low voice:

"This humble slave of yours thinks a crown prince should be chosen from among the virtuous and able of the near imperial relatives of the generation designated by the word *pu*."

Ci Xi was displeased at this suggestion and gave

Wen Xiang a cold stare. As if feeling a whip on his back, Wen Xiang cowered before the empress dowager, then hung his head and said no more. Another man stepped forward to offer his idea: "Of the *pu* generation, Pu Lun is the oldest and might be a good choice as heir to the throne." But Yi Cong, a noble entitled Prince Dun, at once expressed his objection to Pu Lun as a possible successor.

The exchange of opinions ended as Ci Xi concluded: "No proper successor can be found among men of the *pu* generation." After a pause she added: "Zai Tian, the oldest son of Yi Xuan, our Prince Chun, is a 4-year-old boy of high intelligence. As a close relative of the imperial house, he is cut out for continuing our great cause. My idea is that he should be heir to the throne."

As a matter of fact, Zai Tian was the son of Ci Xi's own sister. In Ci Xi's mind, this nephew of hers, if chosen as heir to the throne, would better suit her purpose for controlling state power. If one of the *pu* generation should be chosen, she would be a step farther from power, although she would be honoured as the grand queen mother because the *pu* generation is younger than her son's generation.

What Ci Xi had just said stunned all present, especially Prince Chun. He began to sob and in a moment fell unconcious to the floor. As it was, the prince was in fear of his own son suffering the same hapless fate as Emperor Tong Zhi. As Ci Xi had treated her own son so cruelly, it was hard to imagine that she would treat his son any better. To put his son on the throne would be to put him in the mouth of a tigress.

Prince Gong, as a trusted supporter of Ci Xi, voiced displeasure at Yi Xuan's ungraceful reaction: "What's coming over you? It's a shame to behave so!"

Then he told some eunuchs in attendance to help Yi Xuan out. Now no one else had the courage to say otherwise. It was decided that Zai Tian would be named heir to the throne.

By this moment, Ci Xi declared in a sharp tone: "The emperor is dead!" Although this came as no surprise, noisy weeping arose in the hall.

On the day of the coronation, four-year-old Zai Tian was quietly asleep when a royal sedan-chair carried him to the gateway of the imperial audience hall. He had to be energetically shaken awake by his mother accompanying him before he was helped onto his throne. The child emperor, who was later formally known as Emperor Guang Xu, began crying with fear when the courtiers kowtowed to him and shouted with devotion: "Long live the emperor!" The ceremony over, the newly-enthroned emperor was found to have wetted his pants. This was the first act performed by Emperor Guang Xu: *Wetting the Throne*.

Empress Yi

Emperor Tong Zhi's first lady Alute, who was entitled Filial and Wise Empress Yi, had always incurred Empress Dowager Ci Xi's disfavour. Ci Xi had hoped her son would marry Fucha, the daughter of a high court official. But the emperor decided on Alute against his mother's wish. Ci Xi was so resentful that she vowed to herself: "Whoever makes me miserable for a time will be miserable all the time."

Consequently, the imperial couple fell prey to a bitter fate settled by the ruthless queen mother. Being upright in character, Alute would not go out of her way to please her powerful mother-in-law, who soon regarded her as a thorn in her flesh.

Ci Xi was always very fond of theatrical performances. Given to pretentious display, she would have Empress Yi and a troop of palace maids keep her company in watching such performances. She was especially interested in operatic dramas of the obscene kind, which the empress often found so distasteful that she could not help turning her eyes away. In Ci Xi's mind, such behaviour on the part of the empress would amount to disrespect for, or an insult against her dignity as queen mother. The empress often received stern reproofs on this account, but she had no desire to mend her ways as Ci Xi wished.

Those close to the empress all feared she was treading on thin ice and advised her to take steps to win Ci Xi's affections. But the empress had this to say:

"It's all right for me to respect her, but it's out of

the question for me to flatter her. I was honourably married into the imperial house in conformity with ancestral rules. I mustn't fall an easy victim to any evil designs on me."

But Ci Xi was determined to remove the thorn in her flesh, constantly watching for the chance for action. Cunning as she was, such a chance was hard to find. At no time was the empress acting counter to palace rules or in breach of imperial etiquette. Ci Xi had to resort to faultfinding tactics in her feud with the empress. Whenever the empress smiled in seeing the emperor, Ci Xi would accuse her of attempting to bewitch him with a seductive intent. The empress saw clearly her mother-in-law resented her intimacy with the emperor, so she kept aloof from him of her own accord, just to avoid family troubles.

Ci Xi was also adapt at calling white black. Once she came to see her ailing son and found the empress absent from the bedside. This gave her a chance to bring her daughter-in-law to book. When the empress was summoned before her, she said sternly: "How can you be so indifferent to your husband sick in bed? You must have a heart of stone."

"Without the permission of Your Highness," the empress replied in a calm but firm tone, "this humble slave of yours dare not venture here."

This retort rendered Ci Xi speechless and her face red with rage.

When Emperor Tong Zhi was dying, Empress Yi came boldly to his bedside without waiting to be summoned. Seeing the miserable plight he was in, she fell to weeping without restraint. Then she started to clean his festered lower body of pus and blood with her own hands. At that juncture Ci Xi came in and found the empress touching his penis with her hands.

"You shameless bitch!" exclaimed Ci Xi, gnashing her teeth. "You are still trying to seduce him even at this hour. You wouldn't let him be till his death, would you?"

At once the empress received a shower of slaps on the face and was ordered to leave. A little while later the emperor breathed his last without the empress at his side.

The succssor to the throne turned out to be Zai Tian instead of Zai Shu as named by Emperor Tong Zhi in his deathbed will. Empress Yi sank into despair and protested when she found the will was not dully administered. As this came to the knowledge of Ci Xi, she had the empress brought to her for a stiff lesson given in the form of face-slapping. The pointed gold caps worn on Ci Xi's finger tips drew blood from all over the face of the empress. And Ci Xi added insult to injury by saying: "You vixen have bewitched my son to death. How can you still have the effrontery to claim vainly for yourself the right as empress dowager?" The helpless empress could only go down on her kness and weep her heart out before she went back to her own quarters.

After Zai Tian came to the throne as Emperor Guang Xu, Empress Yi became his widowed sister-in-law by relationship determined by the imperial family line. She felt she was far removed from the new emperor either in political bonds or in blood relations. In her short married life she had suffered all sorts of humiliation and distress. Now with the death of Emperor Tong Zhi, she lost all hope of living a normal life. All day long her eyes were suffused with bitter tears. It seemed to her that only death could put an end to her wretched life.

One day her father Chong Qi came to see her and

found her so inconsolable that she would rather die than live. Then he presented Ci Xi a memorial pleading for more tolerant treatment of his daughter. But Ci Xi only remarked coldly: "If the empress still nurses such great sorrow for the emperor's death, she might as well leave this world with him."

Well aware of the consequent fate of his daughter, Chong Qi went to see her for the last time. When asked by her what she was to do, he wrote on a slip of paper a single word: "death." On seeing the word, she stared at her father for a moment, then said calmly with a bow: "Thank you for having brought me up in this world. Now please forgive me for my failure to have shown you enough filial devotion." With this, she disappeared into her inner chambers.

Less than 100 days after the death of Emperor Tong Zhi, Empress Yi suddenly died in the Chuxiu Palace at the age of less than 19.

The Origin of the "Old Buddha"

Buddhas are renowned for their mercy, and those who are kindhearted and find pleasure in helping others are often said to "have the soft heart of a Buddha." Why then was the cruel and merciless Empress Dowager Ci Xi of the Qing Dynasty known to her servants and officials as "Old Buddha"?

In the closing years of the Qing Dynasty, Ci Xi, who had ruled the country from the inner court for more than 40 years, ordered princes and important ministers to be executed and drove empresses and imperial concubines to commit suicide. Eunuchs and servants were randomly put to death, and even her own son was illtreated. How could such a woman be associated with the venerable Buddha?

It is said that in her 60s, Ci Xi often worshipped Buddha, and liked to sit in meditation after administering affairs of state. In her mind, however, the Buddha was not particularly sacred, and she did not think of him as superior to herself. Ci Xi liked to impersonate Guanyin, the Goddess of Mercy. Clad in a Buddhist coronet and Manchu robes, she would pose with her left hand on her knee, holding a string of beads in her right hand. Alternatively, she would stand in front of a horizontal scroll inscribed with the words "Goddess of Mercy on Mt. Putuo," a water-bottle in her left hand and a willow twig in her right. Her favourite eunuch, Li Lianying, Prince Yi Kuang's daughter, and her servants were often ordered to join her play acting. A photograph, which once hung in Ci Xi's bedroom, has recorded her activities for posterity.

Li Lianying excelled at flattery. To ingratiate himself with Ci Xi, he would often play the fool, and encourage her impersonation. On these occasions he acted as her servant, and would often refer to Ci Xi as "Old Buddha." This pleased her greatly, and he was richly rewarded. Others were ordered to follow suit, and ironically the term "Old Buddha" soon became a common form of address for the empress dowager.

Calling the Empress Dowager "Real Father"

In feudal China, women could not rule directly, only a man could wear the "dragon's robes." Ci Xi considered this unjust and constantly tried to wrest power from the emperors who ascended the throne during her lifetime.

Her treatment of Emperor Guang Xu, who entered the imperial palace at the age of four, was particularly harsh. Emperor Guang Xu was virtually a prisoner in the palace, and was not permitted to have any contact with his real mother.

Every morning he was forced to pay his respects to Ci Xi by kneeling down before her. She often kept him kneeling for long periods of time, and when in bad mood would curse him soundly. Guang Xu was terrified of Ci Xi and became too frightened to eat anything in her presence. The empress dowager took her revenge by serving the uneaten food again and again until it became rotten. Guang Xu, as a result, was often hungry and lived a miserable existance.

Whenever Ci Xi heard Guang Xu call her "Empress Dowager" she flew into a rage. Guang Xu was at a loss to understand her anger until one day eunuch Li Lianying offered him some good advice.

"Your slave has seen that 'Old Buddha' is displeased when Your Majesty calls her 'Empress Dowager.' Does Your Majesty know why?" Guang Xu hurriedly replied, "I wondered why. Please explain frankly."

"Excuse your slave's audacity. In my humble opinion, although 'Old Buddha' is a female, what men can compare with her? Your Majesty's father is the younger brother of the late emperor (the husband of Ci Xi), so 'Old Buddha' is like Your Majesty's father; Your Majesty's mother is the younger sister of 'Old Buddha,' so 'Old Buddha' is just like Your Majesty's mother. Is that right?"

"You are right. But what should I call her?"

"Excuse your slave's audacity again. In my humble opinion, calling her 'Real Father' would be better. She might be pleased to hear that."

"Real Father, Real Father." The emperor practiced the phrase, but felt false and uncomfortable. He frowned.

Seeing that the emperor did not wholly accept his advice, Li Lianying turned to him sternly and said: "Your Majesty, if Your Majesty does not want 'Old Buddha' to be unpleasant, it would be wise to address her in this way."

Guang Xu remembered that Ci Xi had repeatedly referred to him as her own son, and decided to accept Li Lianying's advice.

Next day, when paying his usual respects to Ci Xi, however, Guang Xu forgot his resolution and greeted her with the words "Good morning, Empress Dowager." Ci Xi responded coldly and turned her head. The young emperor knelt for a long time, until finally Ci Xi shouted, "Do you want to kneel until you die?" Emperor Guang Xu hurriedly stood up, and plucking up his courage said, "May my Real Father be happy!" Ci Xi immediately turned to face him and smiled, "Your parent accepts your good wishes, you may leave."

Emperor Guang Xu rapidly retreated to his own

palace, and from that time on always called Ci Xi "Real Father."

Selecting an Empress

When Guang Xu reached the age of seven, Ci Xi chose two reading companions for him. One was a grandson of Prince Gong, the other, Jing Fen, the daughter of Ci Xi's younger brother Gui Xiang. Traditionally the emperor's reading companions should be boys, and the selection of Jing Fen was unprecedented. Ci Xi's explanation that no suitable boy could be found was merely an excuse, her real motive was to make Jing Fen, three years older than Guang Xu, the emperor's wife. According to Ci Xi, the emperor was her sister's son, and the future empress her brother's daughter. If the two were to marry, Ci Xi would be in a position to seize power.

Emperor Guang Xu, however, disliked Jing Fen, considering her taciturn and humourless. She did not like play with toys, and seemed indifferent to everything. Not daring to show his true feelings, Guang Xu said to Ci Xi: "Real Father, I'm seven years old. Confucius said that on reaching the age of seven, boys and girls should not sit face to face. How can I study with her?"

Ci Xi, without revealing that she knew the emperor disliked her niece, replied, "My son, you deserve praise for remembering the sage's teachings, but Confucius's words are only for officials and the common people. You are the Son of Heaven, and therefore not restricted by his words."

Guang Xu continued to tease Jing Fen and treated her coldly, but Ci Xi was determined to bind them together. She ordered the emperor to teach Jing Fen to use a bow and arrows. Although Guang Xu thought her weak and stupid, he was afraid to be too critical.

When Guang Xu reached the age of ten, Ci Xi summoned him and asked what he thought was the most important task for an emperor. Guang Xu replied that it was the administration of the country. Ci Xi disagreed. This could be done by others, she said, hinting that she herself could manage state affairs. Ci Xi informed him that to marry and produce a male heir was the most important task which could not be performed by others.

The ten-year-old boy failed to understand the importance of marriage, and, seeing that he was reluctant to discuss it, Ci Xi hastened to explain. "I don't mean that you should marry immediately. I mean that you should become engaged according to the tradition of our ancestors." She then told him that she had selected a suitable candidate for empress from among thousands of young girls. "The girl has been with you for several years, she is none other than your cousin Jing Fen." Guang Xu was speechless. Ci Xi, seeing that this news was a blow to the emperor, said, "You entered the palace at the age of four, I have raised you for these years. You should listen to what I say. You must not let me down," she cried with tears streaming down her face.

Moved by such emotion from the usually cruel and indifferent empress dowager, Guang Xu's heart softened. "I will follow the instructions of my Real Father," he said. "The matter is now settled according to your wishes."

As he left Chu Xiu Hall, Ci Xi's living quarters, Guang Xu could not hold back his tears. However, on hearing from a eunuch that once engaged, the couple were not permitted to meet until the wedding, the emperor's spirits rose. For the first time in six or seven years he could avoid meeting the girl he disliked so much.

According to the tradition of the Qing Dynasty, the emperor was required to take several concubines before he officially married. Ci Xi, however, decided to ignore tradition for fear that the concubines would further alienate the emperor from her niece. She also wished to avoid quarrels between the concubines and the new empress.

As the wedding approached, time passed all too quickly for Guang Xu. He became anxious, and his tutor, Weng Tonghe, tried to calm him, "Your Majesty, the date for your wedding is approaching. You have reason to be happy."

"Why?" replied Guang Xu, surprised that his tutor could not understand his concern.

"Because, according to the regulations of the dynasty, you will take over the reigns of government once you are married. Your Majesty has always wanted to administer state affairs well and bring life and energy back to the country."

Emperor Guang Xu realized the truth of this, and his anxiety disappeared. He quickly bowed to his tutor, saying, "Thank you for your invaluable advice. I was thinking of trivial things and had almost forgotten the important issues." From that time on, Guang Xu eagerly awaited his wedding day. When the emperor reached the age of 18, Ci Xi unexpectedly postponed his wedding for a year, giving the excuse that the year was inauspicious. Her true motive, however, was to postpone handing over her power to Guang Xu.

The wedding was held the following year. The bride and bridegroom, however, did not share a bed and in fact seldom saw each other. Guang Xu read alone in his study, while Jing Fen--the Empress Long Yu--lived the life of a widow, meanwhile spying on Emperor Guang Xu for Ci Xi.

The Imperial Lady Zhen Fei

When Emperor Guang Xu was seven years old, his tutor Weng Tonghe told him of a girl in Guangdong province who was fond of toy trains. She could take them apart to mend, and planned to build trains and steamboats when she grew up. The emperor was impressed, since he shared her interests. He believed that she must be clever and beautiful. His empress, and the many concubines offered to him seemed dull in comparison.

At a time when the court was busy selecting a consort for the emperor, General Chang Xu and his two daughters travelled from Guangdong to Beijing on business. His friend Weng Tonghe went to visit him at his home. He saw two girls in the family's courtyard taking pictures of each other. One was sligtly plump and dressed in traditional Manchu costume, wearing a *qipao* and wooden soled shoes. The other, who was dressed in western clothes, was slim with a gentle face tinged with red, and large, intelligent eyes. Her long hair cascaded over her shoulder like black satin. These were Chang Xu's daughters. The elder girl was 17, and the younger, who was none other than the girl who had fascinated the emperor when he was a boy, was only 15. Weng Tonghe learned from Chang Xu over tea that Wen Tingshi, a gifted scholar from Jiangxi province, was giving them lessons. The girls learned quickly, and the younger one had already read many books about the West. She longed for China to be rich and strong. Chang Xu sighed, and declared to his friend that if she were a man she could do a great deal for the country.

Weng Tonghe told the emperor that the girl from Guangdong was in Beijing. The emperor was excited and wanted very much to see her, but he immediately realized that this was impossible since his fate was in the hands of the empress dowager.

Weng Tonghe asked one of his close friends to suggest to Ci Xi the two girls become the emperor's concubines. Everyone was surprised when the empress dowager agreed, and asked to see them for herself.

The empress dowager, escorted by eunuchs and palace maids, summoned the two girls to the Hall of Mental Cultivation. Everyone watched as they walked in to pay their respects. Emperor Guang Xu stared at the younger girl. She was graceful and unaffected, the very incarnation of beauty and wisdom. He had seen many pretty girls, but none had attracted him as she did. To him she was sunshine and spring wind.

Ci Xi later asked the emperor and the empress how they liked the two girls. Realizing the emperor was attracted to the younger girl, the empress said she preferred the elder sister. Guang Xu said he liked the younger girl. Ci Xi compromised by making both sisters imperial concubines. The elder sister was given the title Jin Fei, and the younger sister Zhen Fei.

The first time that the emperor summoned Zhen Fei to his room, the court maids spread a woollen blanket over her bed, and told her to take off all her clothes. She was then made to wait for a eunuch to carry her, wrapped in the blanket, to the emperor's living quarters.

"Why must I take off all my clothes and be carried to the emperor's living quarters?" Zhen Fei asked.

She was told this was a rule established by the court after someone had tried to assassinate a former emperor.

Highly displeased, Zhen Fei replied that since they didn't trust her, why sent her to the emperor. However, she loved the emperor, and decided to obey the rules. As the emperor reached out to touch her, she asked him, "Is Your Majesty afraid that I have hidden a sword somewhere?"

Surprised, the emperor asked what had made her ask such a strange question.

"I must come to you naked," she answered. "Does this mean that Your Majesty is afraid I might assassinate you?"

"This is merely a court rule," Guang Xu explained, "and not my idea. Since you don't like it, you need not to obey." He ordered a eunuch to give Zhen Fei her clothes, and announced that in future she could come to his quarters fully dressed.

When the emperor explained how he had felt about her for so many years, Zhen Fei was moved. She took the emperor's hand, and laying it on her chest, vowed that she would care for him for the rest of her life, leaving him to concentrate on running the country and being a virtuous ruler.

The court code was required that concubines attending the emperor at night must leave him before daybreak. However, the empress was informed that Zhen Fei had stayed throughout the night with the emperor, and for several days he saw no one but his beloved Zhen Fei. The empress was extremely jealous. She frowned upon Zhen Fei and created discord between her and her sister. Unaware of the empress' intentions, but feeling neglected by the emperor, Jin Fei became estranged from her sister. She and the empress even sang a duet before the empress dowager reproving Zhen Fei.

Zhen Fei was unconcerned about this, but became anxious that she might bring trouble to the emperor. Guang Xu told her not to worry, an emperor should be able to protect his beloved concubine. "If you love me always as you do today," Zhen Fei said, "I won't be afraid of anything."

The emperor's love however only caused Zhen Fei more troubles. Guang Xu once gave Zhen Fei a shawl made of strings of pearls. When the empress learned of this, she took Jin Fei to the Summer Palace to complain to the empress dowager. On another occasion Guang Xu asked an opera troupe to perform in the imperial palace. The empress lied to the empress dowager, telling her that because Zhen Fei had set her heart on one of the actors in the troupe they had invited. Ci Xi knew that the women were fighting to win the favour of the emperor, but since her own interests were not involved, she did not take the matter seriously.

Zhen Fei loved the emperor with her whole heart and was very happy. She shared his concern over the administration of the state and became his invaluable assistant.

One day, Weng Tonghe reported to the emperor that British and Russian troops had invaded the Pamir area west of Xinjiang. Guang Xu immediately went to the Summer Palace to see the empress dowager. Meanwhile, Zhen Fei waited impatiently in the imperial palace. She was anxious about the meeting and refused to talk or eat anything while the emperor was away. She was delighted when he returned, but could see that he was full of indignation. Guang Xu told her that the empress dowager was unconcerned about the invasion. She had told him that the Pamir area was just a tract of barren land, and the foreigners were welcomed to it.

Zhen Fei was surprised and angry. However she comforted the emperor, telling him that there was no point in being angry, the only way to resist the enemy was to make the country stronger. The emperor asked how this could be done. Zhen Fei replied by opening mines, setting up factories and strengthening the navy as the foreign powers have done.

"We have already tried," said the emperor.

"Yes, but Minister of State Li Hongzhang never really took it seriously. If you, the emperor, approach it in a practical way, we are sure to be successful.'

"But how do we get the money? I don't even have enough for Li Hongzhang to establish the navy."

"Our Qing empire has vast land and rich resources. If we extend our sources of income and reduce expenditure, the problem of money can be solved." So saying, she took a porcelain pot and put all the silver she had with her inside. Then she took a writing brush and wrote on a slip of paper the words: "money pot." She pasted the strip on the pot and told the emperor that from that day on she would deposit part of her money in the pot.

The emperor was touched by her gesture. Taking the pot from her hand he said, "I admire your concern for the country, but we need a great deal more money than this."

"Your Majesty mustn't belittle my small contribution. Our ancestors have taught us that tributaries form the sea and sand can be piled into a tower."

At that moment, Weng Tonghe arrived with a memorial from the Ministry of Public Works, stating that they needed 30 million taels of silver to renovate the Summer Palace. Representatives from the ministry had already talked to Li Hongzhang and he had agreed to provide the money from the funds set aside to train the navy.

The emperor, not wanting to hear any more, struck a table in anger. "How could Li Hongzhang ignore the interests of the state in order to curry favour with the empress dowager," he cried. Snatching up the memorial, he went into an inner room to write a reply. Zhen Fei shared the emperor's feelings. "This order certainly needs to be countermanded," she said, "But what if the empress dowager is angry." Realizing the significance of this, the emperor sank despondently into a chair.

"I have an idea," Zhen Fei told the emperor.

Guang Xu looked at her expectantly as she explained that he could tell the empress dowager that the money to establish the navy was a special fund which could not be diverted to any other purpose. They then could take the money for the renovation of the Summer Palace from the Ministry of Interior. Guang Xu thought it a good idea and wrote out the instructions.

On seeing the emperor's reply, Ci Xi grew very angry. "You won't allow me to use the money which is available, but ask me to spend money which does not exist," she sneered. "How dare you treat me like this." She then altered the emperor's instruction to read "The money to renovate the Summer Palace shall be taken from the funds set aside to establish the navy. This matter needs not to be discussed again."

These changes to his edict made the emperor very angry, but he dared not air his grievances openly. Once back at the palace, however, he could contain his feelings no longer. He seized Zhen Fei's money pot and threw it to the ground, where it broke, spreading the silver dollars across the floor. Unaware of what had happened, Zhen Fei looked at the emperor, feeling very hurt. "They spend thousands of taels of silver without restraint," he shouted. "What is the use of our saving money like this?"

"Your Majesty," Zhen Fei said, "I have also considered this, but if everyone adds just a little, we will soon have a large sum of money."

The emperor was touched by her sincerity, and regretted his anger. He bent down and picked up a fragment of the pot. Tears came to his eyes as he said, "If half the people in the court cared for our country as you do, we wouldn't now be in such danger."

Guang Xu was greatly troubled by domestic problems and the foreign invasion. Zhen Fei suggested that the most important step to take was to choose worthy and talented people to help him administer the country. The imperial examination system did not really provide gifted people, she said. The emperor must invite men of insight to recommend worthy people to him. She then recommened Wen Tingshi, an erudite and devoted servant to the emperor.

Guang Xu appreciated Zhen Fei's suggestion, and attempted to find talented people to reform the country. He hated to see the empress dowager and the court officials struggling for power, and indulging themselves in luxury. They were even apathetic about the invasion of the northeast by Japanese troops. Zhen Fei told the emperor that the major problem was the empress dowager, and she asked the emperor to try and persuade her to change her ways.

"That would be like pulling a tooth from the tiger's mouth," the emperor sighed. "It would only be asking for trouble." Zhen Fei couldn't bear to argue with him, but decided to approach the matter with the empress dowager herself.

It so happened that Ci Xi asked Zhen Fei to accompany her to see an opera at the Summer Palace. Zhen Fei, thinking that this would be a good opportunity to talk, went to the opera in spite of the emperor's misgivings. While Ci Xi was watching the opera "Na Zha Disturbing the Sea" with great interest, the eunuch Li Lianying arrived to report that the Qing troops had suffered a defeat in Pyongyang. A few moments later, she was informed that four Qing gunboats had been sunk by the Japanese army. Ci Xi grew impatient, and ordered the messenger not to bother her with such trifles. Angered and hurt by Ci Xi's attitude, Zhen Fei grasped Ci Xi's chair for support.

When Ci Xi asked what was wrong, Zhen Fei knelt and said, "I have something to say to Your Majesty, but don't know whether or not I should speak."

Given permission to continue, Zhen Fei asked the empress dowager to reduce her expenditure on pleasure and limit the scale of her birthday celebrations in the light of the threat of foreign invasion. She begged Ci Xi to unite the court and people throughout the country to resist aggression. She said she believed this was the best way to celebrate the empress dowager's birthday.

Although very displeased with this speech, Ci Xi recognized the truth of Zhen Fei's words. She did not want to be thought unreasonable, and with a great effort managed to control her anger. She told Zhen Fei that she was right and she should tell the emperor to make the necessary arrangements. Zhen Fei was astonished, but before long the emperor did in fact receive an edict from the empress dowager stating that in order to save money for the war, her birthday celebration would be moved from the Summer Palace in the suburbs to the imperial palace in the center of the city.

The Qing troops continued to suffer defeat after defeat. People throughout the country were indignant and demanded that Li Hongzhang be punished for his passive resistance. Wen Tingshi and Zhen Fei's brother, Zhi Rui, in spite of the risks involved, submitted a statement to the throne, declaring Li Hongzhang and Ci Xi responsible for the nation's defeat. Ci Xi was furious and replied that in fact it was the emperor who was responsible. When she learned from the empress and Li Lianying that Zhen Fei had had a hand in the matter, she summoned both Zhen Fei and her sister to her quarters. She accused them of being fox fairies who had seduced the emperor and dared to meddle in state affairs.

"I follow the rules and accompany the emperor," Zhen Fei argued. "I have never interferred in state affairs."

This made the empress dowager even angrier. "You dare to argue with me," she shouted and demanded that Zhen Fei be beaten.

Feeling very frightened, Guang Xu knelt before the empress dowager and begged her to pardon the two sisters.

"They have poisoned your mind, and encouraged you to declare war on Japan," the empress dowager scolded the emperor. "If they are really so good, why don't they themselves force the enemy to retreat?"

Although Zhen Fei had never intended to interfere in the court's decisions, she nevertheless said that every one should share responsibility for the fate of the country. Even those who declared war on the aggressors should not be blamed.

Ci Xi's face turned purple. "Take off this fox fairy's clothes," she yelled, "and give her 40 lashes." The emprss dowager then reprimanded the emperor for having spoiled Zhen Fei. She ordered that the two sisters be demoted to *guiren* (palace officials), and placed under house arrest for three months. The emperor dared not object.

Zhen Fei was imprisoned with two personal maids in Jing Ren Hall. As soon as he left the empress dowager, Guang Xu hurried to see Zhen Fei. She had been beaten and was lying in bed in great pain. Seeing the emperor she tried to sit up, tears streaming down her cheeks. She asked first about the war, but wiping the tears from her eyes, the emperor told her nothing could be done to change the situation. The Japanese aggressors were moving deeper into China, and the empress dowager had ordered him to make concessions to the enemy to force them to stop. "We must cede territory and pay indemnities again," said Zhen Fei bitterly.

The emperor clutched his head in anguish. "Is our great country going to fall into the hands of foreign invaders during my reign?"

Zhen Fei comforted him, saying that as long as he continued to use worthy people and implement reforms China would eventually become a great power.

Three months later, on Ci Xi's orders, Li Hongzhang signed the Sino-Japanese Treaty of Shimonoseki. This treaty, which ceded China's territory and promised indemnities to the Japanese, aroused nationwide protest. By this time, Zhen Fei had been released from house arrest, and the emperor often consulted her on important state matters. In an attempt at reform, he became determined to appoint reformists Kang Youwei and Tan Sitong to office. Ci Xi and others pretended to support the emperor, but were in fact plotting to remove him from the throne.

The emperor's plan to kill Rong Lu, a powerful general and trusted follower of the empress dowager, as a first step towards reform, was revealed by General Yuan Shikai. The empress dowager decided to have

Kang Youwei and the other reformers executed, but before taking action, she invited the emperor and Zhen Fei to accompany her to the Summer Palace, so cutting them off from the outside world. When the emperor learned of her plan, he was greatly concerned. Zhen Fei suggested that he write secretly to Kang Youwei and the other reformers, advising them to leave Beijing immediately to avoid arrest. Unfortunately, the emperor was unable to smuggle out a message. After inviting the emperor and Zhen Fei to see a carved calabash in the Cloud Dispelling Hall, the empress dowager dismissed all her servants except for the chief eunuch, Li Lianying.

"There is a traitor who wants to overthrow our rule," Ci Xi began sternly. The emperor anxiously inquired who it could be. "Kang Youwei," declared the empress dowager. She ordered the emperor to send an imperial edcit to the commander of the Ministry of War for the immediate arrest of the reble. The empress dowager declared that she would personally administer his punishment.

The emperor and Zhen Fei immediately saw a way of smuggling a letter out of the palace. The emperor agreed to issue the order. Taking it from him, Ci Xi left the room, telling the emperor and Zhen Fei to wait for her return.

Once the empress dowager had left the hall, Zhen Fei took the emperor's letter to Kang Youwei and concealed it. As soon as Li Lianying returned, Zhen Fei turned to him with a smile and said, "The emperor's gown is wet. Please fetch a dry one so that he may change."

Li Lianying didn't move.

"Can't you see I'm shivering with cold?" the emperor demanded. Li Lianying left the room in search of eunuch Wang Shang who would provide fresh clothes. Zhen Fei immediately made a triangular cut in the calabash, and carefully concealed the emperor's letter. Li Lianying soon returned with Wang Shang.

"Wang Shang," he said, "the emperor's clothes are wet. Go quickly to the Hall of Jade Ripples and fetch dry ones."

As Wang Shang turned to leave, Zhen Fei asked him to carry the calabash to her residence so that she might practice carving. Wang Shang picked up the calabash and Zhen Fei's knife, but before he could leave, Li Lianying demanded to inspect them. Before he had time to discover her secret, however, Zhen Fei asked him to get some fresh lotus roots for the emperor. Without Ci Xi's presence Li Lianying did not dare to openly disobey the emperor.

Meanwhile, Wang Shang, who had noticed the emperor's tense expression, became suspicious. He examined the calabash carefully and found the triangular cut. He opened it, took out the emperor's letter and hurried with it to reformist Lin Xu who was waiting to be received by the emperor at the eastern palace gate. Aware of the urgency of the situation, Lin Xu left immediately for the Nanhai guild hall in the city. The letter was soon delivered to Kang Youwei who immediately left by train for Tianjin. The following day he boarded the British vessel *Chongqing* enroute to Shanghai, and from there he travelled to Hong Kong. By the time Li Hongzhang arrived at the Nanhai guild hall with Ci Xi's orders, Kang Youwei and Liang Qichao had fled.

Ci Xi returned to the imperial palace and furiously reprimanded the emperor. Zhen Fei, unable to bear her criticism knelt down before her. "Empress dowager," she said, “the emperor has done nothing wrong. Even if he had, you must tell him what it is and not scold him without reason.“ “Be quiet,” yelled Ci Xi. “It is not your place to speak. I intend not only to scold him, but also to dethrone him.”

“The emperor is the ruler of China,” Zhen Fei argued. “He is not your private property, and cannot be dethroned at will.”

Completely outraged, Ci Xi seized Zhen Fei’s hair and began to beat and kick her.

“You wretch,” she shouted, “I didn’t ask for your opinion!”

Kneeling on the floor, Zhen Fei submitted to Ci Xi’s ill treatment.

The empress dowager eventually tired, and ordered that Zhen Fei be shut in a dark room and kept under strict surveilance.

As the guards took her away, Zhen Fei struggled and, turning to the emperor, she shouted, “Take good care of yourself!”

As part of her plan to take over the administration of the country, Ci Xi had Guang Xu placed under house arrest, first in a side chamber near Ci Ning Hall, and then in Yingtai. She also harshly suppressed any attempts at reform.

After Zhen Fei had been imprisoned for some time, Ci Xi decided to punish her further by making her act as her personal servant. Zhen Fei served Ci Xi tea, made her bed, and even swept her floor. Even though almost unconscious after her harsh treatment, Zhen Fei never complained.

She was later locked in a dark, damp room in Beiwusuo, a deserted pharmacy in the palace. Her yard was overgrown with weeds, and often frequented by rats. On her hard bed she had only a thin quilt, and was forced to wear shabby clothes and eat coarse food. Every day Ci Xi sent Li Lianying to insult her and enumerate her crimes. Blind to her own misfortune, Zhen Fei thought only of the emperor.

The imprisoned emperor was also anxious about Zhen Fei. Although they were physically close, it was as if they were living at opposite corners of the world. Learning from Wang Shang that Zhen Fei was imprisoned at Beiwusuo, the emperor sent her candies in the name of her sister Jin Fei. As Zhen Fei took the candies, she realized that the brand name was written in English and that they must have therefore been sent by Guang Xu. She immediately opened the box and found a letter from the emperor. "I am staying at Yingtai," she read. "Don't worry about me. I'm all-right. Take care of yourself." Zhen Fei was so excited that tears ran down her cheeks. The elderly eunuch who guarded her was sympathetic, and he and Wang Shang conspired to help the young couple communicate.

Although comforted to know each other's present situation, their desire to meet again grew stronger and stronger. With the help of Wang Shang, the emperor managed to cross Nanhai Lake by boat, and one night met his beloved concubine. The emperor and Zhen Fei embraced tightly and wept on each other's shoulders.

"You are in trouble because of me," the emperor said. "Seeing you so pale makes me feel as if a knife were piercing my heart."

Zhen Fei shook her head, begging the emperor not to say such things. She told him that even if she were to die, she would be happy, if he could consolidate his rule and enrich the country.

Holding Zhen Fei closely in his arms, the emperor declared his deep love for her, "We are a pair of lovebirds in the sky, like the linked branches of a tree here on earth."

Zhen Fei also recited two lines of poetry to show her devotion to the emperor. "A silk worm stops spinning only when she dies; A candle dries her tears only when she has finished crying."

Time quickly passed as the emperor and Zhen Fei talked of their sorrows and their love. Outside the door, Wang Shang urged them to hurry, but the lovers were reluctant to part. Zhen Fei placed the emperor's hand over her heart and said, "I live only for you." She then persuaded him to leave, afraid that the guards on night patrol might discover them.

As the political situation in China grew worse, Ci Xi became panic-stricken at the invasion of the eight allied powers. She decided to flee in disguise, forcing the emperor and empress to go with her. Before leaving, she ordered Li Lianying to summon Zhen Fei to her presence.

The emperor and Zhen Fei had previously decided not to leave Beijing, but on seeing Li Lianying Zhen Fei knew her last day had come. She changed into clean clothes and combed her hair in a broken mirror. Even though she had been confined for two years, her arrival at the imperial palace seemed like only yesterday. She hated to leave the emperor, and was concerned about the safety of the country. Wanting to leave something behind for the emperor, she took up a pen and wrote out a poem by the great patriotic poet Lu You: "With one's death everything is ended; but I am sad that I have not seen my country unified. When central China is recaptured from the enemy; at the sacrificial ceremony, don't forget to tell me the good news." Zhen Fei studied the poem, and then changed the word "me" in the last line to "the soul of the deceased." With a light heart she then hurried to the Hall of Happiness and Longevity.

Seeing Ci Xi in disguise, Zhen Fei knew that she was ready to flee Beijing. "Do you think I look stupid like this?" she asked.

"No, not stupid, but sad," Zhen Fei replied. "You are running away in disguise while the country is facing foreign invasion."

Zhen Fei's words struck at the empress dowager's heart. Although she trembled, she quickly pulled herself together, and told Zhen Fei that since foreign soldiers had already entered Beijing, she and the emperor had to flee. She asked Zhen Fei to persuade the emperor to leave the city, but Zhen Fei replied, "I think the emperor is right. How can he flee the capital and leave the people to the enemy?"

"But you know that the foreign devils may commit all kinds of atrocities," Ci Xi retorted.

"I know," Zhen Fei said. "And that is why I am in favour of resistance. I am ready to dedicate myself to our country. I can not drag out this ignoble existence."

Ci Xi ordered Li Lianying to escort Zhen Fei to Jin Qi Hall. North of the hall was a small courtyard in which was a well with a stone cover. When Ci Xi arrived, she glanced at Zhen Fei and said, "I won't force you to leave if you don't want to. You are so pretty, the foreign devils won't let you off. If you want to escape them, you can die here." So saying she ordered Li Lianying to remove the stone cover from the well. Zhen Fei was furious. "What is so impressive about killing a weak and defenceless woman?" she cried. "If you want to display your power, why don't you resist the bandits who have invaded our country to murder the people and burn their homes?"

"You are not afraid of death?"

"No. I know you won't let me live. I only regret that I must die so young. But I have a clear conscience, my 25 years have been blameless. You Empress Dowager should examine your own life and see if you can say the same."

Shaking with fury Ci Xi shouted, "Push her down the well."

Li Lianying ran over, intending to push Zhen Fei into the well. "I'll go by myself," Zhen Fei said, stopping him. She turned to Ci Xi and said, "Empress Dowager, I am going to die upon your orders. Before I do I want to give you some sincere advice. I hope you will give back power to the emperor and allow him to run the country well. You may not be concerned about the country, but you have to think of your reputation after death. Don't be condemned by the people and history as a traitor...."

"Push her down the well!" Ci Xi said and stamped with rage. As she was dragged toward the well, Zhen Fei cried, "Empress Dowager, for the emperor's sake, let us see each other one last time!" Ci Xi refused to listen, only urging Li Lianying to hurry and push her into the well. Li Lianying did as he was told, and Ci Xi ordered that the well be covered.

Sixteen months later, Ci Xi and the emperor returned to Beijing. Afraid that Zhen Fei's death might cause trouble, Ci Xi instructed Li Lianying to retrieve her body from the well and bury it in Tienchun Village outside Xizhimen Gate. It is said that Zhen Fei's body was well preserved, as if she had just fallen in sleep. In later life, Ci Xi often dreamed that Zhen Fei was trying to assassinate her with a sword. To conceal the part she had played in Zhen Fei's death, Ci Xi posthumously granted her the title of the highest ranking imperial lady.

Guang Xu Succeeds to the Throne

It is said that before becoming Ci Xi's trusted servant, Li Lianying had served in the mansion of Prince Chun. In his later years, Emperor Xian Feng came to dislike Ci Xi. He told his minister Su Shun in confidence that if she didn't behave herself after his death, further trouble could be avoided by putting her to death. Li Lianying came to hear of this, and secretly passed the information to Prince Chun's wife, who was Ci Xi's younger sister. Next morning, under the pretext of paying her respects to the empress dowager, the prince's wife visited her sister and told her the news. Ci Xi showed her gratitude by making Guang Xu, her sister's son, the successor to Emperor Tong Zhi, her own son died at an early age. Although Guang Xu didn't have a child for several years after marriage, geomancers who examined a large, ancient cypress tree growing in the yard of Prince Chun's mansion, predictd that another emperor might soon be born into the Chun family.

Ci Xi was displeased by this, and visited the Chun mansion to see the tree for herself. A few days later, the empress dowager returned to the mansion and told Prince Chun that she planned to build a large hall in the Summer Palace, for which she needed a good piece of timber. She indicated that the large cypress growing in his yard would be ideal as the main pillar of the hall. The prince at once kowtowed, and said that since the empress dowager had taken a liking to the tree, it was his honour to contribute it to the construction of the palace hall. The prince held a banquet under the tree, and then gave orders that it should be felled. As the great tree fell to the ground twelve enormous snakes flew out, one of them darting toward the empress dowager. Turning pale with fright, Ci Xi covered her face and tried to hide. She left for her own palace immediately and for several days running refused to hold court.

Soon after the cypress was cut down, the prince fell ill. Although Ci Xi sent a doctor and medicines from the palace, his condition deteriorated. The prince dared not consult another doctor, and realizing that he would not recover, began to worry about his son's failure to produce an heir to the throne. One day, he asked the palace doctor why a strong young man had failed to have any children, even after marrying several wives. When the doctor learned that the young man in question was the emperor, he just shook his head and remained silent. Prince Chun then realized that Guang Xu would remain childless.

Every time that Ci Xi visited the prince, she was accompanied by Guang Xu. The visits angered the emperor for he saw how Ci Xi ordered his parents about. Although he tried to hide his anger, it drove him almost crazy, and he would beat the court eunuchs and smashed things in the palace.

An Honourable Eunuch

The eunuch Kou Liancai was first employed to dress the empress dowager's hair at the age of 15. Finding him intelligent and hard-working, Ci Xi soon put him in charge of her accounts and pass memorials to the throne. Kou had an upright character, and often remonstrated with the empress dowager about her extravagant and dissipated lifestyle. Ci Xi at first did not take him seriously, merely scolding him for speaking so boldly. Eventually, she sent him to wait on Emperor Guang Xu and act as her spy. Kou was outraged by the injustice of the emperor's treatment. Although Ci Xi persuaded Li Lianying, her favourite eunuch, to spread rumours that the emperor "had become immoral," it was she in fact who had encouraged him to gamble and smoke opium--part of her plot to remove him from the throne.

Angered and concerned by the empress dowager's actions, Kou Liancai always appeared troubled and some thought him insane. One day, as the empress dowager lay resting, Kou Liancai knelt by her bed and began to cry bitterly. Ci Xi demanded to know why he was crying. Kou Liancai answered: The country is now miserable and in great danger, and yet you venerable Buddha still indulge in an extravagant life, and spend money without restraint. What will happen if you go on like this! Even if you don't consider the people and the country, you should at least consider yourself. Please don't go on like this! Ci Xi swung the net around her bed angrily and cried: "What a mad man, maniac!

Get out!"

Soon afterwards, Kou Liancai asked for five days' leave. He said a final farewell to his parents and gave a notebook detailing the affairs at court to his younger brother. On returning to the court, Kou Liancai sent a memorial to the empress dowager, urging her to return state power to the emperor, to resist the Japanese invasion and to put an end to her extravagance. He also asked her not to renovate the Summer Palace, not to build railways, and to remove Minister Li Hongzhang from office. The last item in the memorial suggested that, since the emperor had no son of his own, he should select a man of virtue to succeed him. After reading the memorial, Ci Xi was convinced that it had been written at someone else's instigation. She questioned Kou Liancai, but he insisted that he alone was responsible. Ci Xi even asked him to recite a few lines which he did without any mistakes. When Ci Xi reread the memorial, she found many wrong characters and grammatical mistakes, which convinced her that Kou was telling the truth. "Do you know that according to our ancestral code, eunuchs are decapitated if they interfere in political affairs?" she asked.

"Your slave knows. But your slave is not afraid of death, otherwise he would not have given you the memorial!"

"Ah, then you should not complain about my unkindness!" She ordered those in charge of the office of imperial household affairs to imprison Kou, who was sentenced to death by the Ministry of Justice. Taking off his jade ring, which he gave to the executioner, Kou asked him to carry out the execution quickly. He then gave a jade pendant and a gold watch to the eunuchs who had come to bid him farewell. Kou Liancai was only 18 years old when he died.

Ci Xi had always regarded a eunuch's life as of no importance. Why then should she bother to question Kou, and not just execute him immediately? Perhaps, some say, it was because if he had begged for mercy, she may have pardoned him.

A Cobbler Becomes Court Favourite

Ci Xi's chief eunuch, Li Lianying, was originally a villain in Hejian prefecture (today's Xianxian county in Hebei province). His parents died when he was young, and he began to loiter around the streets. After serving a prison term for smuggling nitrosulphur, he became a cobbler. Shen Lanyu, who was an aquaintance of Li's, was a eunuch at the court. Li began to court Shen's favour in the hope that he would recommend him to the imperial household. Shen, thinking him intelligent enough for a position, agreed to help him find work at the court.

It happened that a new hair style was then in fashion in the capital. Ci Xi asked several of the eunuchs who dressed her hair to create the new style for her, but none of their efforts pleased her. When Li Lianying heard of this, he thought his opportunity had come at last. He travelled around the city studying various hair styles, visiting in particular the brothels, where the new hair style was most popular. After he had mastered the technique of creating this new style, Shen Lanyu recommended him to Ci Xi. Ci Xi was very impressed with his skill, and Li Lianying was engaged to do her hair. On the death of the Empress Dowager Ci An, Ci Xi took the powers of the court into her own hands. She made Li the chief eunuch. He understood the workings of Ci Xi's mind and went to great pains to please her. Ci Xi came to depend heavily on Li, and when he was away from the palace she was never satisfied with the eunuchs who took his place.

The eunuchs as a result begged Li not to leave. He could sit with Ci Xi watching dramatic performances. When they ate together, Ci Xi would leave the dishes that she knew Li liked untouched. Recognizing his special position, many tried to gain Li's favour. They knew that on his recommendation they would be promoted to more important positions within the court. On his 40th birthday, Li Lianying received many gifts from the emperor and Ci Xi. The gifts included satin robes embroidered with pythons and the characters for "happiness" and "longevity." According to the Qing system, only officials of the second rank could wear the symbol for "happiness," and only those over the age of 50 were awarded gifts bearing the character "longevity." High officials, from the chief privy councillor to governors, all sent extravagant gifts.

After the death of Ci Xi, Li Lianying continued to enjoy the favour of Emperor Guang Xu and the Empress Dowager Long Yu. When he died, his burial ceremony was as grand as those staged for founders of the dynasty. Other eunuchs had long envied his family property, and soon after his death made plans to divide it up amongst themselves. Li had received many bribes during his lifetime, and even embezzled court funds. He had large deposits of silver and gold at banks in his hometown, in addition to his more than three million taels of silver at court. The eunuchs fought fiercely for a share of Li's property. When the Empress Dowager Long Yu heard of this, she ordered that his property be confiscated. The money was later used to erect buildings at the palace and buy Western-style utensils for the court.

The Empress Dowager's "Scholarly Courtiers"

In her later years, Ci Xi developed an interest in art. She learned to paint and practiced calligraphy, and often wrote characters such as "happiness" and "longevity," and gave them to her favourites at court. A large scroll containing the character for "longevity," and a stone tablet inscribed by Ci Xi are still preserved at Confucius's Mansion in Qufu, Shandong province. People regarded it a great honour to receive even a single character written by the empress dowager, and more and more people came to ask for samples of her work. Ci Xi became bored, and decided to have someone else do the work for her. Miao Suyun, a widow from Sichuan province, was recommended to her. Ci Xi received her at court and was impressed by her mastery of painting, calligraphy and music. Miao remained at the court, and was paid handsomely; she was even exempted from kneeling when in the presence of the empress dowager. The widow's son was later appointed a civil official in the cabinet.

Once Miao entered the court, almost all the princes and ministers received paintings or calligraphy, allegedly by Ci Xi, but in fact the work of Miao Suyun.

On the eve of the empress's 60th birthday, she said to Miao: "You have seen the Manchu women's ceremonial dresses, what do Han women wear at festivals?" Miao replied that they wore phoenix coronets and satin robes. Ci Xi asked her to wear a Han ceremonial dress at her birthday celebrations. Within a day, Miao had made a costume and put it on for Ci Xi's approval. Ci Xi found it so funny that she burst out laughing. Pointing to Miao, she said "You look just like an actress."

On the day of her birthday celebrations, Ci Xi asked Miao to stand in a conspicuous place, wearing her phoenix coronet and satin robe. All the Manchu ladies found her dress very strange and laughed a great deal. Ci Xi was pleased and rewarded Miao well. Miao, however, was very tired and unhappy after standing all day.

Some of Ci Xi's "scholarly courtiers," were in fact women sent from Zhejiang province to advise her on the matter of dress. The women, who had been trained to inquire about prices and answer Ci Xi's questions, were allowed to visit their families once a year. Some of them were spoiled as favourites of Ci Xi and became very arrogant. One of them even insulted the county magistrate of her hometown when he rebuked her for her attitude.

When it came time for the woman to return to court, the county magistrate reported that she was ill and could not go back to the capital. Ci Xi asked why she had not returned, and was told by the other women that the county magistrate was deliberately preventing it. Ci Xi became very angry, and ordered him to send the woman back to the capital at once. The county magistrate was so afraid that he begged the woman to forgive him before she took her leave.

Empress Dowager Ci Xi's "Adopted Son"

It is said that Empress Dowager Ci Xi had an "adopted son" called Guan Guoan, who was born in Yanghu (today's Wujin county in Jiangsu province). Although his father was a businessman, the family was not rich. Guan however, soon developed a taste for a luxurious lifestyle. He was handsome, and skilled at painting and singing, being particularly fond of bawdy songs. His father thought him worthless however, and drove him out of the family. Guan left his wife and parents and travelled to the capital. It so happened that at that time a Happy Studio was seeking to enrol painters. Guan applied, and after coming first in the entrance examination, was offered a position.

Eunuchs from the court often acquired paintings from the Happy Studio, and came to greatly admire Guan's work. Guan also made a point of flattering the eunuchs from the court, and soon became acquainted with Li Lianying. On Li's recommendation the empress dowager agreed to meet Guan in private. Ci Xi was impressed with his painting, and immediately made him head of the Happy Studio. Guan thus enjoyed special privileges, and often visited the court.

Guan knew that the empress dowager was fond of dancing, songs and dramas, and often entertained her with decadent tunes from the south. Ci Xi was familiar with songs from the north, but found the southern songs more exciting. She heaped favours upon Guan, and ordered those in charge of the imperial household affairs to find him a house outside Donghuamen Gate. Guan was very grateful to Ci Xi, and she in her turn referred to him as "my son."

Guan, meanwhile, as the empress dowager's favourite, had forgotten all about his wife and parents. He later became a very wealthy businessman in Beijing, and even as an old man, still cut a striking figure, with his bright eyes and long beard. Although he no longer went to court so often, he was still occasionally favoured by Empress Dowager Ci Xi.

An Imperial Abduction

Prince Zai Cheng was a grandson of Emperor Dao Guang and the eldest son of Prince Yi Xin. Even as a young man he was renowned for his immoral behaviour.

One summer's day, Zai Cheng visited Shishahai Park with a group of his retainers. At that time, Shishahai was famous for its beauty. Willow trees surrounded a lake covered by lotus blossoms, while peddlers sold their wares on its banks. Seated in a tea house on the shores of the lake, Zai Cheng found himself next to a pretty and coquettish lady at a neighboring table. She seemed anxious to speak to him, so Zai Cheng asked one of his servants to give her a bunch of seedpod of the lotus and ask her if she would like to meet his master. The lady replied that although she would like to meet him, it was inconvenient for him to come to her home. She said, however, that she would be glad to meet him at some other appropriate place. Zai Cheng was very pleased and arranged to meet her in a private room at a restaurant. As their relationship developed, they continued to meet at their secret rendezvous.

The lady was aware that Zai Cheng was her nephew, but Zai Cheng knew nothing of their real relationship. Once, after they had made love, Zai Cheng said to her: "We love each other so much, but we cannot live together. What can we do? Can you marry me?" The lady replied that she already had a husband and so could not marry him. She suggested however, that if he could adbuct her, that would solve the problem, for who would dare do anything to a man in his position?

"What a wonderufl idea!" Zai Cheng declared, promising to prepare a house at once. At an appointed time, the lady appeared at the tea house in Shishahai Park, and was seized by Zai Cheng's henchmen.

The lady's father-in-law, who had once been an official in Zhejiang province, had become a monk after rebel forces captured Hangzhou. Although her husband was also an official in the capital, he was incapable of taking any action. When he learned that his wife had been abducted by Zai Cheng, he was afraid and simply walked through the streets with his chest naked and his hair in disarray, telling people about his misfortune.

When Prince Yi Xin learned that his son had abducted a lady of the imperial family, he became angry and ordered that Zai Cheng be imprisoned for the rest of his life. Not long afterwards, Zai Cheng's mother died, and he swore to the Empress Dowager Ci Xi that he would wear mourning for his mother if only she would set him free. Even after his release, however, he continued his licentious life. When Zai Cheng became seriously ill, his father secretly hoped that he would not recover. Nevertheless, since he was his own son, he went to bid him a final farewell. He found Zai Cheng dressed entirely in black silk and on which were embroidered white spiders. Yi Xin flew into a rage. "You should have died earlier for wearing this kind of dress!" he said, as he turned and left the room. Zai Cheng died soon afterwards.

The Empress's Marble Boat

When Zai Tian became emperor, his father Yi Xuan was appointed the chief privy councillor. Instead of concentrating on state and military affairs, however, he sought to please the Empress Dowager Ci Xi by constructing Qianhai (Front Sea), Zhonghai (Middle Sea) and Houhai (Back Sea) parks for her enjoyment. As her 50th birthday approached, Ci Xi decided to renovate Wanshou (Longevity) Park, part of the Summer Palace. At that time, parts of China had been occupied by foreign powers for many years. The Qing court had spent money without restraint, and the national treasury was almost empty. Where could the money for the renovations be found?

"Go to the chief privy councillor!" said Ci Xi. In her eyes, the three parks which the councillor had built were inadequate payment for making Yi Xuan's son the emperor.

Yi Xuan agreed to her proposal without a moment's hesitation, but how could he get the money? He finally hit the idea of using funds intended for building the navy. He would say that the money was to be used to set up a naval training base. In the end, the cost of the restoration work was eight million taels of silver, and funds had to be drawn not only from the navy, but also from the taxes for coastal defence and from customs revenues.

To hide the true nature of his work, Yi Xuan placed a sign on the gate of the Summer Palace, which read "Naval Training School," and even organized a display by navy cadets on Kunming Lake. But where were the ships? Therefore to the west of Ting Li (Listening to the Oriol) Hall, Yi Xuan constructed a boat entirely of white marble. The boat was two storeys high, and fitted out with stone cables and a stone cannon.

On her birthday, Ci Xi toured the Summer Palace accompanied by court officials. As she walked along a 700-meter corridor, the marble boat suddenly came into view. Seeing that the cannon was pointing to Longevity Hill, the empress dowager became displeased, and demanded that the boat be dismantled immediately.

Her personal eunuchs knelt down and explained that this was impossible, since the boat had been built with money intended for the navy.

Yi Xuan also tried to appease her: "I have created this boat just for show. It symbolizes that Your Majesty will always stand firm in spite of the wind and waves."

Ci Xi, however, was still annoyed: "You are just teasing me," she said and insisted that the stone cannon be removed. The boat was later rebuilt to form a carved tower with pictures around its walls, and Ci Xi often used it to hold banquets. Before long, she had the sign removed from the palace gate and drove the naval cadets away. She named the boat "A Simple Banqueting Boat," and used it for entertaining.

One Dream Turns to Ten Thousand Taels of Silver

On the Empress Dowager Ci Xi's 60th birthday, all the civil and military officials in the court came to offer their felicitations at the Summer Palace. Among them were Prime Minister Li Hongzhang.

Li was admiring the scenery in the park with other officials when one of the eunuchs dashed up to him saying that he was wanted by the empress dowager to discuss some official business. The prime minister went to see her with joy, reckoning that Ci Xi might be thinking of awarding him for his diverting much of the navy fund to construct this magnificent park.

Just as Li expected, the old woman was all grace and smiles when she greeted him, which was quite a switch from her usual haughty and ferocious glare. She asked Li to be seated. But to his surprise, there was a long and awkward silence before Li Lianying, the dowager's pet eunuch, told the prime minister that he had been invited there to interpret one of Ci Xi's dreams.

To interpret a dream? The prime minister was almost frozen at the news, for he knew that the old woman was utterly subject to mood swings. She would grant you a very high position with momentary delight, then put you to death in a flicker of rage. It would by no means be an easy job to interpret her dream. Sensing the prime minister's apprehentions, the eunuch whispered in his ear, "You needn't be too serious. Just amuse her. You'll entertain her with your interpretation."

"Knowledgeable as you are, Prime Minister Li, can you see if it's right?" Ci Xi asked suddenly.

"Well...right?" Li murmured, unable to make neither head nor tails of it.

The dowager tittered and continued, "In Tang Dynasty, the Empress Wuzetian could sit dignified in her dragon-seat in the imperial audience hall. Yet today I have to sit behind a curtain in the hall although I am running the Great Qing court. It is a so-called 'holding of court from behind a screen," as if I haven't a nose, eyes and a face. See, is it right?"

"Oh, no, no. Not at all!" replied Li Hongzhang.

"It doesn't matter much whether it is right or not now that I'm already 60. It is time for me to retire and return to my native," the dowager said. "I'm lucky to have your filial devotion. It was you who allocated the navy's silver to build this park for me. Otherwise, I might have to go live in a cave upon my retirement!" Saying so, her manner became stormy once again.

"Such a trifling amount was taken," she continued, "and some feel as if I had cut off a pound of their own flesh."

"Your Majesty was certainly deserving of the favour, after all your hard work of mind and body for the state," the prime minister replied gloatingly, knowing that Ci Xi's words were in reference to Emperor Guang Xu. He had nursed a hatred towards the emperor because he had once intended to discharge him.

"Luckily, I have loyal officials like you," Ci Xi said.

"It is my duty to serve Your Wise Majesty in order to show my respect."

In fear of reminding the old woman of some unhappiness by chattering this way, Li Hongzhang turned to the business at hand. "Your Majesty, His Honour Li just now sent for me, your humble official, to interpret one of Your Majesty's dreams," said the prime minister. "This being such an auspicious birthday of yours, I guess, it must be a very fond dream."

"I'm not sure if it's desirable or not. That's why I would like to ask you to interpret it," the dowager said. "Just now I was relaxing in a deck chair and dozed off. Half asleep, I saw a mountain in front of me. I raised my head and found it very high. I stepped up to it..."

"What a lucky dream!" interrupted Li Hongzhang. "It indicates that Your Majesty will be living a long life, just like the Nanshan Mountains, and will prosper continuously."

With a smile, Ci Xi continued, "There were altogether 88 steps leading to the top of the mount. And it rose steeply. My legs ached after some climbing. Suddenly I caught sight of a pagoda built in the Song Dynasty and a temple of the Tang Dynasty. So I increased my effort and went on climbing."

Hearing this, the prime minister became even more delighted, for the mount in the dowager's dream was the very same as the one in his hometown, Wuhu in Anhui province.

"I've got it, Your Majesty! The mount must have looked reddish brown and was named Zheshan Mount. A few hundred yards from the Tang temple, there must have been an archway with scripts reading "Yitianmen"(The Sole Gateway to Heaven) on it."

Ci Xi nodded yes with a meaningful smile.

Li Lianying, who was listening aside, said knowingly, "So that's why Your Majesty sent for Prime Minister Li to interpret the dream. It has turned out that Your Majesty has had a trip to his hometown."

"I'd rather say it was a return to the place. But it

was all in a dream. I can't forget it, you see. There must be some pedestined relations between the mount and me."

Then, she recalled her childhood, a time when she and her family lived in Wuhu, where her father was then in charge of a customs office. Her family's strict domestic discipline prohibited girls from going out of the mansion without the parents' permission.

One day, when the father was out, Ci Xi, a disobedient girl, slipped out the back door of the house with her sisters to climb Zheshan Mount. Just when they were straining to overcome the precipitous steps, they came across an old monk. He told them that the mount was too high for girls to scale, and that they'd better just not waste their energy.

The girls would not listen to the monk and went on climbing. Thus the monk had to tell them the reason for his advice. The Guangji Temple at the peak of the mount was a sacred place where the Dizangwang Buddhist had mortified himself in order to become one of the gods. Pilgrims had to worship on bended knees every three steps on their way to the mount. And they had to kowtow on each step up the mount. One would fail to reach the temple at the summit if he or she was not sincere enough. Even if one succeeded, a slip on the 87th step could hurl one into the abyss of death or great injury, the monk continued.

His words, however, did not scare the girls. They succeeded in topping the mount. On entering the temple, the old monk congratulated them, saying that they were obviously young ladies from some prosperous family, so the Buddha had blessed them. He then showed them the way to the Buddha idol.

"Why not draw a lot and ask the Buddha about your fate, since you have appealed him?" he said, pointing to the pot of fortunes sitting on an incense altar.

Following the monk's suggestion, Ci Xi shook the pot and drew a lot, which read "the very best." The words were subsequently explained by the monk's diviner which said that the girl would enjoy wealth and honour and might be crowned in the future. Ci Xi was overjoyed upon hearing this and thanked the monk.

But just as they were about to leave, the monk produced an account book and asked them to give some alms. However, the sisters had not brought any money with them. They blushed and said,"How about next time?"

Glancing at the fascinated prime minister, the dowager suddenly roared with laughter. Li Hongzhang was really puzzled about the old woman's digression from the interpretation of her dream to such a childhood memory. Seeing that he was still in the dark, Li Lianying had to illuminate her point.

"Maybe I've figured out what Your Majesty means. Since your childhood you have owed the Zheshan Buddha some alms," he muttered, adding that, "but the debt wouldn't be a small sum with all the interest added in that has accumulated for several decades."

"Right. And what do you think of this sum, Xiao Li?" Ci Xi said, unfolding of her palms to show five talon-like fingers.

Li Lianying nodded in agreement, chiming in that "It has to be at least 50,000 taels of silver to buy joss sticks and candles, maitain the temple, clothe the Buddha image with gold, build bridges and pave roads."

Faced by the dowager's icy stare, the prime minister felt as though he had been boxed on the ear: Again the old woman was fleecing him of the state fund. Yet he dared not express a single word of disagreement.

"The hometown of this humble official has been favoured by bounties from Your Majesty. So your benefaction for the Buddha should certainly be served by me," he said.

"I should thank you for your kindness. But 50,000 taels seems insufficient. How about 100,000?" Hardly had Ci Xi finished her words when she stood up from her seat. "Maybe the performance has started, Xiao Li. Let's go and see it," she said to her eunuch, as if ignoring the very presence of the prime minister.

As he watched the dowager sail away, Li Hongzhang felt humiliated and furious. Nevertheless, he could do nothing but carry out this new mission Ci Xi had just appointed him.

He allocated 100,000 taels of silver, of which a 50,000 taels bank cheque was sent to Li Lianying's house. Only 100 taels were sent to the Wuhu county government. From it, the county magistrate granted 50 taesl to the Guangji Temple. The old monk spent five taels to have the temple gate painted and Buddha image clothed with golden powder. The monks in the temple chanted prayers for three days and nights for Ci Xi after a meal of "Long-Life Noodles."

Li Hongzhang's relatives in his hometown bought estates that included vast amounts of land with the unexpected income. In the suburbs of Wuhu city, two rows of buildings were set up with the fund and later given the name "Jiyi Li," meaning "to benefit the native people."

The Royal Bun

There is a famous restaurant in the Beihai Park, Beijing, named Fangshan--An Imitation of Royal Cuisine--because dishes there are prepared similar to those in the Qing Dynasty.

One of their specialties is tiny, soft buns about the size of half an apricot, which taste sweet. This steamed bread, originally made for Empress Dowager Ci Xi, has quite a story behind it.

In 1900, the Eight-Power Allied Forces, aggressive troops sent by Britain, the United States, Germany, France, Tsarist Russia, Japan, Italy and Austria, occupied Beijing. Ci Xi fled westward helter-skelter for her own safety, despite the threat to the country's territory and people.

After several days' flight, the empress dowager and company were exhausted and starved. However they dared not seek food from local governments in town, where aggressors raged and anti-government forces might recognize them. People they had met along the way were mostly disaster refugees. None of them could offer anything for the regime to gorge themselves with.

The dowager could no longer bear the hunger and shouted at her retinues in exasperation, "You idiots! The emperor and I have been starved for so many days. Why haven't you managed to get us something to eat? Are you going to starve us to death?"

Her followers were so frightened that they all knelt down and kowtowed to calm her anger. They comforted the old woman by telling her that they might be able to find some food in a village right ahead.

Before long they came upon a big tree, under which a group of refugees had stopped for a rest in the shade. They were all gnawing on a kind of dry, yellow cake. Upon spying the food, Ci Xi's mouth began to water. How she wished to snatch one of the cakes and gobble it up!

The attendants approached the refugees and found that what they were eating were steamed corn buns. They then forced themselves to beg one for the dowager to taste, saying that they would pay for it.

"But I'm afraid it is too hard for you ladies and gentlemen to eat," an old man said, looking the royal ones up and down. Although the runaway royal force were in their civilian clothes, they didn't look a bit like the emaciated refugees in rags.

Hastily the retinues explained and begged. And the old man reluctantly pulled a yellow bun out of his bag, which one of the attendants offered with both hands to Ci Xi.

The dowager snatched it up and gobbled it down greedily without a thought of her manners. She felt as if she had never in her life tasted anything so delicious. As she ate, her mind cursed the royal chefs for being such a bunch of blockheads. They had made a play for her favour by varying dishes. How could they have neglected to prepare this sweet thing for her! She decided to make those fellows pay for their ignorance.

After the Qing government was coerced by the foreign powers to sign the traitorous Teaty of 1900, Ci Xi swaggered back to Beijing from Xi'an with the emperor and attending company.

Upon arriving back at the palace, Ci Xi immediately ordered the household cooks to make some of the same type of buns as those she had enjoyed on her flight to the hinterland. But this time, after her palate had once again been delighted by all kinds of famous local foods, the buns tasted too coarse and seemed hard to swallow.

"What I want is the kind I had on my way to Xi'an. How dare you to bring such rubbish to me? Kill that irresponsible cook!" She flared up, and the poor chef died a tragic death under the testy despot's power.

Terrified by the incident, the other cooks began to rack their brains as to how to deal with the dilemma. Suddenly a veteran wit hit upon a resourceful idea.

"We could use fine flour, since she complained of the coarseness," the old cook said. "But wheat flour will not do. How about we grind chestnut meat into fine flour? And we could add some honey or sugar if it is not sweet enough."

Everyone in the royal kitchen then set to work. The buns turned out to be both sweet and soft. After tasting them the dowager nodded and said, "This is somewhat like what I wanted. But the colour is not royally golden and elegant. However, I can manage to eat it anyway."

From then on, a new item, "the Royal Bun," was added to the palace cuisine. The Fangshan Restaurant continues this tradition by treating its guests to this unique food. Whenever it is served at one's table, the waiter or waitress will tell this legend.

Ignorant Number One Scholar

Once there were two scholars, one was Cao Hongxun; the other, Wang Shoupeng. Being neighbours, they had learnt to read and write, as well as had fun together, in their childhood. Yet their characters differed a lot.

Cao was bright and diligent. He could recite all of the "Four Books" and the "Five Classics" without a hitch. As a literary talent, he was always praised for his elegant handwriting and articles.

Wang however, saw learning as a perilous undertaking. He was fond of strolling about and used to play hookey. Their master described Wang as a good-for-nothing, a piece of rotten that could not be carved into anything. But he was chosen as a candidate for the imperial examination at the provincial level by local officials because of his wealthy and influencial family. He and Cao went together to the capital to attend the examination.

On seeing the examination paper, Cao Hongxun found the composition topic quite easy. With a sober mind, he started to write. It did not take him long to complete a magnificent article. His handwriting was so neat and beautiful that the examiner could not help but stop to admire it from over the writer's shoulder.

Wang Shoupeng, however, was perplexed by the topic itself for quite a long time. The only thing he could do later on was stare at the topic while chewing the shaft of his writing brush. When the candidates were asked to hand in their compositions, there was nothing but the topic on Wang's paper.

After skimming through the papers, the chief examiner was convinced that Cao's composition was the best of all, while Wang had just blown the exam.

The day when the chief examiner was about to mark the papers happened to be Empress Dowager Ci Xi's 60th birthday. He had to lay aside the papers to attend the celebrations. As he kowtowed his congratulations to the old lady, she took up the matter of the examination. She declared that she was going to choose the Number One Scholar of the Year herself to add some interest to her birthday celebration.

The examiner could do nothing but lug all the papers to the palace and presented them on a big red lacquer tray to the dowager. She snatched one from the pile and was overjoyed to see the name—"Wang Shoupeng." The reason she found such favour in the name was that the character "Wang" in Chinese means "monarch," referring naturally to herself, the real ruler of the country; "Shou," which stands for "longevity," was a lucky word to appear on her birthday; and the character, "peng," which refers to a roc that is able to travel a great distance, is regarded as an omen of a bright future. So auspicious as the name was, the dowager ignored all indications of the candidate's true ignorance. She took up a brush pen and with red ink placed a large dot on Wang's paper, indicating that he had been chosen the year's Number One Scholar.

The examiner panicked at this, forgetting all about the old woman's fierce abusiveness. He knelt down and said hastily, "That won't do, Your Majesty! This Wang Shoupeng has no talent at all. All he has handed in is a blank piece of paper."

The examiner's censure of Wang Shoupeng had already annoyed the dowager, but when he mentioned the word "blank," which was forbidden in the court, the old woman became even more furious.

"Nonsense!" she roared. "Do you intend to curse me on my birthday by making such unlucky remarks?" She called the guards up and pointed to the trembling examiner, shouting, "Strip this scoundrel of his rank!"

"Your Majesty..." the chief examiner began to speak again, and the old lady ordered that he be taken away.

That was how Wang Shoupeng became the country's Number One Scholar. And he was given a nickname, "The Number One Scholar of No Learning."

Governor Yuan Shikai's Snivelling

After the Treaty of 1900, the imperial court of the Qing Dynasty, headed by the Empress Dowager Ci Xi, was reduced to the role of puppet for the foreign powers. They helped the aggressors enslave and loot the Chinese people. What the empress dowager, who was then 67, gained from the traitorous treaty was momentary ease, the chance to return from Xi'an to her home in Beijing.

On the day when the dowager arrived back in the capital, Yuan Shikai, governor of the Zhili province, led a group of civil and military officials to the outskirts of Beijing to meet the dowager's party. The greeters lined up on both sides of the street as if awaiting the return of a victorious army.

Unexpectedly, Governor Yuan burst into wails after a succession of kowtows at the fugitive dowager's arrival. The governor's act amazed both the welcoming and welcomed forces. They wondered what he had up in his sleeves.

Ci Xi herself felt, at first, that this put a bit of a damper on her homecoming. But she held her temper, remembering the governor's great service--how he had helped her strangle the constitutional reform in the cradle two years ago, thus insuring her status as ruling monarch.

"Why are you weeping so hard, my poor governor?" she forced a smile and asked.

"It has been a long time since this official has seen Your Majesty," the governor said, wiping his eyes.

"Just now I found Your Majesty much more emaciated. I see that it must be caused by your concern about the country and fatigue from the arduous journey. It really caused my heart to ache. I beg your pardon for forgetting myself."

Greatly moved, Ci Xi sighed and said, "I appreciate your filial heart, dear governor. Stand up, please."

Yuan's spontaneous act of sentimentality was soon adopted by the snobbish officials as a successful way to ingratiate themselves with the dowager. After Ci Xi returned to the Summer Palace, she found it a routine task for the civil and military ministers to cry loudly before they bagan to say something. Things became even more ridiculous later, when those who came to give their respects to the dowager cried at every cough or sigh of the old lady.

One day, the ministers assembled at the palace to discuss official business in the presence of the empress dowager. As soon as they heard the old woman saying, "I'm already starting to become senile at the age of 70. I find that both my strength and energy are gradually failing..." The ministers began to look at one another and bawl. The hall was filled with a chorus of sobbing, as if a mourning ceremony was going on.

"That's enough!" the dowager finally grew annoyed.

All at once the hall became silent, as, in unison, the ministers stopped their wails and hurried away. Upon viewing the receding herd of black, gray and white pigtails, dangling away just like a swarm of frightened tadpoles moving towards deeper water, Ci Xi, rather depressed, could not help thinking, "Do they really care about me?"

The Hall of Happiness and Longevity

In the Four Books, one sentence reads: "Wisdom Brings Happiness and Benevolence Brings Longevity." Empress Dowager Ci Xi considered herself a person of wisdom and benevolence, and so she named her favourite palace in the Summer Palace "The Hall of Happiness and Longevity." Although it was honoured by such a beautiful name, it actually was a place of crimes.

Once Emperor Guang Xu went to the Summer Palace to report to Ci Xi the Russian occupation of Pamir and asked for counter-measures. Ci Xi, who was playing chess with the palace ladies and princess, acted as if she couldn't care less. Coldly, she said, "There is nothing important about such a remote and desolated place. If they want to occupy it then let them do as they wish."

Guang Xu was shocked at Ci Xi's indifference toward an issue that brought into question national dignity. Assuming that she might have misunderstood, Guang Xu started to repeat his words, "Dear Father (Ci Xi liked to be called with male titles)...."

He had barely opened his mouth when Ci Xi turned her head away and snapped impatiently, "Stop! Didn't you hear what I just said?"

Then she turned to her long tobacco pipe, which was being lit by a small eunuch. Engrossed by the conversation, the eunuch forgot to keep the match away from Ci Xi's clothes after he had fired the pipe, so her clothes were ablaze. Immediately, several eunuchs and palace ladies scurried to kill the flames.

Ci Xi had been very unhappy with Guang Xu's disturbance and this fanned her temper even more. She stood up and gave a hard kick at the eunuch who was cowering on the floor. "Drag this blind bastard out and beat him to death!" she cried.

Guang Xu, a quivering spectator, wanted to plea for the child, but he dared not. It was no use.

"We have finished the matter. Why do you stand there like an idiot?" Ci Xi scolded Guang Xu and left for her Dormitory Palace.

It was nothing unusual for eunuchs to be flogged and even murdered for being in the least bit careless.

Not even honoured scholars were immune to Ci Xi's vindictiveness. At the last imperial examination of the Qing Dynasty, a scholar from Jinan, Shandong province, named Wang Guojun, won the title of Zhuang Yuan (No.1 Scholar). Hearing that the winner's paper was very outstanding, Ci Xi wanted to have a look at it.

When the exam paper was brought to her, Ci Xi instantly fell into a rage at the sight of the scholar's name. The attendants were all dumbfounded and could not figure out what had happened.

Ci Xi took a brush pen and made three red crosses on the name's three characters and wrote: "The Westerners want to ruin my Great Qing Dynasty. This bastard also wants to have the head of the state die. This is definitely calls for capital punishment." (In Chinese, the pronunciation of the scholar's name, "Wang Guojun," coincides with that of a phrase meaning "to kill the head of the state.")

With that, she flung her pen aside and ordered that the new Zhuang Yuan be given some white cloth with which to hang himself. Thus this outstanding scholar died due to his unfortunate name.

Not only in political affairs but also in everyday life, Ci Xi carried a policy of "those who obey me flourish while those who cross me are doomed."

One day, Ci Xi wanted to play chess. But her favourite eunuch Li Lianying was out, and only a young eunuch was standing nearby. After inquiring as to whether he knew the game, Ci Xi asked him to prepare the board and play with her.

All the seasoned people knew that you had to let Ci Xi win no matter how well you could play. Innocent as the young eunuch was, he took it for a real game. Ci Xi, a lousy chess player, soon started to lose. At the same time, unknown to her opponent, her temper began to boil.

"My slave kills Your Majesty's marshal!" the young eunuch shouted joyfully.

Ci Xi found she was badly defeated. In a flaming rage, she toppled the chess board and slapped the eunuch's face. "Servants! Drag this bastard away and give him 40 heavy strokes!"

The poor eunuch could not stand the torture and humiliation. He knew that his future was at the complete mercy of this cruel woman. Therefore, that very night, he drowned himself in Kunming Lake.

The Copper Pavalion

According to one story, when the Summer Palace was completed, Empress Dowager Ci Xi ordered the building of a copper pavalion west of the Fuoxiang Pavalion on Wanshou Mountain. Ci Xi reasoned as follows: Wanshou means "longevity," and the word signifying copper, tong, is similar in pronunciation to the word meaning "young." Therefore, a copper pavalion could also be a symbol of eternal youth.

However, at that time, continued debts and the loss of land to foreign aggressors resulted in serious financial troubles. It was not an easy task to find enough copper. But Ci Xi would have her own way.

Head eunuch Li Lianying heard about Ci Xi's intention and put forth an idea. "There is a proverb," he said, "that claims 'one drop of water makes a vast sea, and from little comes much.' Why not collect donations from the people and officials?"

Ci Xi shook her head and said, "It won't do. First, people do not have that many copper coins at hand, and moreover, even if they have, they will not donate. As for those officials, they are only interested in extorting money."

"Your Great Buddha need not worry about that. The only thing is a reasonable pretext. Poor as they are, they dare not refuse to donate." Ci Xi stared at Li Lianying and encouraged him to continue. "Such a pretext is... a donation for the love of country."

Ci Xi laughed. "Your are truly some help."

"It is merely the result of your instructions," Li

Lianying flattered.

So nine huge vats were placed outside the Eastern Gates of the Summer Palace. All passers-by, common people or officials, were called upon to throw copper coins into the vats. However, the reasons for such an appeal varied. Commoners would be told to donate for the country, and the officials were told to donate for Ci Xi, for mere sentiment would not loosen their purse strings.

The neighbouring people all complained about such an edict. The court has squandered so much money building the Summer Palace, they said, and now squeezes coppers from the poor, who are so compelled to prove their love of country. Who would believe this frank hawking!

But the imperial order was not to be disobeyed. In order to avoid passing by the vats, people had to make a detour. However, the officials, especially those social ladder-climbers, poured into the vats pack after pack of copper coins. Before a year passed, the nine vats were full of copper coins, weighing about 400,000 kilograms.

Then the coppersmiths began to cast the building materials. A geomancer suggested that since it was a pavalion representing youth, the base of the pillars should rest on the top of virgin bodies. So Ci Xi ordered the abduction and sacrifice of two boys and two girls from the Haidian District. Then she had their bodies set in quicksilver and buried under the four pillars of the Tong Pavalion.

Finally, the unique building was completed. The pillars, beams and rafters were all made of copper. But from the outside, the pavalion looked like it was made of hard wood. Ci Xi was overjoyed at the sight of the pavalion that was meant to bring her longevity. However, the beautiful scene was suddenly clouded by the thought of the four children entombed under the four pillars.

The desperate cries and the terrified images of these innocents haunted her. She felt paralysed with fright, and her head began to swim. "Leave here, leave here!" she cried out suddenly. The eunuchs were puzzled but left Wanshou Mountain in a hurry.

From that time forth, the children's cries echoed in Ci Xi's ears, and she was in a constant state of nervousness and anxiety. So she ordered a three-meter-high portrait of a Buddha placed on the cliff behind the pavalion. At the beginning and middle of every month, monks were called to burn incense and say prayers for the dead children.

Ci Xi also built a Wu Fang Pavalion higher on the cliff to serve as a resting place for those wandering ghosts so they would no longer disturb her and she could maintain good health. But this could not save her from death soon after.

The Tragedy of a Storyteller

In the western outskirts of Beijing, there was a village called Dayou where beggars used to live. During Guang Xu's reign, the small village produced an outstanding storyteller. Knowledgeable and eloquent, he could invent and tell many fantastic tales. In slack seasons, the villagers, old and young, would gather around him to listen to his stories. These were so vivid and dramatic the audience was often stirred by them. Sometimes they burst into hearty laughs, and sometimes they wept bitterly. Hence, the entertainer acquired the name "Story Wang."

Empress Dowager Ci Xi had always been a pleasure-seeker, and she had a strong desire to keep everything for herself. When she heard of this amusing man, Ci Xi instantly summoned Story Wang to the Summer Palace to spin tales for her. Story Wang did not disappoint her. After a few days, he won the favour of the empress dowager and listening to stories became one of her favourite recreations. Story Wang's rewards, at the most, reached 6,000 taels of silver per month.

However, Ci Xi was a suspicious person, and she often liked to link fiction with reality. Subsequently, people were frequently punished for rather obscure reasons.

One year, during the Moon Festival, Ci Xi was enjoying herself with wines in a stone boat at the Summer Palace while dozens of small boats moved about idly in the moonlight to enchant her. Having drunk several cups of wine, Ci Xi became joyful and said, "Story Wang, tell me a story."

So Story Wang began to tell the story of Wu Zetian, an empress in Tang Dynasty, which was one of Ci Xi's favourites. Story Wang told how Wu Zetian's beauty and talent won the favour of Emperor Gao Zong and how she dethroned Emperor Zhong Zong and then Rong Zong and assumed the title of Sheng Shen Emperor herself. Every word of the story fit exactly Ci Xi's own impression of herself, as if she had been Wu Zetian. When the story was finished, Ci Xi laughed heartily and ordered her exchequer opened for Story Wang to take what he liked.

Story Wang knew how to behave himself. He kept his fingers away from Ci Xi's favourites because to take them would mean to take a piece of meat from a hungry tiger. In the end, he took only an inkstone, a piece of solid ink and a brushpen. Ci Xi praised him as being very considerate.

Several months later, foreign aggressors began a series of invasions, while in the court, Emperor Guang Xu began calling for constitutional reforms. All this greatly annoyed Ci Xi, and her temper became even more unpredictable.

One day, Ci Xi called on Story Wang to tell her stories to drive away her cares. Because the empress dowager was very pleased last time with the story of Wu Zetian, Wang thought she probably had a special interest in stories about powerful, historical women. So he began to tell the story of Lu Hou, an empress in Han Dynasty.

He started with the capture of Lu Hou by Xiang Yu. He then told of her return to Liu Bang and how she helped him to kill Han Xin, Peng Yue and other non-family clan princes until she made herself emperor. Ci Xi was listening attentatively. However, unaware of the disaster he would invoke, Story Wang continued with the development of the plot. When he told how Zhou Bo, Chen Ping and other veterans overthrew Lu Hou, Ci Xi stood up in a flaming rage and shrieked, "You bastard! Get out!"

At first Story Wang was at a complete loss. But he soon realized that this old woman had again fancied heself as Lu Hou. That was why she liked to hear of Lu Hou's success but not of her failure. Story Wang was driven out and sent home. Ci Xi told the local authorities not to give him any money, and no one was allowed to go near him or offer him any help.

Story Wang found himself in a miserable situation, and soon he fell ill. Some of his neighbours secretly gave him something to eat but could do nothing to save him from his illness. On a snowy night, Story Wang died, and it was a long time before people found his body.

Escape in the Night

When Empress Dowager Ci Xi returned to Beijing after fleeing from her enemies, the first thing she did was to prepare for her 70th birthday. At that time, the splendid Yuan Ming Yuan Palace had been burned to ashes by the foreign aggressors, and the Summer Palace needed repair. Ci Xi gave orders for funds to be diverted from the navy in order to rebuild the Summer Palace.

Such a person, who betrays and humiliates their nation, certainly aroused the hatred of many people, no matter how much they feared her tyranny. However, people had to swallow their resentment. Nevertheless, there were still some who tried every possible way to show their hatred.

Ci Xi ordered the creation of a large screen, which was to be set up in the Palace of Benevolence and Longevity in the Summer Palace. The work involved more than 20 craftsmen and took more than three months to finish. The responsible artist was Li Kuiyuan, a well-known painter from Yantai, Shandong province. He had long nurtured a great hostility in regard to Ci Xi. This task provided him the best opportunity to vent his spleen.

Li and a group of his apprentices took nearly one month to complete the painting. In feudal China, anything made for the emperor must first meet his approval before anyone else can get a glimpse of it. So when Li and his men finished the painting, they covered it with a silk cloth. Having locked the door of their workshop, Li said to his men, "Tomorrow, the old witch is to inspect the painting and she is sure to kill us. So run away from Beijing as soon as possible."

The next day, followed by a large group of civil officials and court painters, Ci Xi came to appreciate the screen. As the yellow silk cloth was removed, the painting's theme came into view. It depicted an immortal kneeling in front of the Noon Gates of the Forbidden City and holding a big, red peach. Behind the immortal are the allied army of the eight foreign powers, complete with flowing flags, smoking guns and horsemen, slaughtering people.

To ingratiate themselves with Ci Xi, the followers highly praised the painting. Some said the picture was meant to show an immortal coming to extend birthday greetings. Others saw in it homage being paid by world powers. The more clever followers, however, sensed the real meaning of the painting but dared not speak out.

At the first sight, Ci Xi was also enchanted by the grandeur, composition and colour of the picture. By and by, her face began to turn to stone, and she fell into a terrifying rage, ordering the painters to be arrested. The officials, not knowing what had happened, all shivered with fear and kowtowed. A moment later, report came that all the painters had run away the night before.

Then in a scornful manner, Ci Xi asked the officials, "Just now, all of you praised the painting. Do you really understand its meaning?"

The officials merely kowtowed and kept silent. Ci Xi gave a cold laugh and said, "Those bastards dare to taunt me. Xian Ren Tuo Tao (the painting's title) implies that I had fled from Beijing ahead of others when the foreign aggressors came." (In Chinese, the pronunciation of Xian Ren Tuo Tao "An Immortal

Holding a Peach" equals that of Xian Ren Tuo Tao, which means "run away ahead of others.") The officials all praised Ci Xi for her prudence and agreed that the painters should be beheaded.

This happened in Baoding city, Hebei province. On her way back to Beijing after fleeing for her life, Ci Xi encountered local officials who went all out to show their loyalty. Some presented her with a great number of rarities, and some built her palaces. Li Hongzhang, then governor at Baoding, decided to build a palace for Ci Xi. The builders all said that Ci Xi did not deserve the honour and after a discussion, they decided to mock this old woman. Within sight from the palace, they set up a sculpture of large lotus leaves on which stood a big peach.

Hardly had the palace been completed when Ci Xi arrived. Li Hongzhang led a long procession to greet her. Entering the hall, Ci Xi displayed great satisfaction in regard to the magnificent palace and exquisite designs.

She turned to Emperor Guang Xu and remarked, "See, Li Hongzhang is such a loyal man. He is unlike some people, who publically call me "Mother," yet react as if I were cutting their own flesh when I use public funds."

Guang Xu felt greatly humiliated while others all said that they would learn from Li Hongzhang.

Just at that time, head eunuch Li Lianying came near and whispered something to Ci Xi.

"What? Louder!" Ci Xi demanded.

"Your Grand Buddha. Your slave personally thinks that the sculpture on the roof has some untold meaning."

"Continue."

"you see, the peach is placed on the lotus leaves-

-we call that "Lian Yie Tuo Tao" (lotus leaves supporting the peach). But that can also mean "to escape in the night" (In Chinese, the pronunciation of the two phrases are the same). Your slave remembered that you snuck out of Beijing at night."

"They are doomed! Vicerory Li, arrest the craftsmen and kill them," Ci Xi snarled through clenched teeth.

Subsequently, the craftsmen from Baoding were arrested and killed.

The painters who painted the screen for the Summer Palace, however, managed to conceal their identities and returned to their hometown after the end of the Qing Dynasty.

The Mother and Son Stone

When Emperor Guang Xu failed in his constitutional reform and westernization movement, Empress Dowager Ci Xi reassumed her power in the court and Guang Xu was imprisoned at the Yingtai Hall. However, the empress dowager knew only too well that the emperor was still a trump card for her to use during her "rule behind the curtain." So she had to keep him in her hands, just like a monkey-charmer kept his monkey.

Once Ci Xi went to the Summer Palace to have a short stay, taking with her Emperor Guang Xu and his concubine, Zhen Fei. The emperor was temporarily confined to a side room in the Yulantang Hall, which was enclosed by tall walls. The poor emperor could only watch the sky in the narrow courtyard or get a glimpse of the woods, flowers and grasses through the window. Concubine Zhen Fei was imprisoned at a house nearby, but they were separated from each other.

Wang Shang, an old eunuch of Guang Xu, was sympathetic with the emperor and his concubine so he decided to risk his life to arrange a meeting for the two. One night, having learned that Ci Xi was in deep sleep, he begged and got the permission of the palace lady who guarded Zhen Fei to take the concubine to the emperor's room. At the sight of each other, the lovers, overwhelmed by both joy and grief, wept bitterly.

But time refused further generosity when Wang Shang, who was waiting outside, passed a message that said someone was coming. The emperor and the concubine lingered, reluctant to part. Just at that moment, a small eunuch rushed in and said, "Her Great Buddha Ci Xi has arrived."

The emperor and Zhen Fei were in a panic, for if they were caught by the empress dowager, they would suffer even crueler persecutions. And what was more, Wang Shang and all the people involved would be beheaded. Grasping the hands of Wang Shang, they said gravely, "We are doomed to die, but we feel so guilty for having gotten you involved."

Wang Shang responded reassuringly, "Take it easy, Your Majesty and Your Madam. Come with me, Your Madam." Wang Shang then hurried to a dressing mirror and gave a push at a certain spot. Like magic, the mirror-cabinet opened. "Hide yourself inside, Your Madam. I prepared this in case of danger." The emperor and his concubine felt only too grateful to their loyal eunuch.

Wang Shang hastily closed the mirror and told Emperor Guang Xu to sit at the desk to read while he attended aside. Hardly had they prepared themselves when the head eunuch Li Lianying announced in his screaming voice, "Her Great Buddha has arrived!"

Guang Xu instantly kowtowed upon greeting the empress dowager. Ci Xi gave a suspicious look around the room as she entered. But what she saw were the open book on the desk, the tea cup beside the book and the half-burned candle--nothing unusual.

After convincing herself that the emperor had merely been reading, Ci Xi said hypocritically, "Your Emperor should take care of your health. Better not stay up too late."

With that, she turned to Wang Shang and asked, "Wang Shang, did yu hear me?"

Wang Shang kowtowed and answered, "Your humble slave understands Your Great Buddha's instructions."

However, in fear of being discovered by Ci Xi, Guang Xu was so upset he kept saying, "Yes, yes, yes...."

Ci Xi became very angry at the emperor who seemed to show so little gratitude for her concern. Pointing to a stone at the left side of the gate, she said to Guang Xu, "You are as heartless as that stone." Then she stormed away unhappily.

As her footsteps faded into the distance of an otherwise peaceful night, the emperor and Wang Shang returned to the room and freed Zhen Fei. Once again in the presence of his love, Guang Xu felt revived. Pointing to the stone at the right of the gate, he said, "She compared me to a piece of stone. I would say that it is her heart that is colder and harder than this stone." Zhen Fei told him not to be troubled by such a trifling matter and to take care of his health.

Seeing it was already late in the night, Wang Shang asked Zhen Fei to go back. The emperor and the concubine embraced each other, wept and parted very unwillingly.

Ever since then, the eunuchs and palace maids privately began to refer to the two stones beside the gate as "The Son Stone" and "The Mother Stone." For although Ci Xi and Guang Xu were mother and son, their relationship was no better than that of the two lifeless stones.

A Strange Prisoner

When Guang Xu failed in his reform, he was imprisoned at the Hall of Yingtai. In order to cut off his contact with the outside world, all the bridges surrounding Yingtai, except for one draw bridge, were removed. As a result, the emperor lived a life no better than that of a criminal. Although all commerce was blocked, some stories still managed to reach the outside.

One day, a local dentist had a rather unusual visitor, who rushed into his inner room. There he unwrapped a bloodstained tooth, asking the dentist to make a false one. However, the dentist insisted on seeing the patient before making the tooth, no matter how the visitor pleaded. The visitor had no other choice but to lead the dentist to a place deep within the sanctum of the imperial palace.

Sitting in the room was a thin, miserable man in a blue robe. His eyebrows were strained with sadness, and blood could be seen on his lips. After examination, the dentist discovered that the lost tooth was not the result of any disease but of force. As he had been forwarned, the dentist said nothing and quickly set in place a false tooth. On the way back, he thought to himself that the patient must be a eunuch.

The next day, the previous visitor came again and told the dentist in confidence that the patient felt much better. Then he took out a wrapped parcel, saying that the patient had asked him to give the dentist this as payment. The dentist opened the parcel and found four taels of silver inside.

A few days later, another person came to the dentist's home. In a state of great vexation, he asked whether the dentist had been to the palace to set an artificial tooth for someone. The dentist nodded his head. Then the visitor sadly told him that his visit had caused great trouble. The previous visitor was his elder brother. As the operation was later discovered, his brother was arrested and beaten to death. His body was then discarded onto the street, and he did not even have enough money to buy his elder brother a coffin. In saying this, the bereaved brother was overcome with tears.

By this time the dentist came to realize that the patient was no other than Guang Xu, the emperor, and that the lost tooth had been the result of Ci Xi's senseless vengeance. When Ci Xi heard that someone secretly had sent for a dentist for Guang Xu, she became furious and ordered thugs to beat the person to death.

But in front of Guang Xu, Ci Xi acted as if nothing had happened. She had heard that a person with a false tooth was not supposed to eat sticky food as this would unseat the tooth. Therefore, she purposely prepared a yuanxiao (sweet dumplings made of glutinous rice flour) meal and summoned Guang Xu to enjoy the feast with her. After eating for a while, nothing apparently happened. However, Ci Xi did not want to give up so easily.

"Do you enjoy it?" she asked Guang Xu.

"Yes."

"Then have some more."

The emperor continued to eat. Then after another period of time, seeing that the emperor meant to stop, Ci Xi queried, "Are you full?"

The emperor hesitated, as he did not want to answer. Then Ci Xi said immediately, "It seems that you need some more. Help yourself."

The same thing happened four times before Guang Xu began to feel that his stomach was full. However, the food Ci Xi prepared was not to be left over. So Guang Xu had no other choice but to secretly spit the food inside his sleeves.

When he returned to Yingtai, his sleeves were full of the dumplings and his body was covered with sticky saliva. He asked a eunuch to bring him a new set of clothes so he could change, but all his garments had been taken away by the empress dowager. So the emperor had to stay in his dirty clothes. Later, a eunuch found a clean jacket and Guang Xu had to manage with that.

The Death of Guang Xu

Emperor Guang Xu had a broad forehead and a big upper jaw, which were said to be the symbols of a long life. But that could not save him from dying at the early age of 38. His death was quite suspicious, and many believed it was not a natural one.

Guang Xu was born with a slight stutter, a condition that became aggravated when he met Ci Xi. Often he trembled, got tongue-tied and spoke incoherently before this imperial tigress. After he was imprisoned at the Hall of Yingtai, he decided to withdraw from state affairs in order to protect himself. He knew that Ci Xi had long been planning to replace him with someone else and that his very life was at the mercy of this old woman.

Longtime sorrow and loneliness brought many diseases to the emperor, but he was still able to lead a normal life. However, in the autumn of 1908, his health suddenly took a turn for the worse. When the doctor came to feel his pulse, Guang Xu laid his hand flat on the imperial table. He refused to say a word but would write his symptoms on a piece of paper for the doctor to see. If someone asked about or spoke of his illness as a general disability, he would lose his temper. So, with no great concern, the doctor would be forced to give a diagnosis: "The pulse feels normal, and there is nothing serious."

At that time, Ci Xi was also in poor health and suffered from dysentery. When she was told that the emperor was in too good spirits to hear of her illness,

Ci Xi clenched her teeth and vowed, "I must outlive him."

On October 16, Ci Xi went to Yingtai. She and the emperor had audiences with ministers Pu Liang and Fu Zengxiang. However three days later, the Imperial Palace was sealed with a heavy guard. Anyone who came or went had to be questioned. The eunuchs who went out by the Donghuamen Gate said that the emperor had already died. But nothing happened for two more days. On the 21st, when Empress Long Yu went to see the emperor at Yingtai, she found only his stiff corpse lying in bed. Long Yu rushed to tell Ci Xi, whose sole response was a deep sigh.

The emperor's body was placed in a sedan to be carried in a procession, followed by the empress and a number of eunuchs, back to the Imperial Palace. When the sedan reached the Qianqingmen Gate, report came that Her Great Buddha's health was critical. On hearing this, the empress and most of the eunuchs abandoned the emperor's body and dashed off. Only a handful of small eunuchs were left behind. Thinking it improper to have the emperor's dragon body deserted in such a manner, they hastily put it into a coffin.

The second day, Ci Xi died. Thus two political foes, one aged 38 and another, 73, eventually put their differences to rest. However, the younger died first. It was said that Ci Xi had known she would not recover from her illness. But even on her sickbed, she was still determined to outlive the emperor, so she sent her eunuch Li Lianying to choke His Majesty to death.

Robbery of the Eastern Mausoleum

Ci Xi lived an extravagant life during her reign. In terms of clothes alone, she had more than 2,000 suits. Even on her sickbed, she did not forget to give an edict demanding that countless treasures be buried with her after death.

It has been roughly estimated that the re-building of Ci Xi's mausoleum cost 3,000 taels of gold and that the burial objects were worth about 200 million taels of sivler. When she died at the age of 73, wood caskets and stone boxes, one for each year of her life, were made. The burial objects were put inside these boxes and placed in her coffin.

At the bottom of her coffin was a quilt made of goldwires and decorated with 12,604 pearls of various sizes, 85 rubies and 203 white jade wares. On top of the quilt were a silk mattress decorated with 2,400 pearls and then an embroidered mattress with 1,300 pearls.

Ci Xi's costume was a gown embroidered with stringed pearls and gold threads. On her head was a crown containing a rare, egg-sized pearl that weighed four taels. Beside her head were 108 statutes of gold, emerald and jade Buddhas. Pillowing her head was an emerald watermelon that had been found on the Kunlun Mountain. The jewelled melon's green stripes, black seeds and red pulp could be seen. Inside her mouth was placed a luminous pearl and a huge ginseng plant of about 500gr.

Her left hand held a jade lotus flower and the right, a demon-quelling wand made of emerald. On the left side of body was a jade lotus root and one coral was on the right. By her hand were eight jade horses and 18 statues of arhats. Beneath her feet were seven lotus flowers made of 7,300 pure emeralds, symbolizing her 73 years of age.

Inside the coffin there was also a nine-storeyed pogoda decorated with 500 big pearls, 2,200 medium-sized pearls, 1,000 small pearls and 400 round pearls, as well as over 100 rubies and pure emeralds. Covering her body was a quilt made of 6,000 pearls. Around the coffin, there were also over 1,000 various rarities of gold, silver and sacrificial objects.

Ci Xi had hoped that these treasures would guarantee a continuation of her extravagant life after death. But she never expected the treasures to become a great temptation for greedy people. Eighteen years after her death, she underwent this great humiliation when her tomb was ransacked by General Sun Dianying.

Sun was originally a division commander under the Shandong warlord Zhang Zongchang. During the war between Chiang Kaishek and the alliance of the northern warlords, he was bribed by Chiang to become a traitor. Subsequently, his former master was defeated in the war. Then he was appointed army commander by Chiang. Later he was stationed in Zunhua County, Hebei province, where he was to wait for reorganization.

When he arrived in the county, Sun got wind of the fact that the nearby Malan Valley nestled the Eastern Mausoleum where Emperor Qian Long and Ci Xi were buried with numerous rare treasures. Sun began to think about robbing the tomb, a scheme that received the tacit consent of his superior, Xu Yuanquan, the commander-in-chief. On the pretext of carrying out military manoeuvress in the mausoleum area, they drove out all the inhibitants and forbad entry to anyone.

They bombarded the underground palace with explosives to open it and took an ax to Ci Xi's coffin. Cold light gleamed from within, and the robbers found it difficult to keep their eyes open. After a long time they were able to see a female figure buried amid the glistening objects. Sun ordered his men to take everything out.

The amount of treasures removed from the gutted tomb was never known. Sun alone laid claim to five big boxes filled with booty. Then two of the plunderers began to undress the corpse. Everything was stripped except for a pair of undershorts made of gold threads. At this final desecration, the two soldiers hesitated.

Then, Sun, who was standing aside, shouted: "Hurry up! I have long desired a look at the nude body of the empress dowager. Hah! Hah! Today, I've finally got the chance." Hence, the undershorts were also removed.

The robbery met with public condemnations. One newspaper in Beijing wrote: "After the robbery, the Eastern Mausoleum was a sight too pitiful to look at. The bones of Ci Xi were scattered and exposed to the elements, becoming the prey of crows and dogs."

Then descendents of the royal family burst into bitter cries when they heard the news. They sent people to inspect the spot only to find that not only the burial objects but also the surface soil of the tomb were nowhere to be found. Sun, in his greed, had hoarded the topsoil in order to sieve for more treasures. So then Ci Xi's bones were roughly collected and re-buried.

The Last Empress Dowager

Guang Xu's wife, Long Yu, was the last orthodox empress. Although she was neither a beautiful nor capable woman, she liked to put on an empress's airs. Because of her close relation with Ci Xi, Guang Xu disliked his wife from the beginning. After his failure in the Wuxu Reform (1889), Guang Xu was imprisoned, and Ci Xi ordered Long Yu to stay with him. The emperor could not help feeling disgusted at the sight of her.

One day, Guang Xu got so angry that he threw her valuable hairpin to the floor and broke it into pieces. This hairpin was an heirloom handed down from the Qian Long Period. Therefore, Long Yu reported this to Ci Xi. Realizing that she was powerless to reconcile the two, Ci Xi could do nothing but have Long Yu moved to another room. In order to pass the time, Long Yu devoted all her interest to raising silk worms. She did all the work from beginning to the end, such as incubation, collecting mulberry leaves and reeling.

As Guang Xu was only fond of his concubine, Zhen Fei, Long Yu actually became a titular empress. Consequently, she despised her husband and was on Ci Xi's side in the struggle between the emperor's party and the dowager's party. However, she was also discontent with Ci Xi's despotism so her support was only half-hearted. As a matter of fact, her brief 20 years of life were spent dangling between narrow allegiances.

When Guang Xu died, Ci Xi decided to choose Pu Yi as emperor-designate, and Pu Yi's father, Zai Feng, as Regent Prince. On her sickbed, Ci Xi appointed Long Yu Empress Dowager. An edict from her will stipulated that the Regent Prince must consult Long Yu on all important matters. Zai Feng was an indecisive and incompetent person, thus Long Yu became one of the decision-makers during the last years of the Qing Dynasty. She considered following Ci Xi's example of "rule from behind the curtain," but she dared not do it harshly because of the Regent Prince.

Although Long Yu was not in the same league as Ci Xi in terms of intelligence and tactics, she did inherit some of her bad habits. For instance, just as Ci Xi was fond of and trusted eunuch Li Lianying, Long Yu favoured Zhang Lande.

After Zai Feng, the Regent Prince, appointed Yu Lang and Xu Shichang Chief Privy Councillors, Long Yu chose to assert herself by forcing him to remove the two from their positions. This case ended in a battle of words.

With the bourgeois revolution in its infancy, Long Yu wanted to suppress it. However, her trusted eunuch Zhang, who had received a large bribe from General Yuan Shikai, persuaded her to favour the Republic. This he did by telling her that the dignity and life of the empress dowager would be guaranteed and only the Regent Prince was to be abolished.

Long Yu, who had long considered Zai Feng as one of her obstacles, intended to accept Zhang's advice. At the imperial conference, Pu Wei, the Prince Gong, was severely opposed to it. On the next day, Pu Wei wanted to have an audience with Long Yu to further state his opinions.

Long Yu became indignant at this, saying. "They have made a mess of this country. What else do they want? I do not want to meet him." Then she announced the abdication of the emperor and entrusted General Yuan Shikai with full power to organize the provisional Republican Government. Long Yu's decision only helped Yuan to usurp the state power.

Hence, the more than 300 years of Qing rule came to an end. According to the Articles Providing for the Favourable Treatment of the Great Qing Emperor after His Abdiction, the emperor's title and dignity were retained, and the emperor and empress dowager could temporarily live in the Forbidden City,

From then on, Long Yu actually became a housekeeper of the court. She either said prayers or played with the eunuchs and palace ladies. She also developed a bad eating habit and was always thereafter trailed by attendants holding bowls of fruits and other foods. Her unrestrained appetite eventually brought her stomach disease.

When she was dying, she likewise lost the ability to talk. Eunuch Zhang whispered to her, "While Your Highness is not well, the court affairs are being taken care of by Prince Chun." He repeated his sentence three times before Long Yu nodded approvingly.

After a long pause, she said in a weak voice, "Bring me the Emperor." The eunuchs hastily brought Pu Yi. Long Yu pointed to the emperor and said, "He is still a child. Don't bully him," and died.

Great Enthronement Ceremony of the Last Emperor

Ci Xi contracted dysentery while celebrating her 73th birthday at the Summer Palace. Because of her age, the disease grew serious in a few days. On the tenth day, she gave an edict, appointing Prince Chun, Zai Feng, as regent, and his son was taken to the court to be taught. As Guang Xu had no heir, this meant that Pu Yi was to become the emperor-designate.

When the chief privy councillors and eunuchs came to take the future emperor to the palace, the household of Prince Chun was glum. Pu Yi's grandmother fainted away, for she was unwilling to let her grandson go to Ci Xi, and the little emperor himself was howling and hitting the strangers who tried to pick him up. In the end, it was his nurse who carried him to the Zhongnanhai Palace.

However, when the child found himself before a drab form and staring at an emaciated and hideous face, he quaked and burst into howls. Ci Xi told someone to give him a string of candied haws, but Pu Yi, to Ci Xi's great displeasure, threw it onto the floor. "What a naughty child," she said, "Take him away to play."

The next day, Guang Xu died, and on the third day, Ci Xi also passed away. After another fortnight, the great ceremony of enthronement took place. According to the traditional practice, before the ceremony began, the emperor had to receive the obeisance of the commanders of the palace guards and ministers of the inner court in the Hall of Central Harmony and the homage of the leading civilian and military officials in the Hall of Supreme Harmony.

It was already early winter and cold. The three-year-old emperor, who was still a baby at the breasts of his nurse, had found all this long and tiresome. So, when he was carried into the Hall of Supreme Harmony and perched upon the enormous throne, he began to show his temper, struggling and crying fiercely.

His father, who was kneeling below the throne for support, told him not to fidget, but Pu Yi still carried on: "I don't like it here. I want to go home! I want to go home!"

His father, desperate and pouring with sweat, tried to soothe his son by saying, "Don't cry. Don't cry. It will soon be finished. It will soon be finished."

As the officials went on kowtowing to the emperor, his cry grew louder and louder. In this way, Pu Yi was enthroned and the dynastic name was changed to Xuan Tong.

When the ceremony was over, the officials asked each other superstitiously: "How could he say 'It will soon be finished.' " They grew very gloomy, considering it a bad omen.

Within three years, the Qing Dynasty in fact was finished and the boy, the last emperor of Chinese feudal society and the 219th emperor of China, who wanted to go home, did go home. Someone joked that although Pu Yi was a small child, he had already forseen his end at his ceremony of enthronement; so the emperor was by no means an ordinary person.

The Pedigree of the Aisin Gioro (Qing) House

Huangtaiji (the 8th son of Nuerhachi 1592-1643)
  Reign title Tian Cong (1626-1636)
  Reign title Chong De (1634-1644)
Fu Lin (the 9th son of Huangtaiji 1638-1661)
  Reign title Shun Zhi (1644-1661)
Xuan Ye (the third son of Fu Lin 1654-1772)
  Reign title Kang Xi (1661-1772)
Yin Zheng (the 4th son of Xuan Ye 1678-1735)
  Reign title Yong Zheng (1722-1735)
Hong Li (the 4th son of Yin Zheng 1711-1799)
  Reign title Qian Long (1735-1795)
Yong Yan (the 15th son of Hong Li 1760-1820)
  Reign title Jia Qing (1795-1820)
Min Ning (the second son of Yong Yan 1782-1850)
  Reign title Dao Guang (1820-1850)
Yi Zhu (the 4th son of Min Ning 1831-1861)
  Reign title Xian Feng (1850-1861)
Zai Chun (the son of Yi Zhu 1856-1874)
  Reign title Tong Zhi (1861-1874)
Zai Tian (the first son of Zai Chun 1871-1908)
  Reign title Guang Xu (1874-1909)
Pu Yi (the son of Zai Feng 1905-1967)
  Reign title Xuan Tong (1909-1911)

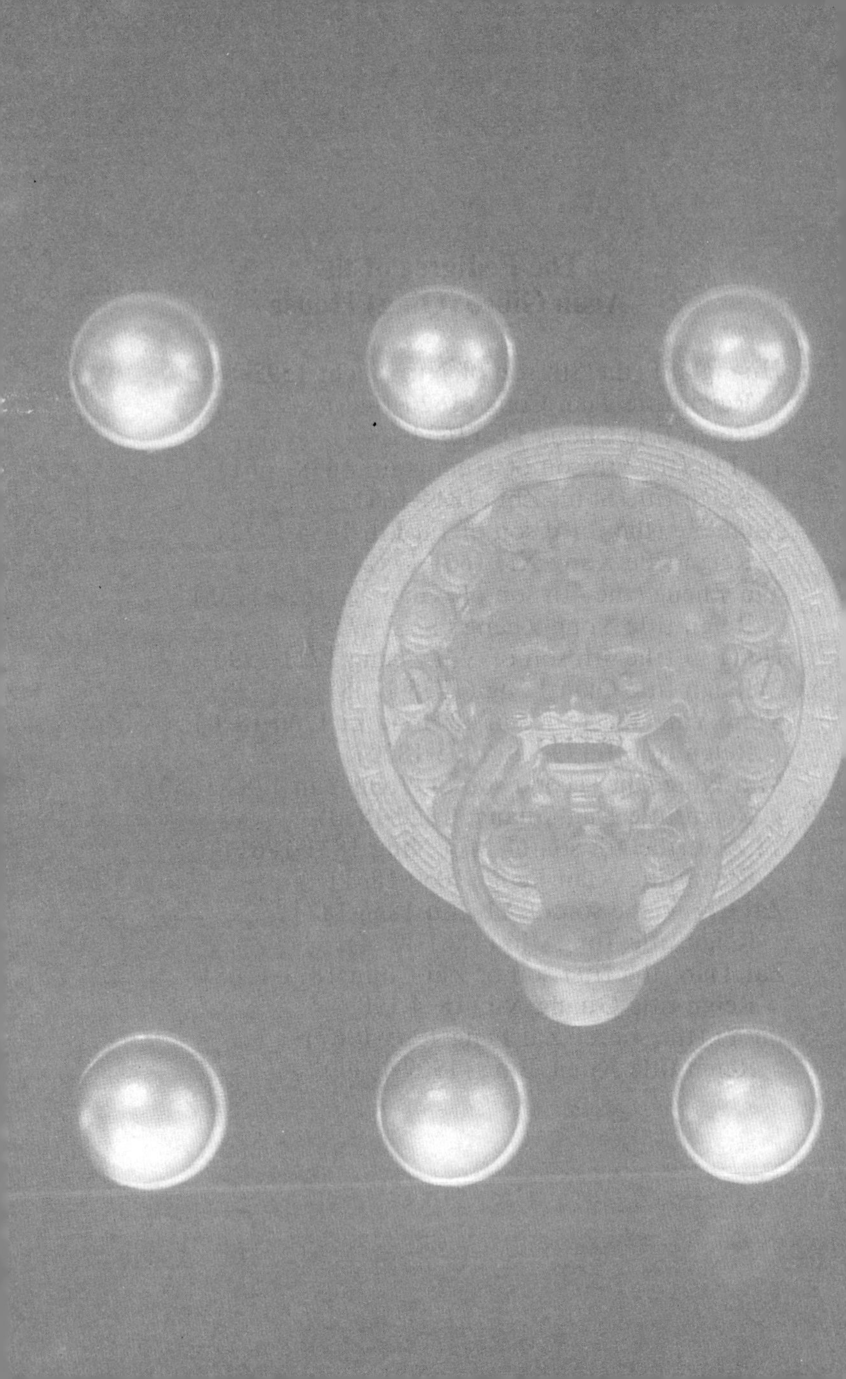

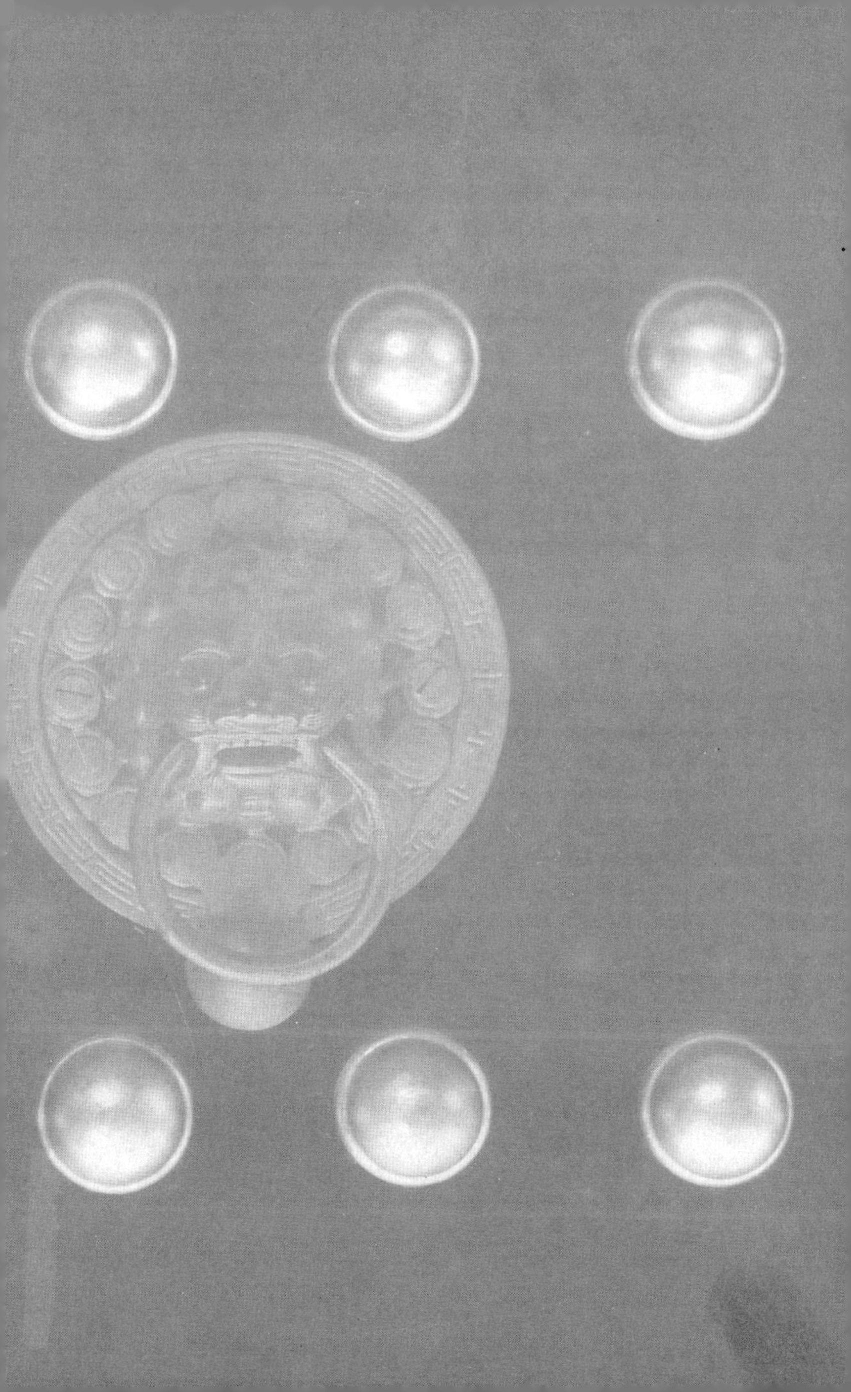